PRAISE FOR

Case Critical

Case Critical successfully weaves Indigenous and settler scholars' perspectives into a braid that challenges ongoing oppressions in Canada. The authors provide an alternate path towards liberation.
— **Michael Anthony Hart**, Fisher River Cree Nation, Canada Research Chair in Indigenous Knowledges and Social Work, Associate Professor, University of Manitoba

The authors of *Case Critical* – two who are Indigenous and two who are not – show how the ongoing effects of colonization are not just a problem for Indigenous peoples, but rather for *all* who live in Canada today. Although social workers continue to practice in times that are indeed "case critical," these authors also plant seeds to re-imagine a better future.
— **Cyndy Baskin**, Associate Professor, School of Social Work, Ryerson University, and author of *Strong Helpers' Teachings: The Value of Indigenous Knowledges in the Helping Professions*

Case Critical is an outstanding resource for learners, educators, and practitioners. This revised edition offers us all a poignant lens for critical social work practice. I applaud with a standing ovation the authors' collaborative scholarship, which exemplifies truth and reconciliation, and which fuels consciousness-raising so that we can all take our place as transformative change agents working to restore humanity in Creation and in our practice.
— **Kathy Absolon**, Associate Dean and Associate Professor, Faculty of Social Work, Wilfrid Laurier University, and author of *Kaandossiwin: How We Come to Know*

Case Critical disrupts those past preconceived views of Indigenous peoples and sets the Canadian social work perspective straight with Indigenous truth and knowledge throughout the whole book. . . . This book is a must-read for all Canadian educators and students in the field of Social Work, especially in this time of honouring truth, action, and social

justice for Indigenous peoples. *Nya:weh* (gratitude) for this valuable publication!
— **Bonnie M. Freeman**, PhD, Algonquin/Mohawk from Six Nations of the Grand River Territory, School of Social Work, McMaster University

To this Indigenous social work graduate and practitioner, the seventh edition of *Case Critical* offers incredible medicine. Under colonial rule, beginning in the 1700s, many of my Mi'kmaq people began to starve to death. In 2016, it still feels as though we are starving, particularly in academia – still waiting for the basic nourishment that comes from respectful recognition – from a sense of being valued and belonging. The traditional teachings of Banakonda (Ojibwe Elder, Scholar, Artist) that open this book speak to this 300-year-old hunger in a deep, spirit-nourishing way.
— **Bagamiayyaabikwe Michelle Sutherland**, MSW, RSW, Executive Director, White Owl Native Ancestry Association

Well-articulated with real life anecdotes, this book unveils the finicky inside stories of social welfare in Canada, and the potential perils in the social work profession, but leaves us with hope for positive change. *Case Critical* is a clarion call to reconnect to our roots, to deconstruct structural paradigms and seek alternatives, and to learn from diversity. Reading *Case Critical* makes you a better person, and then a better social worker.
— **Baiju Vareed**, PhD, RSW, instructor in Social Work, Red Deer College

This seventh edition of *Case Critical* – coming at a time when many of us are thinking about responding to the Truth and Reconciliation Commission of Canada's Calls to Action – is a beautiful example of teams of individuals from diverse backgrounds coming together to dialogue, write, teach one another, teach us, challenge us, and demonstrate how we can work together in respectful, transforming ways.
— **Judy White**, Dean, Faculty of Social Work, University of Regina

Case Critical asks us to examine our lives, families, and communities to look for sites to decolonize and to act in a just, fair, and balanced way in our relationships with one another. In Canada, we face willful ignorance of the ongoing colonization of Indigenous peoples combined with white supremacy, racist and homophobic attacks, and widespread poverty. Until the helping professions admit there is a problem, decolonization alone will not be the solution. We would be wise to consider how each of us can be transformed by kindness, honesty, sharing, strength, and love in our social and political practice.

— **Dr. Patricia D. McGuire**, Kishebakabaykwe, Carleton University

Case Critical should be required reading in every school of social work across the country. It continues to be an important tool to help inspire social justice. It is a must-read.

— **Shari Brotman**, Associate Professor, McGill School of Social Work

This is a wonderful addition to the expanding literature on progressive social work practice. With its co-authorship of Indigenous and non-Indigenous scholars, it is unique in its critical and intersectional engagement with neoliberalism, colonialism, and privilege. This important book moves beyond critique to provide inspiring examples of transformative practices within traditional social services, as well as in social justice movements, labour unions, alternative social services, and Indigenous communities. It offers critical hope and practical strategies to resist the onslaught of increasing inequality, marketization, and oppression.

— **Bob Pease**, Professor, Social Work, University of Tasmania, author of
    Undoing Privilege and co-editor of *Doing Critical Social Work*

It is indeed exciting to see this expanded revision of *Case Critical*'s seminal Canadian work. This seventh edition adds considerably to the growing literature on decolonizing social work. In theorizing beyond mainstream structural social work, *Case Critical* will resonate with Indigenous peoples' issues, further their political cause for justice, inclusion, and better access to services, and validate the experiences of Indigenous social workers in Canada and beyond. It is essential reading for all social workers who share in these causes.

— **Mel Gray**, Professor, Social Work, University of Newcastle, Australia

The four collaborative authors of the seventh edition of *Case Critical* offer social work students and practitioners a text that combines a critical analysis of social services and social work history, skill application with real life examples, while emphasizing the ongoing pursuit of social justice for all marginalized populations. A must-read for all progressive social workers and students.

— **Elizabeth Radian**, PhD, RSW, Social Work instructor and consultant

Case Critical
Social Services &
Social Justice
in Canada

Seventh Edition

Banakonda Kennedy-Kish (Bell)
Raven Sinclair
Ben Carniol
Donna Baines

Between the Lines
Toronto

Case Critical, Seventh Edition

© 2017 Banakonda Kennedy-Kish (Bell), Raven Sinclair, Ben Carniol, Donna Baines
© 1987, 1990, 1995, 2000, 2005, 2010, Ben Carniol

First published in Canada by
Between the Lines
401 Richmond St. W., Studio 277
Toronto, Ontario M5V 3A8
1-800-718-7201
www.btlbooks.com

Library and Archives Canada Cataloguing in Publication

Kennedy-Kish (Bell), Banakonda, author
Case critical : social service and social justice in Canada / Banakonda Kennedy-Kish (Bell), Raven Sinclair, Ben Carniol, and Donna Baines. – 7th edition.
Includes bibliographical references.
Issued in print and electronic formats.
ISBN 978-1-77113-311-1 (softcover). – ISBN 978-1-77113-312-8 (EPUB).
ISBN 978-1-77113-313-5 (PDF).

1. Social service--Canada.   2. Social workers--Canada.   I. Sinclair, Raven, author
II. Carniol, Ben, author   III. Baines, Donna, 1960–, author   IV. Title.
HV105.C39 2017   361.30971   C2016-907415-3
                                                                     C2016-907416-1

Cover design by Jennifer Tiberio
Front cover image: "Third Fire" concept and drawing by Banakonda Kennedy-Kish (Bell).
Co-creative graphic illustration by Banakonda Kennedy-Kish (Bell) and Michelle Sutherland.
Text design and page preparation by Steve Izma
Printed in Canada

We acknowledge for their financial support of our publishing activities the Government of Canada through the Canada Book Fund, the Canada Council for the Arts, which last year invested $153 million to bring the arts to Canadians throughout this country, and the Government of Ontario through the Ontario Arts Council, the Ontario Book Publishers Tax Credit program, and the Ontario Media Development Corporation.

CONTENTS

Preface xiii

A Note about Quotes, Co-authors, and Formatting xiv

1 Ntamkidwinan First Words 1

Welcome 1
   Four voices

An Anishinaabe Elder's Perspectives 3
   Four foundational principles: Kindness • Honesty •
   Sharing • Strength • ingredients for wellness

2 Power, Ideology, and Social Services 11

Ongoing Colonialism and Its Consequences 11
   Indigenous voices • Doctrines of Discovery

Canadian Apology for Residential Schools 14
   Indigenous leaders respond • ongoing Treaty violations •
   colonial privilege

Indigenous Child Removal System and the
"Sixties Scoop" 18

Today's Colonialism 21
   Corporate elites & today's colonialism • neoliberalism •
   rich-poor gap • social service cuts • conservative ideology
   or equity?

Individualism and Privilege 23
   Illegitimate privilege • social problems & systemic
   inequalities

Progressive Social Work 27

3 Naming and Resisting Injustices 28
   Bad news • good news

Colonial Privilege 29
   Violent conquest • theft of land • genocide • colonialism
   today • how we benefit • how we lose • ethical violations
   • racism

Racism and Privilege 32
*Hidden privilege of whiteness • racist domination •
individual racism • institutional/systemic racism •
cultural/ideological racism • anti-racism & social services*

Class Privilege 35
*Special interest groups of big business • Business Council
of Canada • tax cuts: who gains? who loses? • shredding
of social safety net • global links: IMF & World Bank •
class privilege versus democracy*

Patriarchal Privilege 37
*Devaluation of women • male violence • women's feminist
movement • shelters • feminist counselling • intersections
of oppressions • gendered ageism & poverty • long-term
care • nursing homes • a universal caregiver model •
Indigenous approaches*

Heterosexual/Cisgender Privilege 43
*Heterosexism • homophobia • violence • Queer
communities • social service barriers • public opinion •
Trans Pride Canada guide • two-spirited people*

Ableism and Privilege 47
*Medical model • disabling conditions • anti-oppression
model • challenging stigma • (dis)Ability • sanism •
activism & change • intersections*

Social Justice and Social Services 49
*Dismantling injustice • social transformation • resistance
• social services as contested terrain • including ourselves*

4 **Roots: Early Attitudes** 52
*1492 & colonialism • genocide of Indigenous peoples •
African slaves • flogging European "valiant beggars" •
witch hunts • workhouses*

Early North American Social Welfare 55
North American workhouses

"Survival of the Fittest" – Social Darwinism 56
*British enclosure of the commons • "genetic superiority" of
the rich • social Darwinism • normalizing poverty wages*

Social Work: The Beginnings 58
*Charity Organization Society • friendly visitors • moral
uplift*

Oppression and Resistance 60
Jane Addams, social activist • "stern charity" • caring as women's "natural work" under patriarchy • politics of starvation against Indigenous communities

Indigenous "Assimilation" and Resistance 62
Indigenous "assimilation" • author Thomas King: "What do Whites want?"

Inuit and Métis 64
Indian residential schools • coercion against Inuit communities • Métis rebellion • theft of land

Early 1900s Unrest 67
1930s extreme unemployment • police repression

Social Programs and Social Injustices 69
Fear of revolution?

Resistance and Progressive Movement 72
Social programs grow • social injustices continue

Neoliberal Backlash 74

5 **Diverging Schools of Altruism** 76
Eager to help

Conflicts inside the Social Work Curriculum 76
Similar to contested terrain in social services

Conventional: Ecological-Systems Theory 77
Adaptive capacities • ignoring systemic inequality • evidence-based practice • evading social justice issues

Anti-Oppression Perspectives 78
A structural approach • feminist social work • civility in classrooms does not mean neutrality • homo-"phobia" critiqued • anti-oppression critiqued • priority on anti-racist education critiqued • social justice practice as work-in-progress • abandon the teaching of social work skills? • table comparing conventional & progressive practice

The Controversy about Competency Models 86
Promise of high quality • social workers becoming technicians • promise of accountability • employer-imposed tasks • social justice & diversity?

From Aboriginal Circles in the Classroom to Indigenizing
Social Work 88
    Indigenous approaches to helping & healing • Indigenous
    worldviews • different knowledges • meaning of
    "Indigenizing" • avoiding cultural appropriation •
    Indigenous Teachings

Four Principles of Good Practice 92

6 Social Workers: On the Front Line 95

Where Social Workers Work 95
    Social services • voluntary sector • welfare & other sectors
    • taking Indigenous children • private practice • rural
    social work

How People Become Social Service Users 99
    Voluntary & involuntary sectors

Hierarchies and the Stratification of Social Services 100
    Bureaucracy as "natural"? • top-down power • supervisors
    & managers • impact of racism & white supremacy • child
    protection workers

The Challenge of Social Work 104
    Different kinds of help • responding to racism •
    Association of Black Social Workers • responding to needs
    of Queer people • high caseloads & burnout • better
    service models • Indigenous voices • a mirage

The Bottom Line: Managerialized Social Services 113
    Private market-like management models • funding cuts •
    computerized check box forms • deskilling • beholden to
    neoliberal funders

Privatization of Social Services 114
    Contracting out • lower wages • competitive bidding •
    fewer services • advocacy excluded • attacks on collective
    bargaining • a better direction

A Challenge: This Story Must Change 119
    Indigenous call for accountability & reciprocity

7 Reality Check: Service Users' Experience 123
    Are we listening? • survivors of residential school speak •
    intergenerational impact • voices of welfare clients

Welfare "Reform": Smoke and Mirrors 129
Decades of neglect • barriers to service • slick evasions • precarious jobs • criminal record?

Different Shades of Social Coercion 134
Workfare – jobs at poverty wages, or lose stingy financial aid • family tensions • incest • group homes • prisons • solitary confinement • resilience

Caring Social Services: Take a Deep Bow 137
"Helpful social workers" • constructive practice

8 Challenging Feeling Hopeless 139
"Enough!"

Social Justice Movements 139
Anti-colonialism • Idle No More • Arthur Manuel, author & Indigenous activist • each "ism" & social movements • Workers Action Centre • coalitions across movements • SOS (Surpassing our Survival) • Black Lives Matter • Cindy Blackstock, social work advocate & executive director of First Nations Child & Family Caring Society of Canada

Labour Unions and Social Work 147
Why unions? • working conditions • social policies / programs • solidarity work • making a difference

Dealing with Challenges: Tiny Miracles 150
Social workers' resilience / values • example of good practice • a therapeutic relationship

Alternative Social Services 152
Indigenous alternatives • feminist alternatives • (dis)Ability alternatives • Queer-positive alternatives • an inverted hierarchy • generous funding necessary

An Activist Agenda by Progressive Social Workers 156
Social workers as social activists • previous "nay-sayers" defeated • creating new universal social programs • support for Indigenous Treaty & human rights • creating spaces for excluded voices • reaching out to Indigenous Nations

9 Toward Liberation 160
"We are not alone"

Challenging Multiple Oppressions 160
*Multiple "isms" • multiple identities • links to privilege •
social location • subjective responses & resistance*

Themes for Liberation in Social Work Practice 162
*Finding voice • finding oppression • finding resilience •
raising critical consciousness • standing up for client rights
• developing solidarity for emancipation*

Indigenous Healing and Liberation 167
*Sources & nature of lateral violence • Raven's
Transformative Accountability Model • grief work •
historical trauma • ethical Indigenous lifeways •
transforming rage, guilt, & shame*

Liberation and Social Services 170
*Global context • advice from two service users • advice
from Queer activists • Jim Albert, Indigenous Elder*

The Pendulum of Practice: A Tool for Assessing
Cultural Competence 173
*Christine Fejo-King, Warramunga / Larrakia social work
educator • combining Indigenous knowledges with critical
practice • from harmful to helpful practice*

Completing a Cultural Competence Self-Audit 174
Visual assessment tool • honesty required

Competence Matrix 177
*Diverse description of practice • awareness levels • wide
application*

Supporting and Actualizing Transformation 178
*Beyond the job description • "we did it" • support groups
• meaning of "resources"? • conflicting appeals •
reciprocity of support • inclusive of Indigenous nations •
away from elitist democracy • reaching for participatory
democracy*

10   Nawây-pîkiskwêwina After Words 185
Raven, Donna, Ben • Closing words by Banakonda

Can we go where we have never been? 189

References 196

PREFACE

I would like to lift up my gratitude to Ben for inviting me to participate in the seventh addition of Case Critical, for being the one who held space and persevered in gathering together our contributions. I thank my fellow travellers, Ben, Donna, and Raven for sharing your learning, and for your openness throughout the writing process. Further I would like to express gratitude to Michelle Sutherland for her most generous technical know-how, creative problem solving in translating concepts and images into this format. I am full of love and gratitude to my beautiful children, Shoshona, Shehnon, and Sarain, to my beloved grandchildren, Skye, Shanaki, Nadia, Waas, and Sebastion, to my extended family, especially James Dumont and Shelly Charles. This has been a rewarding journey filled with kindness.

– Banakonda Kennedy-Kish (Bell)

I would like to give thanks to Ben for the invitation and for displaying wonderful leadership, to Donna for modelling excellence, to Banakonda for spiritual guidance and kindness, and to the many educators who have been inspirational and supportive. Thanks to my students, and especially to my daughter, Mercedes, for teaching me how to be a better person, making me laugh, and keeping me on my toes.

– Raven Sinclair

I want to express a huge thank you to this seventh edition's superb writing team: Banakonda, Raven, and Donna. To facilitate our process Julie Faubert at Ryerson University kindly interrupted her own work whenever we needed help to navigate around barriers posed by computer technology. I am also grateful to numerous mentors, friends, co-activists, and colleagues for helping to centre my spirit, my feelings, my understandings, and my actions. This edition would not have been possible without encouragement from my siblings, my extended family, and from the ongoing emotional inspiration I receive from my immediate family, Rhona, Mira, Naomi, and Brian.

– Ben Carniol

I would like to thank the following: all the research participants through the years who contributed to my projects; all my research colleagues in their many places and countries; my fellow social and union activists; this marvellous writing team for drawing on their collective learnings and contributing to social justice; and to my wonderful family – Jim Stanford, Chè Baines, and Thea Baines for putting up with me, tolerating my singing, and for being my inspiration.

– Donna Baines

We gratefully acknowledge Shari Brotman for her assistance in bringing greater clarity to the use of terms in chapter 3. In addition, all four of us express our deep appreciation to our publisher, Between the Lines Books, and to its welcoming, supportive team: Amanda Crocker, Matthew Adams, Renée Knapp, Dave Molenhuis, and Jennifer Tiberio. Special mention must be made of the exceptional editorial and communication skills of this edition's copy editor, Mary Newberry.

A NOTE ABOUT QUOTES, CO-AUTHORS, AND FORMATTING

We are fortunate to have supportive circles and networks of social workers, colleagues, students, service users, social activists, and many others. Throughout this book we have consulted with them for advice and support. Occasionally, with permission, we make use of their words. Quotes from individual consultation, interviews, and other various communications are identified in the usual way by enclosing them in quotations or indented blocks for longer passages, and are further identified by being placed in italics. If we have permission to use their name, we identify them. Others have given us permission to quote them without identifying them.

Also, at various places in the book, one or other of us, the co-authors – Banakonda, Raven, Ben, and Donna – have something to say on a specific topic. We identify these individual comments by stating who is speaking, using their first names. We do the same when Banakonda is speaking but when she is providing teachings or other commentary, we add a rounded border to reflect her distinct voice as an Indigenous Elder. We hope you will find these pages helpful to your work.

1 NTAMKIDWINAN FIRST WORDS

WELCOME

For this seventh edition of *Case Critical*, I invited three social work colleagues, all people I greatly respect, to join with me in this work.

In our work together on this edition, we are engaged in a cooperative, consensual process of gathering together our observations, reflections, experiences, and research. In envisioning our work together, we address the following questions:

- Why is it, at a time when social work education is deepening and strengthening its progressive approaches to helping, there are so many social services moving in the opposite direction?
- How can we engage more deeply with the reality of social interdependence and the goals of inclusiveness, in the context of: (a) genocide and contemporary colonialism against Indigenous people in Canada, and (b) governments carrying out the wishes of the richest and most privileged Canadians for more tax cuts, austerity policies, and underfunding of social programs, causing a steady deterioration of social services?
- What knowledge and understanding will move us toward a society that implements political, economic, and social justice?
- What action can we take to contribute to this change? Within social services, what action can we take to clear the way for respectful, anti-oppressive, wholistic practice?

– Ben Carniol, 2017

Banakonda consulted with Anishinaabe Language Carrier Lorraine McRae, who helped find "Ntamkidwinan" to correspond with "First Words" in the title.

Banakonda: My name is Awnjibinayseekwe Banakonda Kennedy-Kish (Bell). I am Bear Clan, and third degree Midewiwin. I was born on the outskirts of Sault Ste. Marie, Ontario. I am an Ojibway woman with Irish descent. As a Traditional Practitioner and Teacher, I have worked and taught within Indigenous communities for over forty years. For a significant amount of that time, I worked on the front line, developing as a Traditional Practitioner. That led me to roles of Treatment Director, Teacher, Facilitator, Curriculum Developer, and Elder-Cultural Adviser.

As an Indigenous woman of mixed heritage, I have undergone the gamut of all-too-common interventions of colonization, including the harmful interventions of social services, child welfare, and education. The heavy hand of colonization deeply influenced my sense of self and belonging in the world. These negative influences were tempered by the presence of a Grandmother and an Aunt. The Land and its changing seasons offered food and medicines, informed and strengthened me in the shelter I experienced in our kitchen by the woodstove, which provided safety and love. My beliefs have emerged from Traditional Teachings of the whole person, family, community development as a way of perceiving, experiencing, knowing, and being on this all-too-brief journey. This informs my traditional practice, and my teaching in the academy. I am committed to pass on these teachings.

Raven: I am Cree/Assinniboine and Anishinaabe and a member of George Gordon First Nation of Treaty 4 in southern Saskatchewan. I came to social work education later in life so I have experience in general labour, the military, and office administration. As a two-spirit woman and transracial adoptee of the 1960s scoop carried out by child welfare agencies, I find myself intrigued with issues of identity and intergenerational trauma. I have been profoundly influenced by the writings of Vine Deloria Jr., Judith Butler, Eduardo and Bonnie Duran, Sandy Grande, bell hooks, and Paulo Freire, among many others.

Ben: I was born in Czechoslovakia, and in the 1940s my parents were victims of Nazi genocide against Jews, causing me as an adult to become a social justice activist, searching for an under-standing of racism and genocidal violence. After social work employment, I became a social work educator. In recent decades, my solidarity with Indigenous people has grown, along with my ongoing journey of decolonizing what I see, what I feel, what I know, and what I do. My evolving perspec-tives are influenced by the writings of Paulo Freire, Abraham Joshua Heschel, Helen Levine, Maurice Moreau, Thomas King, and Kathy Absolon.

Donna: I am White. Our exact heritage is unknown as parts of my family fled their homes in the early 1900s in what is now Poland, leaving behind documents that could have identified them and the religious minority identities that made them vul-nerable to persecution. My journey through social work was interrupted by stints as an organizer in the student, unem-ployed workers, peace, and feminist movements. I bring a com-munity organizing/social justice agenda to social work, and love to muck around in new ways to understand our everyday worlds, not just to analyze, but to change them. Along the way, my thinking and practice has been influenced by groups of scholars and activists including Marxist, socialist feminist, anti-racist, Queer, and union people.

AN ANISHINAABE ELDER'S PERSPECTIVES

Banakonda

I am pleased to participate in this work as an Indigenous Elder and Traditional Practitioner. We are gathering our thoughts onto one landscape, seeking, reaching for con-sensual ways of working together. Respecting, recognizing diversity, we envision ourselves participating in a co-oper-ative journey that lifts up our spirit, strengthens our rela-tionships. We are encouraging each other to commit to caring for ourselves, each other, and the land. Through our conversations and reflections, we intend to embrace our interrelatedness, our interdependence, and our reli-ance on each other.

[Banakonda, *continued*]

I am informed by the teachings, ceremonies, and life-ways of the Midewiwin Lodge in all that I see, feel, know, and do. During my forty years of practice, I have been deeply influenced by Onaubinisay James Dumont, Eastern Door Chief of the Midewiwin Lodge, Elder of Elders, who has long been a spiritual leader, an inspiring teacher, mentor, colleague, and friend. I am forever grateful for his work, translation, and Anishinaabe theology, central to the cultural frameworks and models that are widely used by Indigenous people throughout the Americas.

Other teachers who have influenced me are Peter O'Chiese, Dan Pine, Fred Wheatley, Art Solomon, and Albert Lightning. I have also been influenced and encouraged by Ron Conlon and Paul Zakos, whom I worked with for over twenty-five years. It is their respect, value, and belief in our people, the willingness to invest a very large part of their life journey to facilitate and advocate for Indigenous thought and practice that I will be forever grateful for. Last but not least, my family, my children, and my grandchildren have been true teachers of compassion, patience, and enjoyment in my life.

The following teachings are informed by Midewiwin Traditional Teachings and by the work of Onaubinisay James Dumont. I have developed Indigenous methodologies of social work that are informed by teachings, ceremonies, and practices that emerge from our relationship with each other, in family, in community, and with the land. In sharing my interpretation and application of my traditional teachings and practices, their relevance is ever present and continues to inform my work.

The Four Foundational Principles of Indigenous Traditional Practice are presented in a four-directional framework; Kindness in the east, Honesty in the south, Sharing in the west, Strength in the north. Development and growth unfold in a circular manner. Kindness is the first movement, honesty the second, sharing the third, and strength the fourth. Each movement moves into the other. Wholeness includes each of these principles and each are a part of each other, essential and inseparable. The seed sprouts into the stem, from stem the leaf, the flower. In the flowering the circle ends and begins, for the seed is in the flowering. Wholeness is always unfolding.

This interconnectedness is central to understanding how these principles are inseparable. The strength is in the flowering. Here is new life, and the ability to pass on life. The life yet to come is present in all of these transactions. Wholeness also speaks to and includes the life that is before and to the life that is yet to come. In these principles we are being informed by our ancestors at the same time we are caused to be mindful of future generations. We are not only addressing the teachings of these four principles to those who are present now. As we pass them on, we honour and recognize our ancestors who held onto and passed them on to us. By teaching them now, we assure that they are passed on to the generations who are on their way here.

The Anishinaabe believe that the human being was the last to be created and therefore the youngest relative in creation. We are dependent on the rest of creation for life, and therefore charged to learn co-operation, experience our mutuality, our interdependence, and practise co-existence.

Elder and Eastern Door Chief of the Midewiwin Lodge, Onaubinisay James Dumont often talks about this as "a personal (person-all) kinship relationship as one that is with all of creation." Dumont goes on:

> The most desired and appropriate behaviour for the human being is a kind, caring acceptance that embraces a co-operative, sharing co-existence. An interconnectedness, inter-personal relationship to all life must be maintained to be true to a harmonious co-existence. (Dumont 2006 Nipissing Social Service Worker Diploma Teaching Session)

The motivational principles of harmony and balance cause the first principle to be central and key to Indigenous

[Banakonda, *continued*]

practice. *Kindness* is foundational: valued for itself and unconditional. Kindness is essential in seeking, protecting, nurturing, and sustaining life. Ideally kindness is experienced and taught in the first stage of life. We value life because it is life. Kindness is a seed full of everything that is possible in regard to life. Kindness has intention that is life promoting and life sustaining.

Here, at the very beginning, the concept of gratitude emerges. We are instructed and encouraged to be grateful. Humility is at the core of gratitude and the ability to restore ourselves, to realign and find balance.

Therefore, kindness is the central, driving principle in the helping relationship. It is not possible to engage wellness without kindness; we cannot even be respectful without kindness. Nurturing kindness is a living, breathing challenge to employ. We have to see it to be able to reach for it, experience it, express it, to be able to know and understand it. Our ability to conceive of kindness is always expanding, unfolding, and deepening. It is a lifelong process. In principle, we are forever reaching for and engaging kindness.

The second principle, central and key to Indigenous practice, is *honesty*. The four-directional framework is a design that seems to be present in all of life. Within this design there is this built-in intention that causes us to engage, to experience life with increased consciousness. The centrality of relationship is foundational and is expressed through kindness and honesty. Right at the moment that we each emerge as life we have a desire for life. That desire itself moves us into relationship: we see, we reach for, we feel, and experience. These operational connectors lead us to knowing life, and then to understanding, which then emerges in our behaviour.

In relationship the mystery and wonder of life emerges. Relationship is the doorway to life, and is life itself. It is a journey of seeing and seeking, of connecting and experiencing through time. Change happens when life is set into motion. There is no change without time, and no time without change. As Anishinaabe, we believe Spirit is at the centre of all life. We believe we are spirits in physical form, experiencing this life through relationship.

In helping relationships we find the principles of kindness and honesty present or absent in one degree or another. This is true for the people we are working with; it is true for the practitioners as well.

We, as human beings, are engaged in finding our way between our experiences of ourselves and others. Throughout our life journey, we are navigating our expectations of ourselves and of others. Here the state of incongruencies can and often does emerge. Taking care of incongruencies within ourselves is essential for our own growth and wellness. This is equally essential when we engage others in a helping relationship.

In relationship, we can only bring the kindness and honesty we carry. We cannot bring more than we have; we can and we do bring our desire for more kindness and honesty. This desire and need for kindness and honesty fosters our growth in relationship which in turn increases our capacity for kindness and honesty.

Kindness and honesty are living, breathing, meaning-making experiences that enrich and challenge each of us to employ kindness and honesty on behalf of ourselves and on behalf of others. When these two principles are experienced and expressed, they nourish, engage, move us to growth and healing and to knowing and understanding.

The third principle, central and key to Indigenous practice, is *sharing*. In the third principle, the foundational principles of kindness and honesty emerge into and unfold as knowing, as understanding. Sharing is wrapped within the very concept of knowledge and understanding. It is the intention of knowledge and understanding to be shared. Knowledges are not to be hoarded or squandered. They emerge from our beliefs, values, in relationship, and

[Banakonda, *continued*]
through our experience. The principle of sharing in its highest form is attached and inseparable from kindness and honesty.

Kindness and honesty are inherent in sharing. Within the principle of sharing is the vision of the good life, a life abundant with kindness, honesty, and sharing. At the same time, sharing is a value in itself. In helping relationships we find the principles of kindness, honesty, and sharing present or absent in one degree or another. This is equally true for practitioners and for those who we work with.

Sharing also has an intention that embodies the belief and value in the principle of sharing itself. The ability to carry out the principle of sharing is tempered by the kindness and honesty that we carry or do not carry.

As teachers, helpers, and seekers we are in need of receiving and sharing the knowledge and understanding of kindness and honesty with ourselves and our fellow travellers. Some of us come in pieces, weary and in need; we all come for understanding. This is not knowledge, as might be seen today by the academy. This knowledge that is about belief, place, belonging, value, and relationship. This knowledge and understanding is about the human need to be seen, heard, to come to know, understand, and contribute.

Knowledge and understanding is about seeking, protecting, nurturing, and sustaining life. It is about discovering our purpose, our place in community, in society, and in creation. Elders and Traditional Practitioners employ healing processes that engage each of these principles and values in work with others.

The fourth principle central and key to Indigenous practice is *strength*. Strength is the result of valuing, experiencing, knowing, and being able to apply the three principles: kindness, honesty, and sharing. Carrying these gifts within ourselves and within our relationships cause us to carry strength. We are strong because we are kind, honest, and sharing.

For the Traditional Practitioner, strength resides in the commitment to the four principles. Practice is weakened if these principles are compromised. However, making this commitment causes one to cultivate and mind the vision of those four principles, and in doing so renews our relationship with ourselves and our practice. In the application of kindness, honesty, and sharing we are preserving and maintaining these principles. The doing itself causes and strengthens integration and growth.

The human condition is one that unfolds in a journey through time. One of ways the human journey is seen, experienced, and understood is through the stages of life. Each of us experience unique challenges within our life journey, within each stage. We grow and develop as we balance and align ourselves in relationship with each other and with creation. Strength is also about keeping balance. At each stage of life, we need to realign and re-balance ourselves. That back and forth interaction responds to change in our relationships and in life in general. All life is impacted by those changes: the individual, the family, the community, society, and the land.

Here again, is a pattern that seems to engage us in movement, in growth to become more of who we are, and to support others in doing the same. Movement is life, growth is life, and this is the continuous work of life. We are not *done* with growth, with healing, until we are done with life. It is important to remind ourselves of this as Elders, Traditional Practitioners, helpers in general, and as human beings. As helpers, it is especially incumbent on us to refrain from putting ourselves above others.

Our journeys are individual, yet we do not make them alone, nor can we. We do not develop individually, we are nurtured and influenced by our families and care-givers, by our spiritual, emotional, mental, and physical environment. We excel in some areas, and not in others.

[Banakonda, *continued*]

In our helping relationship we share our beliefs in wellness, our experiences of wellness, our understanding and knowledge, and our methodology through our practice. When it is our turn to seek help or guidance for our own hardship, we will benefit from a practitioner in the same way as those we help. Our work includes helping others come to know that a person is not *less than* if they are in need. No one does it alone. And we are not made to or meant to do it alone. The human condition is one in which relationship is a central and necessary ingredient to life itself on every level, in every way.

Unfortunately, we are being told that we should be self-sufficient, do it alone. This not only suggests that it is possible but *necessary*. It is misleading to give one person credit for success when it has involved so many to hold up that one person. It truly does take a village to raise a child, to lift up a scientist, a dancer, a writer, a social worker, an Elder.

– Awnjibinayseekwe Banakonda Kennedy-Kish (Bell)

2017

2 POWER, IDEOLOGY, AND SOCIAL SERVICES

ONGOING COLONIALISM AND ITS CONSEQUENCES

I n the first chapter, our first words affirm the principles of kindness, honesty, sharing, and strength, which provide a framework for social work practice that is anti-oppressive and
decolonized. Though our main focus is on social services, we believe
that our comments also have wider application to society as a whole.

These pages present a critical narrative that draws on previous
editions of *Case Critical,* and is supplemented by updated reflections, research, and references, which inform our work. At times the
book will present distinctive Indigenous voices to honour the culture and wisdom of the people who first lived in the Americas. For
2017, Oxford University Press plans to publish *Social Work Ethics:
Progressive, Practical and Relational Approaches,* in which Banakonda
writes:

> The Two-Row Wampum, is a beaded record of the first agreement that
> Indigenous nations made with the early settlers that landed on the
> shores of Turtle Island, that is, North America. It was made in the early
> 1600s, and is referred to as the first covenant. In The Two-Row
> Wampum, settlers and Indigenous peoples both agreed to recognize
> each other, to live alongside each other, and navigate the future
> together, we in our canoes, they in their boats. It outlined a mutual
> commitment to friendship, peace between peoples who would live
> alongside each other, stating "as long as the grass is green, as long as
> the rivers flow, as long as the sun rises in the east and sets in the west
> we will travel two paths, the canoe and the boat representing those
> paths."

It was also said, that from time to time that agreement would be taken out, dusted off, and renewed. It is from this first covenant that Treaties emerged and were articulated. Sadly, the Wampum Covenant was mostly disregarded by the settlers in North America, and ignored in general in the Americas. There were very grave and widespread crimes committed against humanity and against the land on Turtle Island by Europeans. (Kennedy-Kish [Bell] and Carniol 2017: in press)

Settlers came to Canada to escape oppression and after coming to Canada they simply changed places and became the oppressors. The very behaviours that they evaded from their home countries came with them when they settled in Canada. Oppression is in-built into the very fabric of the Americas.

In June 2015, the Truth and Reconciliation Commission signalled the urgency of our need to create a new relationship of equity and respect for each other in Canada, and to move forward and embrace Canadians' stated belief in justice, equity, and sharing.

Banakonda

Ongoing colonialism and its consequences continue to be incongruent with the principles of democracy, freedom, social justice, and equity. For Indigenous people congruencies include all our relations, we believe we are *all* related, the four colours of humans, the swimmers, the crawlers, the four-legged, the flyers, all of creation. We see the earth as our mother, a living, breathing, conscious being, complete and whole, with a spirit, heart, mind, and body. We see the sun as our grandfather and the moon our grandmother. We are all relatives. The concept of congruency includes a central belief in reciprocity, as an essential co-operative engagement that strives toward balance.

Renowned author Thomas King (2009) refers to our collective relatedness as a kinship web that includes all animals, plants, the earth, and the cosmos. Western science confirms that human beings have 92 per cent of the same genes as all mammals: "These similarities reflect a common ancestry shared by all life on earth. Even though human beings share 100% of the same genes, instructions ·contained within their genes are not entirely identical. . . . Although the DNA of any two people on earth is, in fact, 99.9% identical, even a tiny difference can have a big effect if this difference is located in a critical gene." (Scientific Steering Committee Website 2014).

This belief in shared co-existence, respect, and humility was not present in the formation of Canada nor in the creation of the Canadian residential schools system across Canada. Moral principles were abandoned in the pursuit of land acquisition.

> For over a century, the central goals of Canada's Aboriginal policy were to eliminate Aboriginal governments, ignore Aboriginal rights; terminate the Treaties; and through a process of assimilation, cause Aboriginal peoples to cease to exist as distinct legal, social, cultural, religious, and racial entities in Canada. The establishment and operations of residential schools were a central element of this policy, which can best be described as "cultural genocide." (Truth and Reconciliation Commission of Canada 2015: 5)

Residential schools were places where children were placed who had been forcibly removed from their parents, their language, their culture, and their land. The families and Indigenous communities strongly resisted and went to extraordinary lengths, risking everything, to prevent their children from being taken. When these efforts failed, we can only try to imagine not only the trauma, but also the self-blame that these families and communities inflicted upon themselves for being unable to stop their children being forcibly yanked away. When the children arrived at an institution, their hair was cut short or shaved off and they were punished for speaking their own language. The majority of these institutions were like prisons, where there was little love or nurturing. Christian nuns and teachers from Catholic, Anglican, and United Churches taught these children to fear the damnation of hell if they did not accept Christian belief. In most cases, girls were trained for domestic work and boys to be farmhands, and their labour was used to run the institutions.

Centuries ago a Catholic Pope, Alexander VI, in the year 1493, issued an edict *Inter Caetera*, which viewed Indigenous people as possessing no souls, and authorized Spain and Portugal to colonize, convert, and enslave Indigenous people. Combined with this, medieval doctrines of "Discovery" and "*terra nullius*" asserted that explorers discovering "empty" lands had authority over them. These doctrines legitimized full-scale invasion, mass murder, theft of land, displacement, and exploitation, or what is now known as colonialism. This tendency to demonize and dehumanize the original inhabitants of the Americas still influences government policy (Reid 2010).

CANADIAN APOLOGY FOR RESIDENTIAL SCHOOLS

In 2008, Canada's residential schools and their flagrant violations of human rights were the focus of the Canadian House of Commons, on June 4, when Prime Minister Stephen Harper made the following public apology:

> The government of Canada built an educational system in which very young children were often forcibly removed from their homes and often taken far from their communities. Many were inadequately fed, clothed and housed. . . . First Nations, Inuit and Métis languages and cultural practices were prohibited in these schools. Tragically, some of these children died while attending residential schools and others never returned home. . . . On behalf of the Government of Canada and all Canadians, I apologize to aboriginal peoples for Canada's role in the Indian residential school system. The burden of this experience has been on your shoulders for far too long. The burden is properly ours as a government, and as a country.

After this apology, Indigenous leaders who had been invited to the House of Commons were given the opportunity to respond. Phil Fontaine, previously a National Chief of the Assembly of First Nations, in part, had this to say:

> This morning our elders held a condolence ceremony for those who never heard an apology, never received compensation, yet courageously fought assimilation so that we could witness this day. Together, we remember and honour them for it was they who suffered the most as they witnessed generation after generation of their chil-

dren taken from their families' love and guidance. . . . Brave survivors, through the telling of their painful stories, have stripped white supremacy of its authority and legitimacy.

Mary Simon, then president of the Inuit Tapiriit Kanatami, offered a sense of caution:

> Let us not be lulled into an impression that when the sun rises tomorrow morning, the pain and scars will miraculously be gone. They will not. But a new day has dawned, a new day heralded by a commitment to reconciliation and building a new relationship with Inuit, Métis and First Nations.

Similarly, Clem Chartier, then president of the Métis National Council, suggested that the work to be done is by no means finished:

> The Prime Minister and the Minister of Indian Affairs know that although I am very sincere and happy, perhaps, that this is happening, I also feel deeply conflicted, because there is still misunderstanding about the situation of the Métis Nation, our history and our contemporary situation. . . . I am one of the survivors of a Métis residential school. . . . The Métis Nation of western Canada, which has been excluded from many things by the workings of this House and its policies, wants in.

Beverly Jacobs, then president of the Native Women's Association of Canada, made this addition:

> Prior to the residential schools system, prior to colonization, the women in our communities were very well respected and honoured for the role that they have in our communities as being the life givers, being the caretakers of the spirit that we bring to mother earth. We have been given those responsibilities to look after our children and to bring that spirit into this physical world. Residential schools caused so much harm to that respect and to that honour. . . . Now it is about our responsibilities today, the decisions that we make today and how they will affect seven generations from now. . . . What is it that this government is going to do in the future to help our people? (House of Commons 2008)

When reporters asked Indigenous peoples across the country about their reaction to this public apology, responses were mixed. They ranged from "To have a government today say, finally, yes, something

was horribly wrong to treat us as less than human. . . . I needed that,"
to "Residential school wrecked my life and an apology won't fix it"
(Strojeck 2008: A17). This was the first time that the government of
Canada had made a public, unconditional apology to Canada's Indigenous communities. While the federal government has yet to match
this apology with effective action to address the intergenerational
consequences of residential schools, the apology is nevertheless an
important benchmark in the uphill process of obtaining justice.

Significantly, the apology's focus was restricted to the harm
caused by the policies of enforced marginalization. The prime minister was silent about genocide – that is, the killing of Indigenous people by British and French colonial powers who set about to destroy
Indigenous communities to clear the way for the theft of Indigenous
land by European settlers. The prime minister was also silent about
the ongoing violation of Treaties made with Indigenous nations. He
did not refer to the ways in which colonialism and militarism had
produced unjust enrichment flowing into the coffers of business and
government elites in Canada, England, and France. He said nothing
about the flip side of this wealth transfer: the destruction and impoverishment of Indigenous communities in Canada, with continuing
reverberations today, as evidenced by the tragically high rates of suicide, imprisonment, and poverty among Indigenous peoples. Lastly,
successive governments have been silent about the ongoing, underlying purpose of "termination" policies that formally began with the
1969 White Paper, and that seek to divest Canada's Aboriginal people
of historical rights and land title through the dismantling of the
Treaties and the repealing of the Indian Act.

But it is worse than silence. There is also hypocrisy. On the one
hand, there is this apology, but on the other hand, then prime minister Harper and his Conservative Government during the 2010s used
the power of the government of Canada to make sure that First
Nations Treaty negotiations did not result in recognition of Aboriginal title to land in their territories. As Arthur Manuel points out in
the book *Unsettling Canada: A National Wake-Up Call,* the current
Treaty process is flawed:

It is demanding that First Nations be willing to extinguish their Aboriginal title and rights before they enter negotiations. The way the policy works, Canada concedes nothing but gains everything before the negotiations even start. This bears no resemblance to the process of recognition and reconciliation that the Supreme Court has called for, and everything that is wrong with the negotiations flows from this. Since Canada does not admit to the existence of Aboriginal title, there is no recognition that Indigenous peoples actually own the lands and resources within their territories. (Manuel and Grand Chief Derrickson 2015: 203)

If this federal policy is allowed to continue, the mining, lumber, oil, and gas companies can continue their extractive activities as in the past, without paying attention to the needs and perspectives of First Nations people on whose land these companies operate. This approach is in direct opposition to Supreme Court rulings on consultation and illustrates how colonialism is hardly a thing of the past, but continues today in various guises. As we move toward reconciliation we should be mindful of Saul Alinsky's reminder that true reconciliation does not mean that "one side gets the power and the other side gets reconciled to it." (Alinksy 1971: 13)

Most of us are not aware of the benefits we receive every day from colonialism, privilege that can be seen as forms of illegitimate privilege, as we did nothing to earn them.

To understand the nature of colonial privilege, we need to understand that for hundreds of years England, France, Spain, Portugal, and other European nations used a combination of violence, gunboat diplomacy, deceit, and trade to exploit people and territories across the globe. Up to the 1950s, public-school classroom walls in Canada featured world maps showing the British Empire coloured pink across large chunks of different parts of the Earth. Students were taught about colonization in benign terms. For example, "voyages of discovery" brought "civilized" values to the rest of the world. Much later, some of us realized "discovery" really meant conquest, frequently accompanied by blood-soaked legacies of slavery and genocide. Ramesh Thakur (2004), senior vice-rector of the United Nations University in Tokyo, had this to say about the nations that practised colonialism around the world: "In the name of enlightenment, they defiled our lands, plundered our resources and expanded their empires."

Public education content on colonialism was not neutral. It promoted Christianity, competitive, capitalist economics, and legitimized racism around the world. This oppression has been well documented (Royal Commission on Aboriginal Peoples 1996; Sinclair, Hart, and Bruyere 2009; Strega and Sohki Aski Esquao 2009; Czyzewski and Tester 2014, Brittain and Blackstock 2015).

Michael Anthony Hart (Kaskitemahikan) from the Fisher River Cree Nation in Southern Manitoba points out (2009b; see also Hart 2015) that colonialism continues today in Canada. It is

> driven by a worldview and processes that embrace dominion, self-righteousness and greed, and affects all levels of Indigenous peoples' lives – the national, communal, familial and individual – and insidiously interferes with all aspects of Indigenous peoples' lives, including their spiritual practices, emotional wellbeing, physical health and knowledge. (26–27)

Before we get any further, we need to clarify some terms. The Constitution Act of 1982 refers to Aboriginal peoples consisting of Indian, Métis, and Inuit peoples of Canada. Instead of *Aboriginal* in this book, we will usually use the term *Indigenous* as it refers to any location's original inhabitants. Instead of *Indian*, we prefer *First Nations* to remind us who were the first nations to inhabit Canada. The Assembly of First Nations uses this term to refer to their membership, many of whom live on reserves or territory assigned by the federal government. *Métis* are people of mixed European and First Nations ancestry and who identify within a unique Métis culture. *Inuit* generally refers to Indigenous people living north of the tree line, near Canada's Arctic coast. In summary, within Canada, Indigenous people include First Nations, Inuit, and Métis.

INDIGENOUS CHILD REMOVAL SYSTEM AND THE "SIXTIES SCOOP"

Although the crimes against Indigenous children in residential schools across Canada have become relatively well known, less well known are the ways that social workers have harmed Indigenous peoples. For example, the "Sixties Scoop" refers to the widespread practice, starting before the 1960s, of social workers forcibly removing Aboriginal children from their families and sending them to non-Aboriginal foster homes, group homes, or out for adoption, all with the approval of the courts. Some of the foster parents or adoptive parents were indifferent or hostile to Indigenous culture, believing that they were "saving" the children from unhealthy and uncaring circumstances.

One of our authors Raven Sinclair (Otiskewapiwskew) researched the "Sixties Scoop" and notes that even today Indigenous children are still being swept into the child welfare system in disproportionately high numbers (2009a: 94; 2007; 2016). As a result, she is applying a more appropriate term – the Indigenous Child Removal System – which spans the late 1940s to the present day and encapsulates all who were adopted transracially as well as those who were taken into foster care or institutionalized in group homes and institutions. Indeed, Cindy Blackstock, from the Gitksan Nation and executive director of the First Nations Child and Family Caring Society of Canada, finds that the number of Indigenous children in care outside their own homes today is three times the number of children in residential schools at the height of their operation. (Blackstock 2006: 163; Brittain and Blackstock 2015: 60–80). In 2004 Laurie Gilchrist coined the term for child welfare overrepresentation as the "Millennium Scoop," and with the ongoing adoption of Indigenous children by non-Indigenous foster families who use policy and legislation to win their cases, Raven believes we are facing a "Foster Care Scoop" (Sinclair 2016). For Raven, this research is more than an academic inquiry. She was one of the children removed from their homes by child welfare services during this period. In her own research, Raven also finds that researchers and practitioners who focus on Aboriginal children raised in non-Aboriginal homes tend to emphasize the loss of cultural identity as a primary theme. Sinclair challenges that approach:

> From the stories, narratives and testimonials of adoptees, many Aboriginal adoptees have struggled greatly to "fit" into White society outside of their family context. . . . The problem with viewing identity as the issue is that the focus of the problem then rests with the child. The literature thus states that adolescents "no longer fit" rather than "a racialized society does not allow them to fit." (Sinclair 2009a: 104)

Her analysis is affirmed by Coleen Rajotte, a Sixties Scoop survivor who grew up in a white, middle-class home, and who says, "I know the feeling of not fitting in while growing up, the feeling of being alone in a crowded room, of being uncomfortable and ashamed." She and other Sixties Scoop survivors had met with Manitoba Premier Greg Selinger, who on June 18, 2015, formally apologized in the Manitoba legislature for the Sixties Scoop and for "the harm it caused and continues to cause for survivors, their families and descendants" (Kush 2015: A3).

As a collective response to generations of imposed assimilation policies, Indigenous community members are today engaged in an intensive revitalization of their cultural traditions, ceremonies, and spirituality. Along with cultural revival, there has been an upsurge of political awareness that recently galvanized into a cross-Canada Indigenous social movement: Idle No More. Over the last few years, this series of grass roots mobilizations within Indigenous communities from coast to coast took Canadians by surprise. Members of Indigenous communities, especially its youth, are insisting on answers to questions such as, "Why are we being excluded from new government decisions about water, minerals, and land on which we live? Why are the Treaties made by our ancestors being ignored? Who is gaining financial wealth at whose expense?" (The Kino-nda-niimi Collective 2014).

Banakonda

The Truth and Reconciliation Commission's call for action clearly states that the very same tool used to colonialize, violate, and destabilize families, communities, nations, cultures, and the land is the same tool that has the ability to direct reclamation. That tool is education. Indigenous education must become a pathway within all levels of learning institutions. In the academy, such pathways need to include all disciplines, ranging from the physical sciences and social sciences to the humanities. In this way we will navigate restitution, reciprocity, restoration, and recovery.

These challenges place a public spotlight on the fact that business corporations, local and international, after token consultations with the affected communities, continue to do business as usual in planning and implementing the extraction of timber, mining, oil, gas, water, and other parts of nature from traditional Indigenous territories. The main role of governments has been to support these corporations, for example, by dismantling previous environmental protections over rivers, lakes, and other dumping grounds for toxic waste, as in the Canadian Omnibus Bill of 2012.

TODAY'S COLONIALISM

While such trashing of the environment is causing growing opposition among Indigenous people and their non-Indigenous allies, it places a focus on private industries and financial institutions as the force driving forward today's version of colonialism. As we consider the private sector, its major corporations, including banks and their linkages to international trade, we begin to understand the huge power they have to influence Canadian society. These powerful corporate elites have increasingly had the co-operation of governments in dismantling social services and other government supports, cutting taxes for the rich and corporations while encouraging Canadians to turn to the private market for all their needs.

Known as neoliberalism, this form of politics and economy is deeply conservative, and restructures society to be increasingly polarized between a small number of very wealthy people and a growing number of people struggling to get by. Neoliberal ideas and platforms blame people who experience growing social problems and advocate for more tax cuts, resulting in service cuts to social programs and social services. This means funding for the social safety net is drying up at the very time when there is an increased demand for these services due to an economy that does not have enough decent jobs for all. Moreover, neoliberal attitudes stigmatize those unable to get ahead in the cut throat competition of advanced neoliberal capitalism. In other words, more and more Canadians are caught up in the negative consequences of more and more inequality (Ng 2015).

One way to measure inequality is to follow the money; that is, to calculate wealth disparity or who actually has money in this society and who does not. Researchers have done this, providing us with a sense of the gap between the rich and poor. For example, in 2012 the top 10 per cent of wealthy Canadians owned 48 per cent of all the wealth in Canada, while the bottom 30 per cent of people account for less than 1 per cent of all wealth (Broadbent Institute 2014). It's our sense that unless there is a strong public outcry this wealth gap will continue to sow ever deeper division among Canadians. A similar process is happening at the international level where the concentration of wealth has been documented by numerous studies. The share of the world's wealth owned by the richest 1 per cent increased from 44 per cent in 2009 to 48 per cent last year (Oxfam 2015).

But are these growing inequalities really so bad? After all, don't we have charities, social services, and social programs to assist the disadvantaged? To find out how these programs were managing, Canada's federal government, along with the national associations of social work educators and practitioners, conducted an extensive study of the social services sector.[1] Researchers surveyed 109 social service employers and carried out over 300 in-depth interviews of social service managers, educators, and employees. Reporting over fifteen years ago, the study finds these programs not doing well:

> Increased workloads, having to do more with less, and service users who are experiencing more intense, multi-dimensional challenges to their social, psychological and economic survival – all contribute significantly to making social service employment extremely demanding and sometimes very dispiriting. (Stephenson, Rondeau, Michaud, and Fidler 2000: 2)

Today, many years after this report was published, the situation continues to deteriorate. Social justice activists see direct links between the deterioration of social services, the growth of indifference toward

---

1 The terms *social agencies* and *social services* are often used interchangeably. Social agencies and social services are organizations that employ social service providers to deliver programs to people who are called *service users* or *consumers* or *clients*. Social service providers may be social workers or more generally social service workers.

the poor, and the expansion of inequalities in Canada. But there are still those who ask, are these trends really so bad?

The answers vary. In the first place, there are sharply opposing opinions about the sources and consequences of inequalities. These disagreements seem to have less to do with a recognition of "hard facts" and more to do with personal values, attitudes, and views about what is fair. People who see nothing wrong with inequalities point to our different talents. They begin by presenting a reasonable case for rewarding not only different talents, but also hard work and a willingness to take risks. From this position, they take a giant leap and suggest that inequalities between rich and poor are caused entirely by personal choices. In other words, they argue, anyone can become financially successful by choosing to be enterprising, working very hard, and simply having talent.

According to this social construction of "choice," if people choose to be lazy or refuse to work, they will be poor. Poverty, therefore, is a simple matter of choice – and if people live in poverty, too bad, because "they choose it through their irresponsible behaviour." Therefore, the argument goes, social services must be minimal. "Why should we help people, when their poverty is their own fault?"

INDIVIDUALISM AND PRIVILEGE

This way of understanding poverty extols great wealth as a condition brought about entirely through a person's own merits. Sometimes called *meritocracy*, this view justifies huge inequalities as a fair outcome of conditions deemed to be based on either wonderful private achievements or dismal personal failures. In this approach, well-being hinges entirely on individual efforts and making the right choices. This line of thought is also known as *individualism*.

Conservative, neoliberal ideology assumes that everyone has the same choice and therefore everyone has to accept the consequences of the choices they make. Furthermore, this perspective asserts that government should not interfere with these outcomes. Indeed, conservative, neoliberal ideology claims that the "best government is the least government" – a government that allows individuals to remain in charge of their own destinies so long as they do not interfere with the same rights of others. According to this theory of individualism, the incentive to succeed and excel is a positive force that fuels our economy and instructs us how best to avoid poverty.

By contrast, people who challenge the growth of inequalities emphasize values of equity and inclusion. They argue that the huge financial wealth of a small group of elites has little or nothing to do with their individual merit – but a lot to do with systems and attitudes that privilege a few and create disadvantage for many. Those who defend inequality are doing their best to hide the full story about why some people have power over others. In our view, it is not power itself that is problematic. After all, parents have been granted legitimate power over their young children, and social services are sometimes called in when this power is abused. Similarly, teachers have legitimate power over young students; again, if this power is abused, the educational institution or justice system should become involved. However, danger exists when power is illegitimate – power that advances the privilege of one group of people who abuse the well-being of others.

The term *privilege* refers to benefits received by one group at the expense of another group, due to the way in which economic and political power is organized in society. Economic and political power in our society is organized in ways that give advantages to some people at the expense of others, in a sort of zero-sum game, instead of recognizing that if we share things more equally we all benefit and society rises together. The injustices of conservative, neoliberal systems are often not widely recognized as unfair because these unequal power relationships are justified as "normal." To achieve social justice we need to expose and de-legitimate these unjust power inequalities, while simultaneously building new relations and systems that meet people's needs with dignity and fairness.

The word *privilege* is often used in our culture to refer to desirable situations – we say, for instance, "It's a privilege to know you." In this book, we use the terms *illegitimate privilege* and *unjustified privilege* to alert readers to the harmful, divisive, and oppressive sense of the term. The other reason for our using the term *illegitimate privilege* is because conservative ideology tries to convince us that the privileged have earned their greater power and status, and therefore our economic system need not be questioned. By deconstructing the term privilege, it becomes possible to gain fresh understanding about the ways that inequalities are caused and justified. Or, as social work scholar Bob Mullaly observes, "the flip side of the coin of oppression is privilege. . . . If we want to truly understand oppression, we must understand oppression and privilege go hand in hand" (2010: 287).

To understand privilege, we need to recognize the contradictions and serious double standards related to how wealth acquisition, economic production, laws, policies, institutions, subjective perceptions, and populist narratives maintain and legitimize privilege for some people (extensive education, business or employment connections, large inheritances) while creating huge barriers for others (racism, frail health due to childhood poverty, few job opportunities, inadequate housing, etc.). In short, the structures of our society favour some people and punish others (McKenzie 2010; Torjman 2015). These imbalances are called *systemic inequalities* because they are created by society's structures, also known as the "system" within which we live. Here again Banakonda encourages us to reflect back to her opening words about incongruence. Kindness, honesty, sharing, and strength are pathways to congruency. Incongruence, by contrast, is not only hidden but nullified in the belief of entitlement associated with privilege.

Conservative and neoliberal elites do not see, much less recognize, these systemic injustices. Elites tend to be rich, White, heterosexual, able-bodied, non-Indigenous males. By contrast, the people who are systemically deprived of affluence and power tend to be Indigenous people, Black Canadians, Hispanics, and other racialized groups, lesbians, gays, bisexual, transgender and intersex people, unemployed or underemployed young adults, and a disproportion number of women and people with disabilities. Many of these people work very hard, often at more than one job, yet they barely make ends meet or live in poverty. Some people among the affluent class also work very hard, but the excessive financial rewards they gain from doing so are out of proportion to their effort and talents. Chief executive officers of the top 100 Canadian corporations had pocketed "on average, $8.96 million in 2014" – that's 184 times more than the average wage in Canada (Mackenzie 2016).

Unequal incomes and opportunities are part of the picture. Another part is the way that the pressure groups of rich elites have disproportionate influence on government policies, which leads to policies favouring the rich. For example, Professor Emeritus John McMurtry argues that affluent people have influenced our tax system to favour themselves. He calls this a war of the rich against the poor:

> The war is waged at all levels of the tax system. Ever more tax evasion, off-shore banking, tax loopholes, transfer pricing and corporate shell companies combine with ever lower upfront tax rates for the wealthy and big business and extravagant tax and other subsidies to transnational oil corporations, factory agribusiness, weapons manufactures. (McMurtry 2009: 1)

A massive leak of 11.5 million records in 2016 revealed a vast global industry providing off-shore tax shelters for tax avoidance. Known as the "Panama Papers," this leak provides powerful evidence of the ways that rich elites have quietly influenced tax policies. As the *Toronto Star* noted, "Affluent Canadians and corporations have some $200 billion in declared assets stashed away in tax havens, costing government as much as $8 billion a year in lost revenue" (*Toronto Star*, Editorial 2016: A12; see also McQuaig 2016; Mayer 2016). Tax evasion and tax cuts mean less revenue collected, which translates into steep cuts in public services, including harsh cuts in social programs. For people seeking social services assistance, the decrease in funding for social programs means that they encounter less help and more bureaucratic hurdles. Yet, the need for services is always higher when poverty and inequality are higher.

Ruth Latta reports on a project by Richard Wilkinson and Kate Pickett, who study wealth patterns in numerous countries and find that social problems "are related to the distribution of wealth in a society, not to its overall wealth." These researchers conclude that based on data from the world's twenty richest countries, "the bigger the income gap, the worse the rates of mental illness, substance abuse, teen pregnancy, male violence, homicide, incarceration, and short life expectancy" (Latta 2009: 17; Wilkinson and Pickett 2014). In other words, greater inequalities lead to more problems.

PROGRESSIVE SOCIAL WORK

As progressive social work educators and social activists, we strongly oppose the policies, beliefs, and practices that are rapidly creating more inequality in Canada and around the world. Our opposition to this systemic inequality comes from our recognition that greater inequalities are not inevitable, but come from human decisions based on faulty subjective assumptions and harmful systemic structures that cater to only one segment of the population. Better decisions are possible and critically urgent if we want to reverse the current trends, harmful to so many people, and build a more just and caring society.

It is critical to build a future where democracy is strengthened, where no one individual, group or class benefits at the expense of others, and where social services and social programs are able to contribute to social and economic justice. We agree with the values expressed by Indigenous leader Arthur Manuel: "There is room on this land for all of us and there must also be, after centuries of struggle, room for justice for Indigenous people. That is all we ask. And we will settle for nothing less" (Manuel 2015: 12).

3 NAMING AND RESISTING INJUSTICES

The earth has enough for the needs of all, but not for the greed of the few. — Mahatma Gandhi

First the bad news: In Canada and worldwide, social injustices come in many shapes and forms and have deep roots. These roots are extensive and not easily dislodged. Some people reap handsome benefit from injustice and usually work hard to protect, enlarge, and entrench their privilege. They benefit from their privilege being invisible and a taken-for-granted aspect of social life. Those in positions of power often ridicule, marginalize, intimidate, and silence those who expose this unfair privilege. A review of these injustices can be discouraging; we can sense the despair and hopelessness experienced by people trapped in oppressive conditions through no fault of their own and we find ourselves unsure of how to proceed in the face of long-standing inequalities and injustice.

Now the good news: These injustices are being challenged in many ways, and some victories have been won in the struggle for greater equity in our society. Many people on their own or as part of networks and organizations have concluded that equity, inclusion, and democratic accountability are not only possible and desirable, but also critically urgent. These equity seekers, both inside and outside of social services, are joining together to learn and to educate others. They are advocating, organizing, demonstrating, and mobilizing public support for greater social justice. Part of this process is the discovery and naming of various sets of privilege. We will talk more about these struggles in subsequent chapters but now we turn to forms of privilege in Canadian society and beyond.

COLONIAL PRIVILEGE

Progressive people in Canadian mainstream society find it disturbing to learn that Whites considered themselves so "superior" that they forcibly imposed their religions, economies, and racism on people around the world in past eras – including on the Indigenous people in what came to be called Canada. This history of white supremacy, buttressed by racism, has been well documented (Royal Commission on Aboriginal Peoples 1996; Sinclair 2009b: 19–24; Strega and Sohki Aski Esquao 2009; King 2012; Truth and Reconciliation Commission of Canada 2014; Cyzerwski and Tester 2014; Brittain and Blackstock 2015).

One example is found in a report issued by the B.C. provincial government:

> Europeans did not only bring cultural chauvinism to North America. They also brought concepts of land use and ownership that thinly veiled the most systematic theft of land in the history of human existence. Because Europeans had a view of Nature as a thing to be brought under human control, lands that were not so dominated were considered unused. Coupled with that view was the concept of private land ownership. Consequently, "undeveloped" land was unused land and unused land was unowned land. Based on this cultural justification, Europeans were to engage in, and condone, a violation of their own international laws regarding the relations between nations. They confiscated virtually all the territories of the Aboriginal Nations of North America. (Aboriginal Committee, Community Panel 1992: 14)

Nevertheless, most people who immigrate to North America from Europe and other parts of the world generally have a lack of awareness of their colonial privilege. Individuals and families who have migrated to Canada within the past centuries often do not see that, along with their immediate circles of family, friends, and colleagues, they gain benefits from an infrastructure of institutions located in towns and cities and on land that is available to them only because of the violent displacement of the original inhabitants.

When Banakonda outlines the Four Foundational Principles of Indigenous Traditional Practice, in this book's first chapter, she applies its principles of kindness, honesty, sharing, and strength: gifts that students bring with them in their helping relationships. But these principles can also be applied on a larger scale to a process like colonialism. If we apply these main principles, it becomes obvious that when perpetrators of colonialism engaged in invasion, massacres, and theft of land, they violated the principles of kindness, honesty, and sharing. First Nations, Inuit, and Métis communities ended up in positions of marginalization and subordination (Allan and Smylie 2015). Those of us who continue to benefit from this history are also in violation of these principles if we do not make ourselves aware of colonialism's continuing impacts, so that we can engage in decolonization. Colonial privilege, like other forms of privilege, operates on a taken-for-granted level in which the injustice is largely concealed in the day-to-day operations of social life. Those who raise the subject are accused of being disruptive, wrong, rude, and of overstating their cases. This invisibility makes it difficult to confront privilege in everyday life.

The invisibility of colonial privilege can be seen as a form of evasion from honestly facing the history of genocide against Indigenous people in the Americas. The United Nations General Assembly in 1948 adopted the following Convention to define genocide: "any of the following acts committed with intent to destroy, in whole or in part, a national, ethnical, racial or religious group" by "forcibly transferring children of the group to another group" (United Nations 1948). There are different types of genocides; residential schools were the made-in-Canada government genocidal policy perpetrated against Indigenous people. Indigenous leaders and their supporters contend that this genocide is still continuing in the ongoing dispossession, violation of Treaties, and the escalating poisoning of the territorial environment in which Indigenous people live. This includes fracking, tar sands "development," pipeline seepages, polluted lakes and rivers from toxic waste by wood mills and other commercial development, clear-cutting of forests, and further threats from oil and gas companies drilling in the arctic and in other areas.

Colonial privilege is present when those of us in mainstream are able to carry on with our daily lives as if these ongoing incursions on Indigenous lands and peoples were not happening. When we do this, we remain oblivious to the ongoing harm being inflicted upon Indigenous people. A feature of colonial privilege, as well as other forms of illegitimate privilege is that it bounces back against the instigators of such privilege and their backers, and the rest of us who acquiesce. Colonial privilege generates a sense of entitlement causing many of us to remain oblivious to the harm inflicted upon ourselves from the very same activities that create havoc for Indigenous people. As our health continues to deteriorate, we fail to recognize the link to industrial, toxic waste seeping into the water, the soil, and the air.

On the one hand, while scientists warn about the threats to life on the planet from climate change driven by the fossil fuel industries, on the other hand, the owners of these industries, their managers, their distributors, their consumers, and apologists either make excuses or become staunch climate change deniers. Their attitudes gain credibility as mainstream opinion leaders, including many CEOs, politicians, teachers, clergy, and the media, play a key role in constructing narratives that deny or minimize these environmental dangers, and that distort history in ways that obscure the harm from colonialism, past and present.

Until recently students learned little or nothing about this history in school and the popular media. As a result, little has been done to expose or critique the systems that hold colonial privilege in place and to examine who mainly benefits from it. While the Statue of Liberty in New York City may symbolize the successful escape of many Europeans from the political oppression, famine, and high unemployment of their original homes, these newcomers did not share their new-found freedom and improved living conditions with the original inhabitants of this continent. Nor did they all find wealth and freedom.

The rugged individualism that has been glorified as part of early European settlement of this continent usually insulted the original inhabitants by seeing them as subhuman impediments who needed to be removed or absorbed into White society. As a result, Indigenous nations were pushed onto the least desirable tracts of land, and their mobility was restricted by agents of the Canadian government in an attempt to remake the economy and culture of Indigenous communities in forms that met capitalism's need for cheap labour and the private acquisition of land (Baines and Freeman 2011: 67–80). In these and many other ways, the assumption and impacts of colonial privilege violated all the Four Foundational Principles of Indigenous Traditional Practice, as well as contravened international law.

Colonial oppression does not stand alone; it feeds into and is reinforced by other systemic violations, such as racism.

RACISM AND PRIVILEGE

Anti-racist educator Peggy McIntosh learned a key personal lesson about racism in what she was taught not to see: "As a White person, I realized I had been taught about racism as something which puts others at a disadvantage, but I had been taught not to see one of its corollary aspects, white privilege, which puts me at an advantage." McIntosh suggests that each White person write out a list of the privileges they experience based on their whiteness. The purpose is to identify privileges in "taken for granted" areas and move them into critical consciousness. She gives examples of her invisible privilege: "I can be sure that if I need legal or medical help, my race will not work against me," and "I am never asked to speak for all the people of my racial group" (1998: 147–50; see also McIntosh 2007). McIntosh's list also includes noticing that her whiteness is not only well represented in history books but is also prominent among people favourably portrayed by the media.

Inasmuch as McIntosh alerts us to the unearned benefits of whiteness, others, such as author and anti-racist researcher Zeus Leonard, advocate going beyond white privilege:

A critical look at white privilege, or the analysis of white racial hegemony, must be complemented by an equally rigorous examination of white supremacy, or the analysis of white racial domination. This is a necessary departure because, although the two processes are related, the condition of white supremacy make white privilege possible. In order for white racial hegemony to saturate everyday life, it has to be secured by a process of domination, or those acts, decisions, and policies that white subjects perpetrate on people of colour. As such, a critical pedagogy of white racial supremacy revolves less around the issue of unearned privilege, or the state of being dominant, and more around direct processes that secure domination and the privileges associated with it. (Leonardo 2009: 261)

Racism is pervasive in Canada today, and it is a contentious issue. For example, social service managers typically become indignant when critics suggest that they are implicated in what amounts to racist practices. Their indignation implies that they view racism as restricted to the intentional conduct of bigots, however there are many kinds and forms of racism. To unravel its different levels Frances Henry and Carol Tator (2010: 41–46) differentiate between three interactive categories of racism: individual, institutional-systemic, and cultural-ideological. They describe individual racism attitudes and everyday behaviour based on unquestioned beliefs about the superiority of the person's own racial group and about the inferiority of other groups. Individual racism is usually deliberate and expresses itself in glances, gestures, forms of speech, and physical movements.

> Sometimes it is not even consciously experienced by its perpetrators, but it is immediately and painfully felt by its victims – the empty seat next to a person of colour, which is the last to be occupied in a crowded bus; the slight movement away from a person of colour in an elevator; the over-attention to the Black customer in the shop; the inability to make direct eye contact with a person of colour. (44)

Derald Wing Sue et al. (2007) explain these experiences as racial micro-aggressions: the "brief and commonplace daily verbal, behavioural, or environmental indignities, whether intentional or unintentional, that communicate hostile, derogatory, or negative racial insights toward people of color" (271).

Building on individual racism, institutional racism expresses itself in an institution's policies, practices, and procedures in ways that create advantage or privilege for certain racialized people. At the institutional level, racism also does not have to be intentional. Rather, it is the outcome of exclusion – in, for example, the rejection of equity hiring practices or relying on "word-of-mouth-recruitment" that generally excludes racial minorities (Henry and Tator 2010: 44). Systemic racism, although similar to institutional racism refers to laws, rules, and norms woven into society, which "result in an unequal distribution of economic, political and social resources and rewards among various racial groups" (45). Institutional and systemic racism result in dynamics of group subordination that disempower the marginalized and extend the privileges of the White majority (Gutiérrez y Muhs et al. 2012: 4). For example, Canada's political and economic elites remain primarily White, while the general population is increasingly globalized and mixed in colour.

Henry and Tator find a third category they call cultural and ideological racism, which possibly preceded individual and institutional racism and certainly accompanies them. It consists of overarching cultural symbols that reinforce both individual and institutional forms of racism. These symbols include ideas and values expressed through language, religion, the media, and art and are deeply woven – for example, by the mass media and the arts – into the fabric of mainstream culture (Henry and Tator: 2010: 45–46). For example, the words "black" and "dark" tend to be associated with something bad, such as "blackmail," "black sheep," "blacklisted," "dark moods," and "dark motives," while the ideas of "white" and "light" tend to be associated with being clean, pure, and inspiring.

Henry and her co-authors point out that racism is a social construction of difference and serves to reproduce existing power relationships. Similar to colonialism, racism in Canada causes whiteness to remain largely invisible as the "normal" reference point for judging different ethno-racialized groups (Henry and Tator 2010: 46; see also Calgary Anti-Racism Education 2015; Pon, Gosine, and Phillips 2011). In Canada, for example, the deliberate construction of difference through media misrepresentation (Harding 2006) can undermine social support for political or economic assertions made by Indigenous people, who instead become the subjects of harsh social criticism and negative judgments. Needless to say, racial privilege and colonialism go hand in hand. Since one dimension of racism is to dehumanize the "other," it becomes much easier for people acting on their colonial privilege to massacre, subordinate, and exploit Indigenous individuals, families, communities, and nations when they are perceived as subhuman. Plus the overlap between racial privilege and colonial privilege produces narratives that make it easier to "justify" this history by viewing Europeans as more "advanced" and "needing" to expand their economies and empires. Indigenous people were seen, and continue to be seen, as in "need" of the technology, religion, and the new social organization imposed on them by colonial powers.

In addition to the abusive treatment of Indigenous people and African Canadians, which began centuries ago, later examples of racism in Canada include the exploitation of Chinese railway workers, the mistreatment of Japanese Canadians during the Second World War, and the denial of immigration to Jews seeking refuge from Nazi regimes, to name a few. A current and pressing example is racial profiling by police departments (Gillis 2015).

Given that racism pervades all of the country's institutions, it is no surprise that it also infects social services. That is why we recommend that anti-racist education be a regular part of professional development among social service providers to raise awareness about both the hidden and not-so-hidden dynamics of racial domination, so that we can work for change.

CLASS PRIVILEGE

Though some Canadians live opulent lifestyles while others barely eke out a living, there is a huge sense of denial about class privilege and class stratification in our society. This denial creates the illusion of equity – fostered by a conservative ideology that justifies class differences as due to the hard work, talent, and skills of individuals. Similar to the invisibility of privilege derived from colonialism and racism, the consequences of class privilege are often seen as "natural," or are hidden from view. Rich elites have developed elaborate ways of expanding their class privileges and hiding the harmful consequences of their actions. The rich, for instance, benefit from the largely hidden privilege of an undue and undemocratic influence over the direction of Canadian society. Their special interest groups are the most powerful in the country – from the Canadian Chamber of Commerce and Canadian Manufacturers and Exporters to the C.D. Howe Institute and Fraser Institute and a host of other business and right-wing political lobbies. Their messages are further amplified by a repeated chorus of editorials from media outlets, almost all of them managed and owned by wealthy individuals or corporations.

The Business Council of Canada, formerly known as the Canadian Council of Chief Executives, for instance, represents 150 of Canada's biggest corporations, with assets totalling over $7.5 trillion (Business Council of Canada 2016). With its relatively easy access to top public officials, this Council argues that reductions to both corporate and personal income tax rates are essential. We ask, "essential for whom?" Who elected these business groups to be our spokespersons? When they say "we know what Canada needs," we want to know who did they ask, apart from economists on their payroll and other highly privileged CEOs? Yet in the end, what these big-business pressure groups ask for is delivered by governments: significant tax cuts for corporations and for the wealthy.

Meanwhile, tax cuts – in combination with other unfair taxation policies – have a devastating impact on Canadian well-being: they cause a significant deterioration in our public health, public education, public libraries, and other public services. Tax cuts also result in deep setbacks for the delivery of social services, with especially devastating effects on people living in poverty. With big holes in what used to be the social safety net (that is the social services and social supports available to Canadians), more and more people are homeless or near-homeless (Shapcott 2012; Canadian Broadcasting Corporation 2013).

Economist Hugh Mackenzie's review of Canadian statistics on the growing rich-poor gap concludes: "Our provincial and federal governments have been talking tax cuts [for everyone], but those cuts went into the pockets of the richest of the rich. And that tax break only bolstered the unprecedented growth in the share of income going to Canada's richest" (2010; see also Canadians for Tax Fairness 2015). Something is terribly wrong when government policies, such as tax cuts, result in substantial benefits for the rich and privileged few in society, while the same policies cause a great many others to lose the benefit of a variety of public services – and the steepest loss is experienced, again and again, by the poorest of the poor.

These inequitable outcomes are reinforced by so-called free trade agreements that encourage global corporations to shop around for nations that offer the most favourable conditions for profit. These agreements also contribute to gross corporate irresponsibility, environmental degradation, misuse of Indigenous lands and national preserves, and the growing polarization of the rich and poor. Free trade legislation gives corporations even more opportunity to move to lower wage regions in search of higher profits. But lower wage regions are generally very oppressive and exploitive, and sometimes they are environments where labour union leaders and other resisters are assassinated, while governments slash taxes and ignore environmental protection. Supporting this entrenchment of global corporate privileges is the World Bank and the International Monetary Fund (IMF). These non-elected, undemocratic institutions establish global financial procedures that enforce unjust and harsh conditions for loans and credits to poor nations. These processes hurt poor nations by cutting their social programs, selling off their public resources, removing food subsidies and violating other human rights (Lundy 2011: 10; Klein 2014; Hedges 2015a, 2015b).

An eloquent voice for more authentic democracy comes from one of India's leading physicists, Vandana Shiva: "Democracy is not merely an electoral ritual but the power of people to shape their destiny, determine how their natural resources are owned and utilized, how their thirst is quenched, how their food is produced and distributed, and what health and education systems they have" (2002: xv; also Democracy Now 2014). Shiva's advocacy for systemic accountability is a good reminder that greater democracy will mean placing limits on top-down, unaccountable power, including class privilege. Therefore, as progressive social workers, we are on the right track in resisting and challenging class privilege when we push to expand the scope and effectiveness of our democratic institutions (Klein and Yalnizyan 2010; LaBerge 2010; Hedges, 2015c; McGuaig and Brooks, 2012). Whether from within social work or outside of it, social activists find that as we challenge the racialized and colonized privileges of class, we encounter other sources of systemic inequalities.

Patriarchal Privilege

Feminists have taught us that gender inequality is entirely social, not biological. Gender inequality (along with all the other inequalities) is built into the way we organize who takes care of whom, and who participates in what way in paid work, society's structures, and social meanings. In short, we assign different kinds of meaning and status to different activities and develop complex social, culture, legal, and religious understandings around them to naturalize and rationalize patriarchal domination and privilege by males.

The devaluation of women's reproductive and other social roles involves, among other things, a mix of restrictions: legal, economic, social, and psychological. While different waves of feminism have challenged these complex restrictions, gender inequalities remain. One of the most dangerous relics of patriarchal privilege is the belief that men have the "right" to boss women around and to punish them for "disobedience." The Canadian Network of Women's Shelters and Transition Houses report that in one day 242 emergency shelters across the country help 4,178 women survivors of abuse and 2,490 children (Canadian Network of Women's Shelters and Transition Houses 2014).

About a decade ago, approximately 350 shelters existed across Canada where women and their children could seek safety from abusive relationships. As of 2012, Statistics Canada finds that there are 601 shelters for abused women operating across Canada (Mazowita and Burczycka 2014). This survey also finds that hundreds of women and children are being turned away on any given day because many shelters are filled to capacity. Even when women have their day in court, public attitudes are still prone to be one-sided, as this study by Dawn Hemingway, Clarie Johnson, and Brenda Roland, finds:

> With sexual violence, the level of scrutiny is such that the onus is entirely on the victim to prove her victimization and face the court of judgement about her character. Is she moral or immoral? Was she in the wrong place at the wrong time or did she "ask for it"? Myths rooted in the oppression and exploitation of women declare that sexual assault is inevitable and part of the natural order of things; that women are assaulted only because they have poor judgement, put themselves in dangerous situations, follow a particular lifestyle, wear a short skirt, or have a drink or two. Even implementation of the 1983 Rape Shield Law . . . intended to restrict court testimony regarding a woman's sexual history or character, has failed to halt accusations and innuendo that blamed the victim. Women continue to be silenced. (2010: 84; See also Borel 2016; Garossino 2016.)

These painful experiences, sustained by patriarchal privilege, are interwoven with other systemic inequalities such as racism, colonialism, and class oppression. These oppressions are dynamically interconnected in ways that can deepen the sense of hopelessness and often mask their multiple sources. A case in point is the situation of Indigenous women in Canada whose experiences of oppression deeply contradict the roles and power held by women in traditional matriarchal societies. Indeed, Indigenous women are relegated to the lowest social strata of Canadian society as evidenced by the lack of concern, until recently, for the high number of missing and murdered Aboriginal women.

Though excluded from discussion in earlier times, issues identified by women of colour, lesbians, transgendered women, working-class women, and women with disabilities are now being heard in the women's movement and beyond it. While diversity is now part of the women's movement, and while the women's movement has succeeded in pressing for the development of shelters and other support services, women are often excluded from major decision making within large corporate and governmental institutions. The wage gap remains in place. Citing statistics Canada, the Centre for Families, Work and Well-Being notes that on average, female workers earn 72 cents for every dollar earned by a male worker. (Centre for Families, Work and Well-Being 2013). In addition, feminists point out that many women still suffer multiple jeopardy on a daily basis. As Martha Kuwee Kumsa explains:

> Women's multiple jeopardy refers to the double or triple day that most women assume when they take on paid work outside the home, unpaid care work in the home and unpaid, often unrecognized, advocacy, volunteer or activist work in the community. This compounded and often invisible workload can leave women feeling exhausted and exploited. (2007: 114)

Working within the women's movement, women developed innovative, fresh ways of helping women. Helen Levine, one of the early pillars in Canadian feminist social work, highlights features of feminist counselling:

It has to do with an approach, a feminist way of defining women's struggles and facilitating change. It is no mysterious, professional technique. The focus is on women helping women in a non-hierarchical, reciprocal and supportive way. . . . It rests on a critical analysis of the sexism embedded in the theory and practice of the helping professions. (1982: 199)

The women's movement put feminist counselling into practice in shelters and counselling centres for abused women and their children, often on shoestring budgets. As time went on, the movement struggled to make services for women more accessible and inclusive.

Although the silencing of women's voices continues, the women's movement has opened up many arenas in which patriarchal privilege is being challenged. As a result, many women have regained their voices, but there is a long way to go to achieve full gender equality. Along that road, feminists have helped us to recognize the intersections of gender with other oppressions (intersectionist sexism) (Feehan, Boettcher, and Quinn 2009: 64–68; Texler Segal and Martinez 2007; Hulko 2015; Hobbs and Rice 2013). For example, using the lens of anti-racism, feminists have examined the root causes of the government's failure to implement a national child-care program. More specifically, Canadian immigration policies have been complicit by granting only temporary work visas for women recruited from outside the country to immigrate and perform domestic work. This allows "the Canadian state to avoid the costs of a national childcare program" and enables middle-class women to participate in the labour force at the expense of the women of colour who get jobs as cheaply paid domestic workers (Dua 1999: 246).

Gendered ageism is another aspect of intersectionist sexism. Within mainstream society, until recently public policies demonstrated a certain success in improving people's incomes and well-being. In recent decades, the rate of poverty for all Canadians over sixty-five years old declined, though with recent and proposed changes to Old Age Security (OAS), these gains will be rolled back. While the Special Senate Committee on Aging reported (2009: 93) that while the incomes of older people have generally increased over the past few decades, this trend has not resulted in the elimination of poverty among Canadian older people. The intersections between gender inequality and ageism persist, and elderly women are still more than twice as susceptible to poverty as their male counterparts (Canada Without Poverty 2009: 4). Furthermore, according to the Canadian Association of Retired Persons (CARP), an advocacy organization for older adults, "the new StatsCan numbers better reflect what we've been hearing from our members – much more people than previously thought are struggling to get by, especially single seniors and convey a greater urgency to acting immediately to keep people out of poverty" (CARP 2014).

The *Encyclopedia of Aging* presents Robert Butler's definition of ageism "as a process of systematic stereotyping and discrimination" against older adults. Ageism can apply to attitudes toward the young as well as the old. In any case, as the *Encyclopedia* puts it, "Ageism is manifested in a wide range of phenomena (on both individual and institutional levels), stereotypes and myths, outright disdain and dislike, or simply subtle avoidance of contact; discriminatory practices in housing, employment, and services of all kinds; epithets, cartoons and jokes" (Butler 2001: 38). While ageism against older adults is still pervasive in Canada, the Canadian Network for the Prevention of Elder Abuse (2016), has identified ways to resist these harmful attitudes and practices.

Another consequence of ageism has been inadequate government support for social services in the area of long-term care. Sheila Neysmith notes that budget cuts to health and social services have resulted in caring responsibilities for older adults being off-loaded onto families. She warns: "There is no evidence that family members can provide the type of care delivered by a qualified nursing assistant or home-care worker. This off-loading onto families also results in services being moved off the public stage and rendered invisible by relocating them in the private sphere of family responsibility" (2012: 302). Much of the responsibilities for caring work within families are still taken up by women. Furthermore, women experience even greater indignities as they grow older. Neysmith notes: "Aging is a gendered process, so that women experience old age differently than men. One of these differences is that old women inhabit an aging body in a culture that devalues both old age and women" (2012: 301–2).). In opposition to conventional economics, which fails to recognize the financial contribution of women in raising children, organizing their households, and caring for its adult members, Neysmith recommends that we un-gender caring labour and establish a universal caregiver model.

> Under such a model, employment policies and job descriptions would have caring related rights and benefits that complement the health and pension benefits today. Promotion ladders that do not allow for caring responsibilities could be challenged as discriminatory. Doing so is pivotal if women's citizenship claims are to be realized. This will happen only if caring for others is seen as central to the lives of all citizens, as central as holding down a paid job, participating in community affairs, paying taxes, and being a consumer. (309)

Proposals for innovative policy changes are crucial if we are to undo oppression based on gender, age, and other forms of discrimination. The next step is to mobilize support for such changes. This also applies to a second version of ageism: as a condition that creates an illegitimate sense of adult superiority by denying the humanity of young people, relegating them to the state of objects and as targets for manipulation by some adults. This can result in abuse and neglect of young people. In the context of sexual abuse of youth, ageism can collide with patriarchal male privilege, while social workers and social service providers are expected to pick up the pieces.

Aging can be a process of dignity and inclusion, a process white societies have not always done well. For example, older adults in North America are often cast off as "useless" and warehoused in nursing homes that provide little nursing care, almost no attention to the social needs of residents, and are hardly homes. Other cultures have a different and more respectful approach to older adults. In many Indigenous communities, special roles are given to older adults, recognized by their communities as being Knowledge Carriers and as having wisdom that comes from a lifetime of experience. Some Indigenous communities call these older adults, known for their wisdom and for their knowledge of ceremonies, *grandmothers* and *aunties*. Other Indigenous communities use the term *Elder*. These are individuals who continue to learn about their culture, often from other Elders by meeting regularly in Indigenous lodges, longhouses, or other meeting places (depending on their nation). Lessons should be learned from these positive examples to build more affirming lives and supports for the old and the young.

HETEROSEXUAL/CISGENDER PRIVILEGE

Alongside colonial, gendered, and racial privileges – with the interwoven illegitimate benefits that are due to race, class, gender, and age – are sexual orientation and gender identification, which are yet other major sources of oppression and privilege. Marion Brown, Brenda Richard, and Leighann Wichman suggest a starting point for addressing lesbian, gay, transgender, two-spirit, intersex, and Queer issues:

> Analysis of heterosexism and homophobia is where any discussion of the lives and challenges of queer people must begin, because the challenges faced and coping strategies utilized by queer people do not result from individual pathology, deficiency, or weakness, but rather result from the historic and contemporary discrimination, prejudice, and violence levelled against queer people and communities through the exploitative social constructs of heterosexism and homophobia. (2010: 157)

The McGill University Equity Subcommittee on Queer People (2010) provides definitions of heterosexism and homophobia:

> *Heterosexism* is based on societal values and personal belief systems which dictate that everyone is, or should be, heterosexual. Intentionally or unintentionally, our society privileges heterosexuality and heterosexual persons, and devalues, mistreats or discriminates against lesbian, gay, bisexual, two-spirited, queer and/or transgender persons and those perceived to be so.
>
> *Homophobia* involves harassing, prejudicial treatment of, or negative attitudes about lesbian, gay, bisexual, queer, trans-identified, transgendered, inter-sexed or two-spirited (LGBQTT) persons and those perceived to be of these sexual orientations or gender identities. Homophobia includes a range of feelings and behaviours from discomfort and fear to disgust, hatred and violence.

Harassment and violence, in addition to exclusion due to heterosexist domination, has resulted in negative self-image and despair – so much so that Queer youth have a high risk of suicide. For example, in 2010, 47 per cent of trans youth in Ontario had thought about suicide and 19 per cent had attempted suicide in the preceding year (Egale 2011).

Heterosexism also operates within services that are meant to support all Canadians equally. For example, Shari Brotman and a team of researchers gave voice to the caregivers of gay and lesbian older adults who were receiving services from health and social service institutions in Montreal, Halifax, and Vancouver. The heterosexist discrimination experienced by these caregivers made it "increasingly difficult for caregiving partners to show affection, provide care when others were present, or gain recognition as the care receiver's spouse." As a result, the care receivers became alienated from the services offered, and in an effort to protect or avoid discrimination the caregivers sometimes refrained from making the most of the services available. The problem is that "the less care receivers make use of health and social services, the more is demanded of their caregivers" (Brotman et al. 2007: 498, 500).

While many health and social services have adopted policies that prohibit discrimination based on sexual orientation, for the most part these services do not provide services that support the lives of Queer people. According to Brian O'Neill, "the pervasiveness of heterosexism" in health and social services have the effect of silencing the "discussion of sexual orientation, thereby impeding the development of accessible and responsive programs, and leaving decisions regarding service delivery to individual workers. This approach may not only prevent clients from receiving adequate service – but also leave workers without guidance and support in their practice" (2012: 325).

With the growing popularity of Queer Pride parades in certain parts of the country, with same sex marriages being approved in North American and other jurisdictions, and with an increasing recognition that hate laws need to be strengthened to protect Queer people, heterosexist privileges are being increasingly challenged. Some Canadian social agencies have set in place programs that specifically respond to the service delivery needs of Queer people (Todd 2006: 292). Typically, these social services have emerged within visible Queer communities, located in urban environments, and as public attitudes have shifted toward a more progressive direction, these services have gained credibility. The shifts in public opinion did not just happen on their own. They are the result of hard work and dedication by members of sexually diverse community organizations, supported by allies in feminist and numerous other progressive social movements.

Though the term *Queer* encompasses the broad and diverse community of people who identify outside of the heterosexist norm, particular groups within this larger community encounter particular kinds of challenges. Drawing attention to the privilege of identifying with the gender assigned to the biological characteristics we are born with (cis-gendered privilege), transgendered people challenge the notion that the world can comfortably be divided into two genders. Dalhousie University provides this definition:

> Transgender refers to a person who identifies with a gender other than the one ascribed to the biological sex at birth; or a person who views their gender as being more fluid or non-binary than the strictly male or female genders allow. It is also used as an umbrella term for those who identify themselves as transsexual, transgender, gender variant, or a similar term. Gender identity is not the same as sexual orientation. Trans persons may be gay, lesbian, bisexual, queer, two-spirit or heterosexual. (2016)

Trans Pride Canada, a non-partisan network of partners and allies working together for trans rights, has put together a useful guide for appropriate and respectful language for the general public, including social workers:

> SEX (n): The biological classification of people as male and/or female. Sex is usually assigned by a physician at birth and is based on a visual assessment of external anatomy.
> GENDER (n): The social classification of people as masculine and/or feminine. Whereas sex is an externally assigned classification, gender is something that becomes evident in a social context.
> GENDER IDENTITY (n): A person's conscious sense of maleness and/or

femaleness. This sense of self is separate and distinct from biological sex.

CISGENDER (adj): Refers to a person whose biological sex assigned at birth matches their gender identity (the antonym for transgender).

Correct: Cisgender men, cisgender women, cisgender person.

Incorrect: He is a cisgender, she is cisgendered.

TRANSGENDER (adj): Refers to a person whose biological sex assigned at birth does not match their gender identity (the antonym for cisgender).

Correct: Transgender men, transgender women, transgender rights.

Incorrect: He is a transgender, she is transgendered.

The issue of autonomy (the right to name oneself) is of vital importance to trans people. Autonomy begins with the right to name one's gender and continues with the right to be called by one's chosen name. A chosen name is NOT an alias – it signifies one's claim to one's identity. Always use the personal name preferred by the individual, and do so in an unqualified manner.

Correct: Jane is a trans woman from New York.

Incorrect: John (who prefers to be called Jane) is from New York.

Correct: She is a trans woman and this is her life.

Incorrect: He (she) is a trans woman, "she" is a trans woman.

(Trans Pride Canada, Style Guide 2012)

Gerald Hunt (2011) argues that transgendered people absorb a disproportionate amount of the hatred directed at Queer people as a reflection of the notion of gender as unchanging and biologically based. In light of this, it is not surprising that transgendered kids and adults often feel unsafe and alienated, with few services or supports for the multiple challenges they face. Young transgendered people are particularly vulnerable with ninety per cent of transgendered youth reporting feeling unsafe in high school. "Transgender youth and adults have far higher rates of suicidal thoughts and suicide attempts than the average person . . . 41% of transgender adults report having ever attempted suicide, compared to 5% of adults in the general population" (Freedenthal 2015). The right to express their identities as they feel appropriate and to feel safe in the world is one that is often denied this group of Queer people.

Indigenous communities have decolonized heterosexism and reclaimed Queer-positive terms. The term *two-spirit* or *two-spirited* people, as Fiona Meyer-Cook and Diane Labelle point out, refers to Indigenous "gender identity and role, and includes gays, lesbians and other gender and sexuality identification." Coined in Winnipeg in 1990 at a Native American/First Nations gay and lesbian conference, "the term was adopted to reawaken the spiritual nature of the role these people are meant to play in their communities" (2004: 31); in essence, to reclaim traditional sociocultural roles.

ABLEISM AND PRIVILEGE

About 12 per cent of Canadians are disabled in one way or another, and that condition has led to another social movement pushing for much-needed change. Roy Hanes outlines a range of possible disabilities, including sensory impairments, such as blindness or deafness, psychiatric disabilities, developmental disabilities, learning disabilities, neurological disabilities, and mobility impairments. As Hanes indicates: "People can also become disabled as a result of many different factors, such as disease and/or injury. And, of course, many persons with disabilities have more than one impairment and therefore have more complex needs" (2006: 297).

Hanes and others have identified two competing disability theories that inform social work practice (Hanes 2006; Schwartz and O'Brien 2010; Mingus 2010). According to Hanes, the first theory views disability as primarily a medical problem that requires professional and medical assistance focused on rehabilitating the disabled individual. This rehabilitative/medical model also includes helping disabled individuals and those around them to pass through various stages of adjustment, such as denial, grief, and acceptance. This focus on the rehabilitative/medical model is the one most used by social services.

The second disability theory is the social oppression theory. Central to this approach is the recognition that "problems faced by people with disabilities are not the result of physical impairments alone, but are the result of the social and political inequality that exists between people with disabilities on the one hand and people without disabilities on the other." In this view, it is society's failure to accommodate their needs that disables people (Mingus 2015; Poole et al. 2012). These barriers persist in large part because of *ableism*, which denotes the consequences of "the belief in the superiority of people without disabilities over people with disabilities" (Hanes 2006: 310; see also Hanes 2012; Poole and Jivraj 2015).

This belief in superiority produces privilege, such as the ability to construct a dominant set of attitudes and practices that over many years have stigmatized people with visible and invisible disabilities. Judy MacDonald and Gaila Friars write about how people with disabilities have been treated historically: "They have been hidden away in family attics, institutionalized in state-based and private asylums, physically, emotionally, and sexually abused, sterilized against their will, socially segregated, and politically silenced" (2010: 138).

In addition to producing privilege, this belief in superiority contributes to oppression and to barriers against effective help. It is also present in colonial and racist attitudes. Furthermore, a belief in superiority can easily be found among people who possess class and patriarchal privileges. So when a social worker tries to help an Indigenous woman who has a disability and is also poor, we need to be aware of how her self-worth may be eroded under the weight of multiple and intersecting oppressions.

Much of the progress in breaking down the barriers facing people with disabilities is not due primarily to academic research, or to the work of social services, but rather to the political activism of people with disabilities (Barnes, Oliver, and Barton 2002: 4; Withers 2012; Cohen-Rottenberg 2015; Mingus 2013, 2015). Disabilities rights movements in various countries have contributed to a new, and crucial, sense of identity for people with disabilities. This was recognized over a decade ago: "Discovering our identity as disabled people is very, very important," Ayesha Vernon and John Swain (2002: 85) argue. "I think that it is probably the biggest success that the movement has been able to point to. It is our movement, nobody else owns it. We know who we are."

Part of this self-definition is the use of language. People who want to become allies to those who are marginalized for systemic reasons need to be open to the words and phrases recommended by the people most directly affected. More specifically, MacDonald and Friars point out that to be respectful, we need to further shift our language "by deconstructing terms such as mentally retarded, crippled, or mad and replacing them with people-first language. 'People with disabilities' puts the person first while identifying disability as one characteristic, while 'disabled persons' highlights the disability issues" (2010: 140).

MacDonald and Friars (2010: 140) advocate writing the word "disability" as: "(dis)Ability: '(dis)' to respect the person's social and physical connection with disability, and 'Ability' to highlight the creative and innovative ways of dealing with societal barriers."

There is also a growing recognition of how ableism not only intersects with other areas of privileges or oppressions, but also widens its scope, for example to challenge the disparaging yet frequent narratives and practices of sanism against people who are deemed "crazy" (Poole et al. 2012; Meerai, Abdillahi, and Poole 2016). Furthermore, research into the views of (dis)Abled lesbians and bisexual women, for instance, has indicated that many see themselves as being marginalized by lesbian and gay groups; according to Vernon and Swain (2002: 82), they "have experienced alienation rather than nurturing and support from the lesbian and gay community." People with (dis)Abilities and Black and ethnic minority people experience high unemployment rates and concentration in low-paid and low-skilled jobs. To gain awareness of the complexities facing people with (dis)Abilities, progressive social service providers need to take into account the intersecting personal and political barriers that include living in poverty, heterosexism, ableism, colonialism, ageism, and racism (Withers 2012; Chan 2013; Mingus 2015).

Social Justice and Social Services

The privileges and various systemic inequalities generated by society's structures and narratives have an impact on all of us. At the same time, we are not merely passive recipients of these political and personal dynamics. On the contrary, as individuals, we have our own capacity to respond – that is, to accept or to resist, or question, what we are presented. Working for social justice is a continuing, unending process, not just an immediate goal or a once and for all event. Social justice calls for the dismantling of all oppressions and undue privileges.

But we also need to remember that social justice is about more than just dismantling injustice. It is also about constructing equitable personal/political/economic/social realities based on values such as kindness, honesty, authentic democracy, and fairness. This process is sometimes called *social transformation*.

Social services are institutions that are officially supposed to improve people's lives. We help older adults write claims for necessary financial supplements. We help children find their way through difficult family situations. We provide shelter for women fleeing abusive relationships. We support palliative care patients who are facing death. We may also help a service user become an outspoken leader in one of the social movements committed to equity.

But these positives are only part of the picture. Much like other institutions in Canadian society, social services reproduce and perpetuate a variety of systemic privileges and oppressions, ranging from racism to ableism. Most social services are bureaucracies organized along hierarchical lines. They have rules to follow and funding conditions that prescribe the services to be provided. Whether funded by governments or charities, social services are usually answerable to affluent elites who often view their own privileges as entitlements.

That is why social services are more than places that deliver social programs. They are also contested terrain, meaning that a number of service providers, service users, and their allies are seeking social transformation. In this process, many social work educators and social service practitioners are resisting the consequences of multiple oppressions and attempting to address the root causes of domination, exploitation, and oppression in our society (Hart 2015; Baines 2014; Baines and Armstrong 2015; Brittain, and Blackstock 2015; Hick et al. 2010; Czyzewski and Tester 2014; P. Johnson 2014; S. Johnson 2014; Kinewesquao and Wade 2009; Lavallée and Poole: 2009; Torjman 2015; Mullaly 2010; Social Work Action Network 2015; Lundy 2011; Ng 2015).

As Donna Baines notes, in this process, we need to include how to use our privilege: "While addressing where one is placed on a multi-level continuum of privilege and oppression, it is equally important to understand, critique and improve how one *uses* that privilege to challenge oppression in everyday life" (2011a: 7). These new and better forms of social work are emerging alongside other practical initiatives within social services, and alongside grassroots networks and diverse social movements – such as the efforts by Indigenous organizations and their allies to press for justice for First Nations, Métis, and Inuit peoples in Canada. Progressive community-based voices, including those of social workers, are calling for an end of oppressive policies and practices both locally and globally. To better understand what we need to do now, we turn to the past. Are there any lessons from the past that can inform us in how to best proceed in the present to build an equitable future?

4 Roots: Early Attitudes

> Mary Dowding 514 King St. E. and husband. No children. says can't get work. fancy they don't want it. no reason why they should be in want. Recommend a little starvation until self-help engendered, probably drink.
>
> — notes of a volunteer visitor, Toronto 1882

W hen we were students, the history of the welfare state was presented as a peaceful evolution. Society gradually recognized its responsibility to the "less fortunate" or "under-privileged," which meant that governments took on a greater and greater role in the social care for each other. Nowhere in our high school or university education was there any mention of how today's institutions in North America were built on the ashes of two colossal human catastrophes, or that progressive policies tend to result from intense struggle of those fighting for a better world.

In 1492, when the European conquest of the "New World" began, a population of about 100 million Indigenous people lived in the vast terrain of what is now North, Central, and South America. The violent invasion and subsequent European settlement, including extensive massacres of Indigenous peoples, led to the introduction of wave upon wave of disease – smallpox, yellow fever, cholera, and others – to which the Indigenous peoples had previously had no exposure and therefore had little or no immunity. These diseases inflicted a devastating toll. By 1600 an estimated 90 million of the original inhabitants of the Americas had died. Writer Ronald Wright states, "It was the greatest mortality in history. To conquered and conqueror alike, it seemed as though God really was on the white man's side" (2000: 13–14).

The second event, also fuelled by greed, the drive for profits, and racism, was the violent wrenching of African people away from their homes to become slaves in the New World. Historian Donald Spivey argues:

> Europe systematically raped the African continent. Whether one accepts the often cited figure of twelve million Africans killed, taken, or otherwise lost to the slave trade, or the more likely figure of forty million and more killed, taken, or otherwise lost to the slave trade, the impact was catastrophic for Africa and monumental for European coffers and the New World. (2003: 59)

These two catastrophes are strongly interconnected and linked with a third historical phenomenon: the cruel and abusive treatment of poverty-stricken and other "inferior" Europeans at the hands of their rulers. English law in 1531, certainly, was blunt about what would happen to the less fortunate. A person considered to be one of society's "ill-begotten" group of "idle poor, ruffelers, sturdy vagabonds and valiant beggars" was "to be tied to the end of a cart naked and to be beaten with whips throughout the same market-town or other place til his body be bloody by reason of such whipping." As if this was not enough, this unfortunate would "also have the upper part of the grissle of his right ear clean cut off" (de Schweinitz 1943: 21–22).

At the same time as brutality was inflicted on jobless men, women were violently persecuted under suspicion of witchcraft. The accusation was focused mainly on spinsters and widows (that is, those women without male "protection") who might achieve a degree of independence. This posed a threat to the monopoly of male authority in intellectual, moral, economic, and religious spheres. Mary Daly documents (1978: 180) the belief current in 1486 that "all witchcraft comes from carnal lust which is in women insatiable." This belief, combined with the suspicion that some women were in league with the devil, served to justify witch hunts and the subsequent cruelty, torture, and killings of large numbers of women (Daly 1978: 178–222). At about the same time the Inquisition was in full swing, confirming that European leaders did not restrict their cruelty to women or to the poor. Anyone suspected of deviations from official Catholic teachings could be subjected to investigation, with lethal consequences. Furthermore, people who were part of the Jewish community were considered a different kind of "deviant" and could be a target for forcible conversion, be deported, or face death (Paris 1995). The contempt and hatred for Jews has a long history in Christian Europe – a history that became a rehearsal for the genocidal policies carried out when the Nazis rose to power in Germany during the twentieth century.

Periodically, rebellions occurred among oppressed groups in which violence was reversed and aimed at the privileged – as in the French Revolution and earlier. In sixteenth-century France, for example, the general population suffered through bad harvests, extreme hunger, and famine, causing countless people to leave their farms. Many migrated to the city of Lyons, where they begged or found work at low wages. With the poor harvests the townsfolk found the price of grain doubling or quadrupling in a matter of days, and they could not afford to buy bread. Jean Swanson notes: "In 1529 the starving people of Lyons took over the city, forcing the wealthy to flee to a monastery for their own protection. They looted the homes of the rich and sold the grain from a public and a church granary" (2001: 30). In an attempt to avoid further rebellions, the elite developed a crude welfare system, taxing the well-off in Lyons to supplement church contributions for the poor; every Sunday food and money were distributed to the needy.

In time, some European laws softened. In England, instead of being beaten and mutilated, the unemployed were imprisoned and forced to work in jail-like institutions called houses of correction: "There to be straightly kept, as well in diet as in work, and also punished from time to time" (de Schweinitz 1943: 26). Influenced by the church, the state was somewhat less harsh to the "impotent poor," that is, the deserted mothers with children, the "lame," the "demented," the old, and the sick. These unfortunates could, in seventeenth-century England, receive limited assistance from officials who were called the "overseers" of the poor and who had been appointed to their positions by justices of the peace or magistrates. Two centuries later this division between worthy and unworthy poor remained, with both groups often ending up in workhouses or poorhouses, which had replaced the houses of correction. Social critic Charles Dickens attacked these workhouses in his novel *Oliver Twist*.

EARLY NORTH AMERICAN SOCIAL WELFARE

American feminist Mimi Abramovitz examined the impact of U.S. social welfare policy on the lives of women from colonial times to the late twentieth century. Her book *Regulating the Lives of Women* notes that a patriarchal standard about what women should or should not do "has been used to distinguish among women as deserving or undeserving of aid since colonial times" (1988: 40).

In Canada, governments imported the traditions of France and England. While Quebec's government left it to the Catholic Church to provide assistance and education to the poor, the colonial administration in the Maritimes saw to the construction of a workhouse in 1759, where "for many years whipping, shackling, starvation, and other necessary inducements were used to correct the behaviour of the idle, vagrant, or incorrigible inmates" (Bellamy 1965). Public auctions of paupers also took place. In 1816 in the Upper Canada village of Delaware, an indigent widow was auctioned off to the *lowest* bidder. Paupers were "boarded out" in a sort of foster-home system. The auction was to see who would charge the municipality *least* for their keep; the successful bidder would expect to more than make up his cost by the work he would get out of the pauper.

Social historian Allan Irving documented the introduction of welfare to Upper Canada in the 1830s by Sir Francis Bond Head, the lieutenant-governor. He believed that "workhouses should be made repulsive . . . if any would not work for relief, neither should he eat" (1989: 17). Although workhouses were not developed everywhere in English Canada, the local jails served the same purpose: "Jails became a type of poorhouse – a catch-all for a variety of social problems," which included people of all ages who were in poverty, homeless, or had a mental illness, or were found guilty of minor or major crimes (Guest 1980: 12).

This history of Canada's responses to people barely surviving due to poverty or other oppressive conditions evolved on the heels of the horrific dispossession of Indigenous people. Colonial violence, racism, and exploitation not only shattered the economic self-sufficiency of the First Nations peoples, but also created havoc with their communal and family life (Albert 1991).

"SURVIVAL OF THE FITTEST" – SOCIAL DARWINISM

The colonial takeover of land in North America and the attitude of contempt toward the First Nations were echoed in sixteenth- and seventeenth-century England by the enclosures of common land used by peasant farmers. Richard Bocking outlines the seizure of land in England:

> "The commons" was the name used in medieval England to describe parcels of land that were used "in common" by peasant farmers, very few of whom owned enough land to survive on. Their lives depended on access to and use of shared land that provided many necessities: pasture for their oxen or livestock, water in streams, ponds or wells, wood and fuel from a forest. . . . The land was probably owned by a titled notable [who] began to think how much richer they could be if they could remove the "commoners" and use the land themselves. (2003: 26)

These landowners pressured the British Parliament to transfer full title to them. It was no coincidence that when English farmers were forced off the commons, they moved into cities and towns looking for work. During this same time, the factory system was expanding rapidly and had a huge need for workers, but was unwilling to pay fair wages or provide livable working conditions. Hence, it was necessary to push people out of farming, to compel them into factory work. In the nineteenth century, England had brutal factory conditions, including long hours of child labour, trade unions were illegal, women had no vote, and the living conditions of the working class were abysmal, reflecting their near-starvation level of wages and exhausting conditions of work.

The owners of industry and commerce believed that it was their superior moral character, not their economic structures or the starvation wages they paid, that was responsible for the large gap between rich and poor, men and women, Whites and non-Whites. The philosophy of genetic superiority underpinned ideologies of empire building and provided the justification for colonizing the lands and resources of "inferior" peoples. Cecil Rhodes, born in 1854, an ardent British imperialist, epitomizes the privileged, White, European world view in his comment:

"We know the size of the world and we know the total extent. It is our duty to seize every opportunity of acquiring more territory and we should keep this one idea steadily before our eyes that more territory simply means more of the Anglo-Saxon race more of the best the most human, most honorable race the world possesses." (Rhodes, quoted in Flint 1974: 252)

Some of the well-to-do genuinely felt that the pauper class needed only proper moral instruction and self-discipline to raise themselves out of their woeful condition.

True, poor men had few rights during this era, and women even fewer. They were seen as chattels, or as the property of men, with no separate legal existence of their own.

Just as the position of people living in poverty was a subordinate one, the same was true of people of colour. During an age when many people still supported slavery, there were ample theories to justify assumptions about the "superiority" of a highly privileged upper class and indeed of the growing middle class, and the "natural rights" of the men in these classes to subordinate others.

One form of justification was the growing emphasis on "scientific thinking," which by the nineteenth century was used to explain why people occupied different ranks and status. Theories such as Charles Darwin's *natural selection*, with arguments about the extinction of certain animal species and the continuation of other species based on "survival of the fittest," were applied to thinking about people and economic status. Aristocratic men of privilege, as a consequence, were viewed as the "fittest," possessing the most desirable of human traits. This group of "superior" beings included men rather than women, Whites rather than non-Whites, the able-bodied rather than people with (dis)Abilities, property owners rather than servants. The evidence for the aristocracy's "moral superiority," presumably, consisted of their extraordinary privileges and their ability to have their commands carried out (Macarov 1978).

Conversely, it followed that the poor and the powerless possessed the least desirable traits. Those who were paupers, due to either illness or (dis)Ability, or to old age, gender prejudices, low-paying jobs, or unemployment, became viewed as "inferior" – a designation still very much with us to this day.

The brutalities of the workhouses in England brought agitation for change by the working class and reformers in England. A Royal Commission established in 1834 to study the conditions of the poor strongly recommended the continuation of workhouses for the poor, including the continuation of harsh conditions. The reason these privileged commissioners gave: "Every penny bestowed, that tends to render the condition of the pauper more eligible than that of the independent laborer, is a bounty on indolence and vice" (Marcus 1978: 51).

The Royal Commission believed that it had discovered a way of aiding the needy and protecting the system. It would accomplish this by extending benefits to the poor at a level that was clearly less than the wage of the poorest-paid employee, a policy known as "lesser-eligibility." The net effect was to legitimate these lowest wages by focusing on the "need" to make the working poor accept work regardless of wage levels or working conditions. This approach created the illusion of freedom. The poor were to be given "choices" – work at abysmal wages, enter the workhouse, or die of starvation. This policy ensured that there was no room to ask how exploitation of the poor was the product of social and economic systems perpetuating unjust privilege.

To implement that report, six hundred more workhouses were built throughout England between 1834 and 1850 (Corrigan and Corrigan 1980: 14). It was the kind of thinking, fashioned by rich White men of privilege, that still reverberates today within social assistance offices across Canada.

SOCIAL WORK: THE BEGINNINGS

In the late nineteenth century, when social work began as an embryonic profession in London, the notion of the worthy and unworthy poor was well established and a pivotal part of every charity. There was a certain sympathy for the worthy poor, but for the unworthy – the able-bodied poor or the unemployed – it was still felt that the full rigour of the workhouse should be applied. Welfare-state services tended to focus on the unworthy poor, often women, "unwed" mothers, "promiscuous ladies," "irresponsible" wives, and so on. This left the worthy to be aided by the more traditional charitable organizations, outside the purview of the state.

The idea of more systematic social assistance took on an added sense of urgency when members of the affluent class noticed that socialism was becoming more appealing to the factory workers. Some members of the upper class started to accept the idea that one way to prevent socialism was to consent to some services for the poor. In addition, rich people resented being pestered for donations to the many separate charities and favoured the idea of donating to a single organization that could address most social ills. Along with this resentment, there was the suspicion that many paupers were collecting relief from more than one charity and lying about their circumstances in an effort to collect more assistance.

Charity Organization Society (cos)

As a result, a new organization was formed in 1869 in London, the Society for Organizing Charitable Relief and Repressing Mendicancy. It was soon renamed the Charity Organization Society (cos). It offered to coordinate the various charities and advocated a thorough "scientific" investigation of every person applying for charity, thus avoiding fraud or a person receiving benefits from more than one charity. This coordination and investigation came to symbolize "scientific charity," which borrowed ideas from the emerging social sciences and factory management. With these innovations, charity leaders held out the promise of imposing efficiency and effectiveness on the charity process. And for the truly needy, the cause of their poverty would be discovered and their problems addressed (Lappin 1965). The cos approach became popular and spread to other locations. At the operational level, the cos provided "friendly visitors" from the upper class who volunteered to visit poor families. So much importance was placed on developing a co-operative, helpful relationship between the help-giver and the help-receiver that it was the relationship itself that came to be viewed as the best form of assistance to the poor. Since the cos leaders believed that financial aid would be wasted on the poor, their motto became "Not alms, but a friend."

In the late nineteenth century the cos was transplanted to North America (Popple 1983: 75). The following advice was given to friendly visitors regarding how to develop co-operative, helpful relationships with the poor: "You go in the full strength and joy and fire of life; full of cheer and courage; with a far wider knowledge of affairs; and it would be indeed a wonder if you could not often see why the needy family does not succeed, and how to help them up" (Lubove 1965: 13). Given the assumption that the poor were morally inferior, it was logical that assistance was defined as moral advice on how to uplift the poor into becoming better people. It was thought that over time, morally uplifted individuals might even escape their poverty.

At the operational level, the COS format consisted not only of wealthy volunteers, but also of paid employees called "agents" who were often from the working class (Lappin 1965: 64). These "agents" were poorly paid, considered low-status technicians, and initially were few in number. But as the quantity of cases grew and far exceeded the number of volunteers, more agents were hired and carried larger parts of the workload. This group of employees was the forerunner of the modern social worker.

While a humanitarian impulse was present, the early days of social work were also infused by negative attitudes toward the less fortunate. Most thinkers on social questions at the time believed that the proper role of the state was to be minimal – to maintain public institutions for criminals, the "insane," and the "absolutely unfit." Those who were simply poor or unemployed or "handicapped" in some way were to be left to the charitable institutions or, more likely, to their own devices. The prevailing attitude was that most people who were living in poverty and who, for instance, resorted to begging were out-and-out frauds, and that it was harmful to aid these people (Copp 1974: 115).

OPPRESSION AND RESISTANCE

Still, some of the early social workers had a more compassionate social justice view. They refused to accept as a "given" the oppressive living conditions of new immigrants in the urban centres of North America. They believed social conditions could be changed. For example, Jane Addams, who founded Chicago's Hull House in 1889, became legendary for her advocacy for public health, decent housing, peace, and women's rights. She inspired others, both inside and outside of social work, to begin recognizing that the social environment external to an individual was the major cause of poverty. She encouraged social workers to live in the communities they served and to mobilize communities in mutual support of one another. At the same time as progressive thoughts were making advances, injustices continued in many forms.

During this same period of history, scholar and activist Akua Benjamin argues: "First Nations peoples faced genocide. Queers were forced into the closet. During Jane Addams' era and beyond, Blacks were being lynched with the tolerance or participation of the law. Thus, while radical forms of social work resisted oppression in some communities, oppression found expression in the everyday life of many other communities" (2007: 199).

The invisibility of systemic barriers, such as those posed by class privilege, racism, ableism, and heterosexism, reinforced conservative ideologies among Canada's early social workers. The model adopted in social work, as social historian Terry Copp puts it, was "stern charity, charity designed to be as uncomfortable and demeaning as possible." Copp analyzes the case of Montreal, which in 1901 was home to a great variety of charitable institutions organized along ethnic and religious lines: "fifteen houses of refuge, thirteen outdoor relief agencies, fourteen old age homes, eleven orphanages, eighteen 'moral and educational institutions,' and more than a score of other miscellaneous charitable agencies" (1974:106).

Similarly, gender inequities were recreated in the services of the late 1800s. Carol Baines documents how in a world of patriarchal privilege, caring for others was seen as women's "natural work" and was undervalued. Baines also describes how the move toward social work professionalism at the turn of the twentieth century recreated unjust gender relations in new ways, such as increased reliance on male supervisors and more specialization, as well as less emphasis on support networks with other women (1998: 59–60). These early social agencies found themselves answerable to wealthy male philanthropists or politicians who were not interested in empowering women or poor communities. According to Jennifer Dale and Peggy Foster (1986: 38), "the new professions were made up of middle-class women who were very much involved in the social control of working class mothers."

This social control also extended to Indigenous people. During the early years of social service provision, First Nations people received little or nothing of these "benefits." Instead they came under rigid and systematic government control to foster the "settlement" of western Canada. White settlers and rail companies, intent on opening up the land to further settlement, deliberately slaughtered the buffalo, destroying the traditional Indigenous economic systems, based on buffalo hunting. Consequently, Indigenous people who became dependent on government support were manipulated and coerced through starvation tactics to consent to government policies, which led to intense suffering and high death rates (Neu and Therrien 2003; Shewell 2004; Daschuk 2013). Resistance in the form of riots over food and other protests were met with violent force from government authorities.

To solidify the settlers' power, various Indigenous nations were divided through the treaty-making process and forced to accept small and widely dispersed land allotments. For example, the Cree wanted to settle in the highlands area of the Cypress Hills (Frideres 1998), however, the federal government, aware of strength in numbers, divided the Cree into small and separate bands across the prairies.

INDIGENOUS "ASSIMILATION" AND RESISTANCE

Early social workers were complicit in the push toward assimilation through the residential school system, which affected all Indigenous people (First Nation, Métis, and Inuit). One of their roles was assisting police in escorting children to the schools. And, as noted earlier, social workers were responsible in large part for the removal of thousands of Indigenous children from families and communities and their subsequent placement into foster and adoptive care.

Banakonda

The term *assimilation* is a misnomer: It is my belief that assimilation was a means to an end, it did not at any time involve recognition of belonging or being full members of Canadian society. Indigenous people in fact were never allowed to be a part of the fabric of the "New World" vision of Canada, the United States, or anywhere in the Americas. The goal was at best disenfranchisement, but the intent has always been the same, the disappearance of Indigenous people, that is, genocide.

Indigenous history in Canada has by and large been omitted, evaded, devalued, and denied by educational, political, and social narratives, rendering it an invisible history. By contrast, the message we have attempted to assert, at many places in this book, is that to be ignorant of history is to operate in a vacuum (see Duran and Duran 1995). This vacuum, consciously or unconsciously, contributes to the colonial privilege that normalizes the social relations of subjugation, inequality, and mistreatment imposed on Indigenous populations. As social work students, educators, and practitioners, we have an ethical responsibility to uncover injustices that have been rendered invisible. Acting on this ethical responsibility can interrupt colonial subjugation and allow for a new relationship, based on mutual respect between mainstream Canadians and Indigenous nations, communities, families, and individuals. That becomes a first step to correcting the wrongs of the past which continue into the present.

Bob Antone, from the Oneida Nation, is the former executive director of KiiKeeWanNiiKaan – South West Regional Healing Lodge, located in Muncey, Ontario. He presents an overview of history, as it affected Haudenosaunee people, that is a very different history than what is typically taught in Canadian educational institutions (Antone 2013). This conflict in views can result in controversy. Eurocentric historians have become invested in certain views and have made their careers promoting colonial narratives. In light of the pervasiveness of a Eurocentric history viewpoint, we sometimes hear, "So today, what do Indigenous people want anyway?"

Responding from an Indigenous perspective, Thomas King notes:

It's the wrong question to ask. . . . There's a better question to ask. One that will help us understand the nature of contemporary North American Indian history. A question that we can ask of both the past and the present.

What do Whites want? Native history as writ has never really been about Native people. It's been about Whites and their needs and desires. What Native people wanted has never been a vital concern, has never been a political or social priority.

The Lakota didn't want Europeans in the Black Hills, but Whites wanted the gold that was there. The Cherokee didn't want to move from Georgia to Indian Territory (Oklahoma) but Whites wanted the land. The Cree of Quebec weren't at all keen on vacating their home to make way for the Great Whale project, but there's excellent money in hydroelectric power. The California Indians did not ask to be enslaved by the Franciscans and forced to build that order's missions.

What do Whites want?

The answer is quite simple, and it's been in plain sight all along.

Land.

Whites want land. (King 2012: 215, 216).

Such candid comments challenge the prevailing colonial attitudes that have been infused into the popular Canadian narrative of "nation building and ongoing, pleasing development for all." The result is that every field, discipline, and profession has been influenced by these neo-colonial narratives, including social work. Because of this, the work of decolonization belongs to all Canadians, including to all fields of study and to all professions, not just to Indigenous people.

INUIT AND MÉTIS

Today, investigative reporters, various writers, and film documentaries provide glimpses into how the theft of land enriched European settlers, while simultaneously causing the impoverishment and suffering of Indigenous communities. The Truth and Reconciliation Commission of Canada held hearings throughout the country and documented the horrendous abuses that have become synonymous with the residential schools system, begun in the 1870s. While less is heard about the impact of residential schools on northern communities, here is what the Commission notes about Inuit communities:

> In the North, the Residential School program was implemented quickly and often aggressively. Within one generation, Inuit went from a nomadic hunter-gatherer existence, to living in settlements with their children being sent away for long periods of time to Residential School. The abrupt transition from their traditional ways of life were further complicated when the RCMP killed their dog-teams. Left without a means to hunt and provide for their families, whole communities were devastated and forced to depend on a Northern Allowance to purchase food and other necessities. Parents were threatened with the loss of their government assistance if they refused to allow their children to be sent off to Residential Schools. . . . Some students travelled as far as 2,500 miles. For most of the children, the distance created further isolation as they were not allowed to travel home for holidays like other students. Many children did not see their families and home communities for years. . . . For many students, the isolation was further compounded by deprivation of all that was familiar to them. A number of students described a constant hunger – for their country food and a longing for the comfort of their family. (Truth and Reconciliation Commission 2014, 2013a)

Just as many Canadians know little about the terrible pain and suffering caused by the forced relocation of Inuit people, most of us also know little about the details of the attacks against the Métis Nation. While Métis people today are struggling due to being marginalized by mainstream society, they are also marginalized by non-Métis Indigenous people, partly because it serves the interest of dominant elites to foster divisions among Indigenous peoples. Métis concerns have often been relegated to the periphery in political negotiations that have given precedence to Treaty and land claims of First Nations groups. Currently, Métis advocates and scholars are challenging the misrecognition of Métis identity as simply "mixed" White/Aboriginal individuals (Anderson 2014). To learn more about Métis people, we need to acknowledge that their traditional language is Michif, as Cathy Richardson (Kinewesquao) and Dana Lynn Seaborn have documented:

The Métis emerged as a nation in Red River, Rupertsland, in 1816, in response to orchestrated land theft, facilitated by the Saskatchewan Valley Land Company in alignment with the interests of the federal government. This sense of nationhood was strengthened over the next fifty years, as the Métis resisted the Government of Canada's repeated appropriation of their lands and refusal to acknowledge their right to representation. . . . In 1885 the Canadian Government sent its army to clear the Métis from the prairies at Batoche. After the Métis defeat, 1.4 million acres of land were transferred to the Canadian state.

While the Métis community embraced both English- and French-speaking people with equality, as well as having close ties to the many First Nations to which they are related, linguistic and class tensions in European Canada were exploited in the trial, legal process and then state execution of the Métis leader: Louis Riel's trial was moved from Manitoba, and Canada hanged him for treason against the British Crown. This act served multiple functions: to humiliate the Métis and intimidate those remaining who contemplated ongoing resistance, either overtly or in ways that defended the Métis' right to exist. . . . While the history of the Red River Rebellion is presented in Canadian schools, the analysis seldom acknowledges the concerns of empire and colonial violence on which this attack and land theft were predicated. (Richardson and Seaborn 2009: 115, 116)

But that is by no means the end of the story. In 2016 the Supreme Court of Canada issued a landmark decision that "the ongoing exclusion of Métis from all federal negotiation processes cannot be sustained" (Madden et al. 2016). The court ruled that after years of being marginalized, the Métis Nation had a valid claim to be recognized and to be at the table to negotiate with the federal government. While this opens up a new chapter for Métis people, the fact remains that during the 1800s and up to the present, it was colonial violence that killed Métis people, robbed them of land, and undermined their culture. That violence was the heavy hand that created immense pain and suffering for Métis families, communities, and their leaders.

EARLY 1900S UNREST

The ugly violence of militarism, a key instrument of colonial policy throughout the Americas and elsewhere, then again burst into the open during 1914 – 18. In the muddy European trenches of the First World War, huge armies inflicted massive deaths on each other. The war that was "supposed to end all wars" produced casualties and hard economic times, with little economic justice.

Commenting on the first three decades of the twentieth century, Copp notes:

> All of the accepted norms of society were being called into question by the growing complexity and disorder of the industrial system. Montreal was being transformed into a sprawling ugly anthill. Frequent strikes and the growth of labour unions seemed to foreshadow class warfare on a European scale. . . . The fundamental social problem was poverty, massive poverty, created by low wages and unemployment. For individuals, direct assistance limited hunger and prevented starvation, but the small section of the working class which regularly came into contact with organized charity was too often confronted with the "alms of friendly advice" and too seldom helped to achieve security. (1974: 127)

It was not surprising that the anger of the working class bubbled up against intolerable working conditions. In 1919, Winnipeg experienced a general strike when thirty thousand workers left their jobs to fight for better wages, the improvement of working conditions, and the principle of collective bargaining. In this case the state proved only too eager to intervene, refusing to talk with unions, and instead, sending in Mounted Police and federal troops to break up the strike. The state clearly came down on the side of the privileged – manufacturers, bankers, businessmen – and revealed a strong opposition to ideas and actions involving workers' rights.

Police forces were also used against the institutions of Indigenous people – who were still referred to in insulting terms such as "savages," "lacking in culture," and "possessing no worthy structures of their own in the first place." This was far from the truth, as the destruction from colonialism was documented by the House of Commons Special Committee on Indian Self-Government:

The Iroquois (as they were known by the French) or Six Nations (as the English called them) or the Haudenosaunee (*People of the Longhouse*, as they called themselves) have a formalized constitution, which is recited every five years by Elders who have committed it to memory. It provides for a democratic system in which each extended family selects a senior female leader and a senior male leader to speak on its behalf in their respective councils. Debates on matters of common concern are held according to strict rules that allow consensus to be reached in an efficient manner, thus ensuring that the community remains unified. A code of laws, generally expressed in positive admonitions rather than negative prohibitions, governs both official and civil behaviour. . . .

The Canadian government suppressed the Haudenosaunee government by jailing its leaders and refusing to give it official recognition. In 1924, the council hall at the Six Nations Reserve was raided by the Royal Canadian Mounted Police (RCMP). All official records and symbols of government were seized. (House of Commons, Canada 1983)

At the same time as the police and military were targeting Indigenous people and labour unions, they provided security to people of affluence and their private corporations. Yet even that security was no protection against the wild and reckless stock-market speculation, which culminated in the American stock-market crash, plunging the Western world into the Depression of the 1930s. One result was massive unemployment. At the time, social work leaders were suspicious of granting relief payments to the poor. One leader, Charlotte Whitton, argued that instead of paying money to needy parents, the state should remove children from their homes. She believed that many of the mothers were unfit as parents and so "the dictates of child protection and sound social work would require cancellation of allowance, and provision for the care of the children under guardianship and authority" (Guest 1980: 57).

There was also fear among social work leaders, alongside recognition of who exerted real control in society. At a January 1932 meeting, one of the local branches of the Canadian Association of Social Workers reported: "Social workers are paid by the capitalist group, for the most part, in order to assist the under-privileged group. Thus organized support of political issues would be very difficult if not dangerous . . . because of the danger of attempting too radical changes, since we are paid by the group who would resent such changes most" (1932: 117, 119).

In Canada, the growth of government social welfare programs grew unevenly, in fits and starts, due to several converging factors. The dislocation during and after the First World War resulted in the need for support both of injured soldiers and of families left behind, and some services were developed at this time. There were sharp differences of opinions about what should be done when an economy collapses or is in deep recession. Record-high levels of poverty and unemployment resulted in working-class militancy, spawning a series of protests. One such protest was the famous On-to-Ottawa Trek, when four thousand angry workers marched across Canada to present their grievances to Parliament. During this time in the United States, social workers known as the Rank and File Movement joined militant labour activists who, similar to left-wing political groups in Canada, were openly calling for an end to capitalism (Heinomen and Spearman 2001: 16–18).

SOCIAL PROGRAMS AND SOCIAL INJUSTICES

As a result of the intensity and wide scope of this agitation and opposition during the 1930s, leading industrialists began to grant concessions to the labour movement's advocacy for old age pensions and unemployment insurance. Reluctantly, they supported some expansion of the state into social welfare, provided it was understood that capitalism itself would not be threatened. Sir Charles Gordon, president of the Bank of Montreal, wrote to Prime Minister R.B. Bennett in 1934 to support the idea of unemployment insurance: "May I suggest to you that for our general self-preservation some such arrangement will have to be worked out in Canada and that if it can be done soon so much the better" (Finkel 1977: 349). Not everyone in power agreed, but enough of them were persuaded to accept an expansion of social welfare. When the federal government decided it was time to adopt unemployment insurance and other social programs, the same prime minister reminded business leaders why an expansion of the welfare state was necessary: "A good deal of pruning is sometimes necessary to save a tree and it would be well for us to remember there is considerable pruning to be done if we are to save the fabric of the capitalist system" (Findlay 1982: 9).

To further camouflage this "pruning" of the capitalist system, business and government officials began to argue that our civilization had developed a capacity for compassionate responses to the needy, that "humane values" constituted the foundation of Canadian society, and that social programs were the manifestations of the society's concern for helping one's "fellow man" (they were, perhaps, less certain about women).

Within this rationale, political support was consolidated for Canada's income security programs. The first old age pension was introduced in 1927. Its payment of $20 a month was subject, as social policy researcher Dennis Guest puts it, "to a strict and often humiliating means test – proof that poor-law attitudes still influenced Canadian political leaders in the 1920s" (1985: 1723).

In the following years up to, during, and after the Second World War, workers' compensation for workplace injuries, public assistance, child welfare, and public health programs were created or expanded (Struthers 1983; Irving 1981; Moscovitch 1986). The 1950s and 1960s saw a substantial growth in social programs, with the federal government playing a key role in the funding of new universal Old Age Security payments, an expanded unemployment insurance program, an evolving medicare approach, and additional social services geared to low-income Canadians.

Outspoken social workers also criticized the ever-present opposition to social welfare. Bertha Capen Reynolds, a radical social worker in the United States, writes in 1951:

> We have noted that the interests which oppose really constructive social work constitute only a small minority of the whole population, but influence a much larger sector through their ownership of newspaper chains and control of radio broadcasting. Many hard-working folk who sincerely want people in trouble to have a fair break are frightened by propaganda to the effect that the country is being ruined by taxes to support a "welfare state," and that people on relief are "chiselers" and social workers "sob sisters." (1951: 165)

Yet even the years of welfare-state expansion saw severe shortages of social services. Bridget Moran, a social worker based in Prince George, B.C., during the 1950s and 1960s, documented her experience, and, in 1963, she writes to the premier of British Columbia:

> I could not face my clients for yet another year without raising my voice to protest for them the service they are going to get from me. I have no excuse except desperation for what follows. . . . Every day, here and across the province social workers are called upon to deal with seriously disturbed children. We have no psychiatrists, no specially trained foster parents, no receiving or detention homes to aid us. We place children in homes that have never been properly investigated, we ignore serious neglect cases because we have no available homes. (1992: 69–70)

The Canada Assistance Plan, devised in 1964 and implemented in 1966, that sought to remedy gaps in funding for welfare to the needy and children (Osborne 1985), saw an increase in child welfare programming that affected Indigenous people, in particular. As social work was growing as a profession, child welfare agencies hired social workers to protect children who were abused or neglected – which led, among other things, to another shameful chapter in social work history known as the "Sixties Scoop" of Indigenous children (see chapter 1). Feelings of resentment against social workers by Indigenous people are echoed by many people in low-income neighbourhoods, where social workers were called child-snatchers.

These dynamics prompted social critics to weigh in. For example, U.S. community organizer Saul Alinsky argues, over sixty years ago, that social workers "come to the people of the slums under the aegis of benevolence and goodness, not to organize the people, not to help them rebel and fight their way out of the muck – NO! They come to get these people 'adjusted'; adjusted so they will live in hell and like it too" (1946: 82). An extreme view, perhaps, but one shared by many critics who see the conservative and colonial values of the past – the values of the poor laws, for example – as being simply recycled, modernized, and institutionalized within Canadian social services. These critics argue that such beliefs about helping are expressions of an unjust system rather than challenges to it, and that social programs are shaped by capitalism, male domination, and colonialism and other power relations based on inequality.

Canadian history provides all too many examples of how such power relations have shaped "assistance" to the detriment of the people being "helped." For example, people with (dis)Abilities were certainly not "helped" by the sterilization laws introduced by most Canadian provinces in the 1920s and 1930s. As part of the eugenics movement, which assumed that "better" breeding would create a "better" society, thousands of people with (dis)Abilities, often people with intellectual (dis)Abilities, were sterilized (MacDonald and Friars 2010:139).

In the 1950s women were not "helped" by the psychiatric treatment of families, a treatment that highlighted faulty mothering as the key cause of emotional disturbances. Helen Levine documented sexist and oppressive assumptions made by psychiatrists at that time: "The message is that if mothers/wives were doing their motherwork of meeting the personal and sexual needs of men and fathers, incest would not occur" (1982: 196).

Gay men, lesbians, and bisexual and transgendered people were harmed rather than "helped" by professionals who diagnosed them as being mentally ill due to their sexuality. Children were definitely not "helped" in various Canadian orphanages and institutions where they had to endure all kinds of abuse. When these children were Indigenous, and/or female, or Queer, and when some of them had (dis)Abilities, the intersecting vulnerabilities combined as targets for further harm.

RESISTANCE AND PROGRESSIVE MOVEMENT

But the social services provided by the state have been more than a method of social control. They also represent battles fought and sometimes won over the years by many people. Side by side with domination came resistance. Frances Fox Piven and Richard Cloward studied the mass protests and strikes by the labour, civil rights, and welfare rights movements in the United States during the twentieth century. They concluded that when there is wide public support for protest movements, the privileged may offer an expansion of social programs in a bid to restore stability (1979: 4). According to this analysis, the growth of the welfare state can be understood as stemming in part from a militant labour movement and a consequent fear of revolution. Together these create concessions to a population that needs to be convinced that capitalism is capable of caring for its social casualties and of curbing its worst excesses. In this sense the welfare state played the role of legitimizing a political and economic system under attack.

During the 1960s and 1970s the system was increasingly challenged not only for its racism and economic exploitation but also for its exclusions based on gender and sexuality. As a result of these challenges, further progress toward equity, though limited, was nevertheless achieved. Feminists and the women's movement broke occupational barriers and created women's shelters and feminist counselling centres that influenced social work education. In 1973, the American Psychiatric Association removed homosexuality from its list of mental disorders. Gay, lesbian, bisexual, trans people, and other sexual minorities created networks of social services, and in 1982 parts of the Queer community won some rights under section 15 of the Canadian Charter of Rights and Freedoms (Bielmeier 2002: 208). That same year people with physical and mental (dis)Abilities were also included in the Charter of Rights (Dunn 2003: 206). (Dis)Abilities rights organizations engaged in court battles; in 1997 the Supreme Court of Canada states:

> Historical disadvantage has to a great extent been shaped and perpetuated by the notion that disability is an abnormality or flaw. As a result, disabled persons have not generally been afforded the "equal concern, respect and consideration" that Section 15(1) of the Charter demands. Instead, they have been subjected to paternalistic attitudes of pity and charity, and their entrance into the social mainstream has been conditional upon their emulation of able bodied norms. (*Eldridge v. British Columbia* 1997)

In 2010 Canada ratified the United Nations Convention on the Rights of Persons with Disabilities, calling on its signatories to change or abolish laws, policies, and practices that permit discrimination against individuals with (dis)Abilities. But while this ratification may seem like major progress, as newspaper columnist Carol Goar cautions, "Canada has failed to live up to the standards of other UN conventions it has ratified: on climate change, the rights of the child, the elimination of discrimination against women and the protection of the rights of migrants workers" (2010: A15).

These limited victories, often won through the courts and other institutions, are the culmination of sustained educational and political campaigns by social movements that had minimal contact with each other. During the 1970s and 1980s these separate formations began to change. Instead of competing about which oppression was the most damaging, social activists came to recognize the value of analysis and action that drew on the interconnections among various oppressions.

By the 1980s many feminists were making these links explicit. In their book *Feminist Organizing for Change*, Nancy Adamson, Linda Briskin, and Margaret McPhail (1988: 98–99) develop a synthesis of major forms of domination: "Neither class, gender, nor race is privileged as *the* primary source of oppression. Rather, the fundamental interconnections between the structures of political and economic power – in our society, capitalism – and the organization of male power – what we might refer to as 'patriarchal relations' – [are] emphasized." That is why these authors highlight the term *patriarchal capitalism*, to illuminate "the class nature of women's oppression, the impact of racism and heterosexism, and the role of the state in reinforcing women's oppression" (99).

NEOLIBERAL BACKLASH

Just when there seemed to be a new potential for the diverse networks, including social service providers, to consolidate their limited gains and work closer together to achieve greater equity, these hopes, with a few exceptions, have been shattered by a countervailing force known as neoliberalism. Some of the main features of neoliberalism include an intense suspicion of governments and government services, widespread demands for tax cuts and deregulation, and narratives that insist everyone needs to take care of themselves, rather than depend on collective or shared social solutions. These features were directly and indirectly promoted by the richest .01 per cent of the population, who used their influence to mount an attack on social programs, but also clearly recognized that tax cuts and other regressive policies would consolidate and further expand their power, their benefits, and their privilege.

Generally thought to have started in the 1980s, neoliberal policies laid the conditions for speculative investments and an artificial financial bubble that burst in 2008, sending the world's economies into a tailspin and recession. Social programs, which had already been squeezed due to tax cuts, became even more vulnerable as political leaders used public funds to prop up teetering business corporations. Despite these efforts, unemployment worsened along with an increase in precarious, part-time, and low-paying jobs, all of which contributed to greater poverty and greater economic insecurity. Pursuing policies known as austerity, the financial cuts to social programs by various levels of government put considerable pressure on social service providers to carry higher caseloads to deal with more service users trapped in more desperate situations. Some social agencies were shut down due to a lack of funds; others continued to barely limp along and many, many services were restructured and downsized. Social work education, in a new century, was presented yet again with new challenges. The next chapter discusses some of the ways it has responded.

5 DIVERGING SCHOOLS OF ALTRUISM

> Social workers advocate for change in the best interests of clients and for the overall benefit of society, the environment and the global community. . . .
>
> Human rights and social justice are the philosophical underpinnings of social work practice.
>
> — Canadian Association of Social Workers, Code of Ethics

M ost students who enter social work are eager to help others. In addition to social work degrees and diplomas, colleges and universities offer diplomas and degrees in a whole series of social service specializations, such as disabilities studies, youth and child welfare work, gerontology, addictions counselling, correctional officers, women's shelters, and community work. When asked why they choose these programs of study, students frequently say, "I want to help people."

CONFLICTS INSIDE THE SOCIAL WORK CURRICULUM

Just as the push and pull of domination and resistance within society generally result in social services being contested terrains, similar conflicts exist within social work education. Indeed, conventional and progressive approaches often co-exist uneasily within the same college or university. "Progressive" means working toward an understanding of the root causes of social problems, and taking actions, along with others, to address these sources. This has also been called a radical approach to social work (Galper 1980). By contrast, the conventional or mainstream approaches reflect top-down approaches that attempt to legitimate social work as an efficient and credible profession in the eyes of the powers-that-be, and do little to address underlying social relations and privileged groups who benefit from these inequities (Baines 2011a).

Conventional: Ecological-Systems Theory

A prominent example of a conventional approach is the ecological-systems theory. Though this theory sounds like it should be progressive, in reality, it leaves systems of dominance and relations of injustice unexamined. Within this theory the "environment" includes the social systems of family, community, and institutions such as the workplace, school, and social services. According to the theory, individuals "both change and are changed by the environment" and are also assumed to be constantly changing. Part of the social worker's job in addressing social problems, is to "strengthen the adaptive capacities" of both individuals and social environments (Germain and Gitterman 1980: 10).

On the surface, much of this approach sounds promising, however, it over emphasizes the individual's responsibility to adapt to often very oppressive and unresponsive systems. This is unlikely to be helpful in the long term and may cause serious emotional distress. A substantial power imbalance exists between individuals and their social environments – an imbalance that is not effectively addressed by ecological-systems theory's notion that social workers can successfully encourage systems to be more constructive and receive a positive response. If it were this easy, most systems would already be caring and responsive. Social work would have generous support and could shift its focus to help individuals, families, and communities to reach their full human potential. In short, the ecological approach largely ignores questions, such as: Why is there inequality? Who benefits from it? Who is harmed and what keeps it in place? What are the implications for social services and for helping social service users?

Another example of a mainstream practice is evidence-based practice (Bates, 2011). Though on its surface, the idea of social work practice that is based on evidence sounds like a good one. In reality, evidence-based practice values only evidence from research that has been produced in random clinical trials and by other tightly controlled "scientific" methods. Though this evidence may be helpful in some situations, it is collected in such controlled environments that it tends to be divorced from the diverse and multi-problem contexts in which most social problems exist.

Because they cannot be easily measured in random clinical trials, evidence-based approaches also discount practice knowledge or knowledge that comes from doing social work and social justice work, and other knowledge traditions such as Indigenous, social activism, grassroots community development, and so forth. This narrows social work practice, as will be discussed in chapter 6, and makes it easier to manage, measure, and cut back. In the words of one front-line practitioner with experience in evidence-based approaches, Michelle Bates observes that evidence-based practice pushes "a certain kind of 'scientific' professionalism . . . undermining our personal and collective ability for social justice-oriented practice" (2011: 146). Progressive practitioners criticize the "ecological" adaptation and exclusively "scientifically approved" approaches for dealing only with the symptoms of social problems (Baines 2011a; Lundy 2011; Mullaly 2010; Murray and Hick 2010; Sinclair, Hart, and Bruyere 2009).

ANTI-OPPRESSION PERSPECTIVES

Anti-oppressive social work, also known as "structural social work" or "critical" forms of practice, provides an umbrella for a whole series of progressive practice approaches, from decolonization to feminist, each of which has its own distinct conceptual and practice approach. Common to all of these approaches are theories and practices that oppose the systemic inequalities that create so much grief for social service users and many other people. Since social services and social work educational institutions are an integral part of the very society that has generated oppression for multiple reasons, ranging from colonialism to capitalism, it is no surprise that systemic inequalities are also found within social work education and practice (Smith and Jeffery 2013).

In response to these system-created inequalities, feminist activists established social services to challenge the assumption that expertise is the exclusive domain of professionals. Feminists used consciousness-raising approaches to redefine social work and help service users recognize themselves as experts in their own lives. This redefinition integrates the personal and political aspects of social problems and their remedies. An early and very influential feminist social worker, Helen Levine, notes, over three decades ago:

> Personal stress and distress are seen as a barometer, a kind of fever rating connected to the unequal and unhealthy structures, prescriptions and power relationships in women's lives. There is a rejection of the artificial split between internal feelings and external conditions of living and working, between human behaviour and structural context. A feminist approach to working with women involves weaving together personal and political issues as causes of and potential solutions to women's struggles. Women's troubles are placed within, not outside their structural context. (1982: 200; see also Church 2016)

Around the same time, educator and clinician Maurice Moreau expanded the scope of radical social work in Canada by recognizing the diversity of oppressions. He argues that multiple oppressions are interwoven into the structures of systemic inequality (Carniol 2005a, 2005b, 1992: 4). These insights, linking diversity to personal and political issues gave an impetus to social work educators taking a wider view of power relations. For example, in *Social Work, Social Justice and Human Rights: A Structural Approach to Practice*, Colleen Lundy notes that with a wider view of power relations, social work "can illuminate the obstacles to, as well as the strategies for, achieving advocacy, providing education, and promoting social change. Too often the social, political, and economic underpinnings of people's problems are not considered" (2011: 18).

We agree that multiple oppressions are harmful, and each one must be dismantled. At the same time, we recognize that some oppressions have received more attention than others. In truth, all of these oppressions need far more attention so that they can become a greater part of awareness by the general public. Part of an anti-oppressive social work approach is to bring forward those oppressions that in the past have received insufficient attention. In our chapter 3, we address a number of different injustices in a spirit of being as inclusive as possible. In this edition of *Case Critical* we are paying more attention to the injustices that are caused by colonialism and by colonial privilege, as well as by neoliberal policies that have buttressed class privilege. This does not mean that the other forms of injustices and illegitimate privilege are less important, but rather it is our attempt to bring forward what in our view needs further attention today.

As an Indigenous educator who is, like most academics of colour, subject to challenges by students on multiple fronts (Gutiérrez and Lewis 2012), Raven notes that civility in the classroom is not only important, but critical for creating the necessary classroom spaces for students to feel relaxed enough to engage freely and learn. She utilizes a framework designed to equalize power differentials among students, to have students engage authentically with each other and the professor, and to integrate their authenticity into their future personal and professional encounters.

As we reflect on how to achieve respect and constructive discussion in the classroom, it seems to us that instructors also need to be partisan. By partisan, we don't mean that instructors should single out and embarrass a student who makes, for example, a heterosexist slur. We do mean that such a situation is a teachable moment. Instructors need to point out that heterosexist abuses and stereotypes are extremely common, to the point where we may be unaware of how we ourselves hold oppressive stereotypes, often coming from media and popular culture. We are flooded with images that devalue people, on any number of axes of oppression (intersecting or overlapping areas of oppression). As instructors, we need to pause and interrupt society's harmful narratives. We need to invite students to brainstorm about how things would be different in a society that accords full human rights to Queer persons and other oppressed groups. What would be different in how we think, feel, and act toward lesbians, gay, bisexual, and transgendered people, for example? What would be different in our laws, policies, and institutional practices? Equally important, what could each of us do to contribute to such a transformation?

In widening the focus to address a diversity of oppressions, we are striving to become more inclusive. To ensure that Queer students feel they can participate fully in the learning experience, progressive social work educators have to raise Queer issues in the classroom, or as one student put it, "make Queer issues speakable in this space." This is true for instructors who identify as Queer and those who do not.

Educators committed to equity periodically critique the meaning of words and definitions that were originally intended to advance social justice. For example, Queer activists Marion Brown, Brenda Richard, and Leighann Wichman point out,

> Homophobia has been widely defined as the irrational fear and hatred of people whose intimate relationships are with members of the same sex. The original intent of creating this definition was to remove the focus from the queer person and emphasize the illogical reaction aimed toward him or her. Lived experience and further analysis of this term over the years, however, has led to the critique that the suffix "phobia" suggests a psychosocial condition, which absolves the homophobic person of social responsibility and obscures the legitimization of homophobia throughout social processes. (2010: 158)

These activists also point out that describing the fear of Queer persons as "irrational" ignores the history and contemporary context of how this fear has actually been "rationalized" by so-called scientific evidence (when medical science defined homosexuality as pathology) and by punitive religious dogma and cultural norms. To put it another way, using the term homo-"phobia" without a larger social analysis results in "diverting attention from the systemic discrimination toward queer persons that the culture of homophobia perpetuates." (159). It narrows the focus to individualized thoughts, feelings, and behaviour as the sources of heterosexist abuses.

Just as individual terms are being critiqued in the quest for more effective progressive practice, similar critiques are happening at the larger level of conceptual frameworks. Anti-oppression itself is being critiqued for having lost its critical edge by becoming mainstreamed and by downplaying the history of white supremacy, anti-black racism, and white privilege. Some critics have advocated a shift from anti-oppression toward "critical race feminism and anti-colonialism." They suggest, "while it is important to grapple with intersectionality, race must serve as the 'entry point' or 'lens' through which one acquires insights into inequalities of class, gender, ability, and sexuality and how these sources of oppression interact with race" (Pon, Gosine, and Phillips 2011: 386).

Such critiques are passionate and healthy. They are usually in response to anti-oppressive theorists watering down or excluding areas of inequality, in contradiction to the initial intent of anti-oppressive perspectives. A similar process, this time critical of anti-racism, was made by Bonita Lawrence and Enakshi Dua, who point out that anti-racist scholars and activists have ignored the importance of Indigenous realities and Indigenous sovereignty, thereby colluding with the colonial project in North America (Lawrence and Dua 2005).

These critics of anti-racism go on to say: "At the core of Indigenous survival and resistance is reclaiming a relationship to land. Yet within antiracism theory and practice, the question of land as contested space is seldom taken up. From Indigenous perspectives, it speaks to a reluctance on the part of non-Natives of any background to acknowledge that there is more to this land than being settlers on it, that there are deeper, older stories and knowledge connected to the landscapes around us. To acknowledge that we all share the same land base and yet to question the differential terms on which it is occupied is to become aware of the colonial project that is taking place around us" (Lawrence and Dua 2005: 126).

In these debates, there is a genuine quest for inclusion and for developing the most effective analysis and action toward achieving social justice. It seems to us that the test for the viability of any innovative critique of progressive practice is whether the critique is able to move outside of the confines of academic journals, conferences, and classrooms. To what degree are such critiques succeeding in motivating more widespread personal and political change? How are the proposed innovations contributing to practical victories against modern-day colonialism, white supremacy, neoliberalism, and other forms of oppression?

All this is to indicate that educational initiatives addressing the multiple sources of domination are proceeding, even if in an uneven fashion. Our understanding is evolving about the intersections of privilege and oppression and the complexities of teaching this material (Friedman and Poole 2016). At the same time, gains have been made. For example, schools of social work across Canada are expected to follow the Accreditation Standards of the Canadian Association for Social Work Education. Those standards state: "The core learning objectives for students include addressing the structural sources of inequity . . . by having knowledge of how discrimination, oppression, poverty, exclusion, exploitation, and marginalization have a negative impact on particular individuals and groups and strive to end these and other forms of social injustice" (Canadian Association for Social Work Education 2014: section 4.2).

Some progressive educators have given up on teaching social work skills. This is somewhat understandable in light of conventional approaches in social work that over-emphasize practice skills while totally ignoring the political context, such as the unjust power relations that harm all of us. We take the position that progressive social work education does need to include a focus on practice skills, so long as such skills are infused with a critical analysis that pushes back against oppression, including contemporary colonialism, and the neoliberalism that reinforces it.

We acknowledge the different versions of progressive social analysis, just as there are different sources of knowledge. We agree with the merit of teaching various versions of progressive analysis and different pedagogies that disrupt systemic inequalities. As part of this diversity of knowledge, we seek to identify skills of practice that respond to disenfranchised individuals, families, and communities by helping them to move away from being silenced, devalued, and oppressed. But progressive social work skills do not only struggle against unjust barriers. They also reach for finding the resilience and the voices that lead to personal, familial, and communal growth, wellness, and caring relationships in the context of advocating for social justice.

See table 5.1, Social Work Skills in Social Services, where we have illustrated the contrasting knowledge and application of structural, critical, anti-oppressive perspectives from the more conventional systems and cognitive approaches to practice. Generalist social workers are influenced by different viewpoints ranging from conventional (e.g., ecological, cognitive, systems theory) to progressive (e.g., anti-oppressive / anti-racist / structural / critical) perspectives. Table 5.1 applies different perspectives to a sample of practice skills. A printable copy of this table is also available free for download at btlbooks.com/book/case-critical-new.

Table 5.1
Social Work Skills in Social Services (2017)

Assessment skills	Empathy skills	Reframing skills
Social workers applying conventional ecological, cognitive & systems perspectives		
Use ecological, cognitive & systems theory: 1. to analyze dysfunctional interactions among individuals, families, groups, communities & formal systems; 2. to identify areas for new beliefs, new behaviour, new services & new policies; 3. to prioritize professional interventions appropriate to meeting client needs.	• Communicate an understanding & appreciation of the client's feelings, subjective experience & narratives (as part of developing trust within a professional relationship). • Use these skills in working directly with individuals, as well as with individuals in families, groups & communities. • Develop anticipatory empathy by tuning in, as part of preparing to work with specific client systems.	• Aim to reduce clients' sense of hopelessness by encouraging new, more hopeful ways of thinking about & re-storying the situation. • Congratulate clients for achievements that are ignored or devalued by others. • Invite clients to identify unrecognized strengths within themselves & in their interactions with other systems. • Help empower alternative, harm reduction responses that contribute to emotional growth & systems change.
Social workers applying anti-racist, anti-oppressive, structural & critical perspectives		
Use structural, critical & liberation narratives: 1. to analyze power & privilege associated with colonialism, whiteness, patriarchal capitalism, racism, heterosexism, ableism, & other systemic oppressions & their intersections with each other & with environmental contamination; 2. to identify urgent survival needs & next steps toward goals of emancipation.	• Communicate efforts to learn about & appreciate the service users' feelings & meanings (as part of trust evolving within a non-elitist professional relationship). • Honour individuality but not individualism. • Widen focus on emancipatory empathy: i.e., dialogue about subjective & systemic barriers faced by others similarly oppressed & about the courage to name & to address such barriers.	• Aim to reduce self-blame by co-investigating with service users: 1. external & internalized oppression; 2. external & internalized privilege; 3. systemic change & service users' growth. • Facilitate new, more hopeful (e.g., decolonized, feminist) ways to build on service users' resilience in light of social justice inspirations & initiatives & solidarities.

Social Work Skills in Social Services (continued)

Communication Skills	Spiritual Sensitivity Skills	Advocacy Skills

Social workers applying conventional ecological, cognitive & systems perspectives

Communication Skills	Spiritual Sensitivity Skills	Advocacy Skills
• Listen. • Encourage options for crisis dissipation & stress reduction. • Explore ways that clients could function better with family members & others. • Focus on access to available services / resources, while affirming client strengths. • Offer respect & support client self-determination. • Mediate / guide client systems into problem-solving & solution-finding processes.	• Validate religious / meditative / spiritual pluralism. • Support spirituality by clients as a strength to cope with stress (e.g., life transitions, trauma & crises caused by painful losses). • Honour / appeal to spiritual / meditative / religious values including compassion, charity & generosity of spirit to support clients & others within / across multicultural communities.	• Work at convincing formal & informal systems to better meet client needs, by urging more generosity & goodwill toward disadvantaged populations. • Be active with others in lobbying governments for better policies, coordination, integration & delivery of social programs. • Seek support from private, public & charitable sectors for additional resources to alleviate social problems.

Social workers applying anti-racist, anti-oppressive, structural & critical perspectives

Communication Skills	Spiritual Sensitivity Skills	Advocacy Skills
• Listen. • Encourage options for crisis dissipation & stress reduction, using narratives that explore ways in which clients may be victims & survivors of oppression. • Model power-sharing with service users. • Focus on unmasking illegitimate privilege. • Support & suggest narratives pointing to personal & political emancipation.	• Validate religious / meditative / spiritual diversity. • Oppose religious beliefs & practices that are oppressive. • Learn about / honour spirituality rooted in diverse cultures, including its role in Indigenous people's helping & healing. • Find spiritual / meditative / religious inspiration for personal / political / economic / global liberation.	• Become allies with Indigenous people & other oppressed populations, including service users in challenging: 1. neoliberalism, colonialism, racism & other systemic oppression; 2. environmental decisions that harm people, communities & the land. • Participate in social movements that demand local / global human rights & justice & democracy.

THE CONTROVERSY ABOUT COMPETENCY MODELS

These different approaches lead us to ask: Who should define social work competency? The debate about progressive versus conventional perspectives has become focused in this question. During an era of neoliberalism and its cutbacks to social programs, competency models were introduced by conservative social workers as "the" framework to define social work practice. They argue that competency frameworks "will permit regulators to identify the beginning competencies of social workers to ensure the delivery of high quality services and the protection of the public." They believe such competencies would standardize social work skills and advance the profession (Birnbaum and Silver 2011: 302).

While many of us oppose their competency approach, we certainly do not oppose competency in social work practice. We are concerned about the proposed competency approach's attempt to freeze a small number of practices in place as the only acceptable form of social work practices. In effect, these limited number of practices remove open-ended, hard to define social justice practices, leaving little room for practice to grow and change in response to rapidly changing social conditions. We oppose social work professional decisions being deflated into the role of technician. Furthermore, by reducing social justice practices, while increasing the number of rules social workers have to work within, progressive social work educators warn that ethical practice would become difficult or impossible to carry out (Weinberg 2010).

Jane Aronson and Dawn Hemingway note the pressure on social workers during an era of growing inequity and injustice:

> Social workers experience these regressive trends in multiple ways: in the narrowing of entitlements to service, in the offloading of responsibility for care to families and communities, and in the downloading of systems' shortcomings to individual workers. Pressed toward more fragmented and superficial practice, they face dwindling support for collective advocacy or community development and the squeezing out of the very language of social justice and systemic change." (Aronson and Hemingway 2011: 281)

Aronson and Hemingway are critical of the actual list of social work competencies produced by the Canadian Council of Social Work Regulators:

> The listed competencies are an assortment of behaviours stripped from any basis in knowledge, theory and values, from their relational contexts, from their full social contexts, and from an analysis of power inequities, or the expectation that – in accord with the Code of Ethics – social workers seek to contribute to the enhancement of social justice.
> (Aronson and Hemingway 2011: 282)

Carolyn Campbell points out that a major flaw with competency models is that they are the result of a top-down, bureaucratic approach being imposed by managers: "This 'picture of the profession' is based on employer and organizational constraints and possibilities, not on the interpretations, aspirations and imaginations of social workers themselves" (Campbell, 2011: 312). Campbell further notes that over the past century social work has been characterized by strong differences about social work's mission, fundamental values and beliefs, theoretical foundations, and practice methods. These differences have "given rise to multiple 'social works' and this diversity is one of our professional uniqueness and strengths. This diversity is denied by competency profiles as they entrench and privilege one particular understanding of social work . . . reflect[ing] a conservative political discourse and movement within social work" (313).

Competency models have been traced as an offshoot of international free trade agreements, when "provincial regulatory bodies were quietly given authority to determine the recognition of social workers via competencies" (Rossiter and Heron 2011:305). If this process succeeds, it will mean a major shift in who will be defining social work. Instead of social work practitioners and educators and their organizations making decisions about the nature of social work to be taught and practised, these decisions will be made elsewhere by competency boards with little or no ties to local communities and concerns. Instead of supporting such a conservative view of social work, we celebrate diversity, which we affirm by presenting Indigenous knowledge and Traditional Indigenous ways of teaching / learning how to become effective helpers.

FROM ABORIGINAL CIRCLES IN THE CLASSROOM TO
INDIGENIZING SOCIAL WORK

At the same time as there are efforts to trim back the scope of social work, there are promising initiatives to shift away from a profession that has been mainly White, Eurocentric, and rooted in the middle class. Some schools of social work in Canada have given greater curriculum space to emphasizing Indigenous approaches to helping and healing, while many others have begun the process of Indigenizing the social work academy (Hill and Wilkinson 2014). The shift from including content to integrating Indigenous world views and teaching methods and approaches has taken place gradually, since the inception of the first Indian social work program in 1972, at the Saskatchewan Indian Federated College (now the First Nations University of Canada). Other early Native social work programs included Maskwachees College in Alberta, Laurentian University (Sudbury, Ont.), and Nicola Valley Institute of Technology (Merritt, B.C.). Wilfrid Laurier University (Kitchener, Ont.) was the first to offer a Master of Social Work degree specializing in Aboriginal Studies, and several universities have developed similar programs in the ensuing years. Numerous other Canadian universities and colleges have taken initiatives to invite First Nations Elders and Aboriginal instructors to share their Indigenous knowledge as part of the social work curriculum.

An example of an early effort to introduce Indigenous knowledge to a mainstream school of social work was by Fyre Jean Graveline, a Métis (Cree) social work educator.

> In most Aboriginal Traditions, prior to ceremony, procedures are followed in order to prepare the mind and the body to be receptive to knowledge and insight, which may come from anywhere. Smudging, the use of burning herbs for purifying space and one another, has many effects on the individual and collective psyche. It serves as a demarcation of time, notifying everyone that "Circle Time" is beginning. It is a signal for the mind to be still and in present time; it provides everyone in the group with a shared embodied experience. As the sweet-smelling smoke encircles the area, it is easy to feel the calming presence of our plant sisters, entering and filling all of those present. (1998: 133)

An Indigenous student in Graveline's class comments on the profound effect of these practices: "As class ended tonight, I reflected on the wonderful experience that it was! I was so happy to finally be able to express my Native identity as part of my being. It was the first time that my Voice was actually being heard, not only by others but by myself" (Graveline 1998: 73,124).

Non-Indigenous social work educators are starting to learn from Indigenous ways of helping – nudged along by Canadian social work conferences that over the past decades have included an increasing number of papers and workshops on Indigenous topics. Over twenty years ago, one of the presenters at these conferences, a respected Anishinaabe teacher, Elder Waubauno Kwe (whose English name is Barbara Riley), provides teachings about the Anishinaabek Traditional Counselling Wheel:

> Unlike mainstream culture, spirituality is at the base of all (our) teachings and values. This view emphasizes balance, harmony and unity amongst all things – in particular within humankind and between each race. Aboriginal people are not an ethnocentric people. We are taught respect, kindness, generosity and humility. Because of our holistic world view, we see the interdependency, inter-relatedness and interconnectedness of all things among human beings, animals, plants, elements, and the universe. (Riley 1994: 8)

Social work educator Cyndy Baskin of the Mi'kmaw Nation summarizes how Indigenous world views apply to social services:

> An Indigenous approach to social work and being a helper is one that seeks harmony and balance among individuals, the family and community. In using the teachings that have been given to Indigenous peoples, the worldviews strive to re-balance all aspects of an individual, family, community and society. This is done with the recognition that when the physical, emotional, psychological and spiritual aspects within an individual are out of balance, the rest of the family and community are also out of balance. This is one of the most fundamental teachings and is the basis for learning to work from an Indigenous worldview. (2009: 137)

Baskin notes that Western ways of helping may not fit with Indigenous world views because, for example, Western ways emphasize individualistic rather than community-based approaches. In addition, Anglo-American social work typically ignores spirituality, rather than placing it at the core of the helping process (2009:136). The foundation of Indigenous spirituality is vitally important to cultural understanding as well as to helping strategies. Spiritual knowledge contains guidance, expectations, insights, and ethics that guide human behaviour.

As one example from the Cree culture, social worker-turned-lawyer Sylvia McAdam, in her book Cree Cultural Teachings (2009), explains the four Cree laws that guide verbal and physical conduct for humans and non-humans alike. For Indigenous clients suffering from trauma, addictions, lateral violence, and cultural dislocation, learning about the natural laws of their culture can be a critical starting point for Indigenous-based social work intervention (McAdam, 2015).

The conflict of world views that Baskin highlights, and its impact on what is taught and how it is taught, has been experienced in multiple disciplines in the social sciences. In the mid-1990s, Indigenous academics in North America, through Devon Mihesuah and Angela Wilson's (2004) critiques about Indigenous representations in academia, were mobilized to challenge the dominance of Euro-American and Euro-Canadian pedagogies.

Indigenous academics have pushed for moving beyond the addition of a few teachings or helping strategies in curriculum to more basic Indigenizing approaches to teaching, research, and program delivery. This means "integrating and centering Indigenous peoples and their knowledges within programs, curricula, and administrative structures, while simultaneously increasing the recruitment and retention of Indigenous faculty and students" (Brealey 2012).

In this sense, "Indigenizing" means removing colonial narratives, but also inserting Indigenous content in what is being taught, while avoiding cultural appropriation. This includes attention to who is appropriate to teach what content, and how to do research using Indigenous research methods (Brealey 2012). Though in mainstream the term "knowledge" is typically singular, we use the term "knowledges" to acknowledge the diversity of Indigenous nations and communities that results in very different knowledge bases, depending on the region, nation, and community.

National and international gatherings since 2012 have focused on Indigenizing academia, which in turn resulted in many universities finding ways to include Indigenization as part of their strategic plans. Though "academia" usually refers to universities, we note that a number of community colleges are also responsive to and taking up these changes. Because of the move toward Indigenization for social work, we are starting to see generalist social service and social work programs that no longer merely pay lip service to Indigenous helping and healing strategies. Indigenous knowledges and approaches are being established in curriculum development and content so that students engage with more accurate historical knowledge, and develop more insight into ways to respect cultural differences. Consequently, students graduate with a wider and more culturally relevant skill-set in helping Indigenous clients.

These forward-looking approaches are just beginning in social work (Kennedy-Kish [Bell] and Carniol 2017, in press). Of course, decolonizing education must involve more than social work. As Justice Murray Sinclair points out in an interview with the *Globe and Mail*, the Truth and Reconciliation Commission of Canada is greatly concerned "over the fact that universities continue to graduate people into important professions – legal, medical, social work, even science, including engineering – who don't have an understanding, education and respect of who aboriginal people are and what they have to contribute in those areas" (Chiose 2015: A7; see also Kennedy 2015).

Anglo-American and other non-Indigenous social workers can learn from Indigenous-based programs to develop a better balance between the individual and the community. Our social work can also be more attentive to spirituality. To the degree that we are open to learn from Indigenous culture, it also becomes important that we avoid stealing Indigenous knowledge. As Baskin warns, "appropriation is the new tool of colonization. . . . To appropriate Indigenous spiritualities or other practices into Western forms of social work without consultation of Indigenous people and without acknowledgement of Indigenous knowledge is no different than the theft of our land" (Baskin 2013: 150).

FOUR PRINCIPLES OF GOOD PRACTICE

Awnjibinayseekwe Banakonda Kennedy-Kish (Bell)

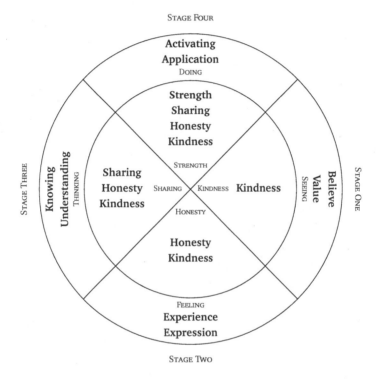

Stage 1

In teaching Indigenous social work, the very first principle of good practice is kindness. Kindness is not a value in itself; it is inseparable from belief, location, and belonging, to land and creation.

Kindness is a way of seeing and being in the world. It is a landscape, an essential framework, a foundation that directs and informs relationship. Kindness would not exist without relationship.

We experience self and the other simultaneously. The principle of honesty emerges in that experience and in self-expression.

The belief in kindness, the reaching for kindness, the expression and experience of kindness cause a knowing of kindness that leads and furthers knowledge and understanding, enabling and facilitating practice.

Stage 2
Honesty emerges in relationship within and from kindness. Seeing and valuing kindness moves us into experiencing and feeling kindness, leading to the expression of kindness. This can and often does engage us in a struggle when kindness is compromised or diminished. We struggle with our beliefs and our values when kindness is not expressed and experienced. The principle of honesty itself may be compromised if we have seen and experienced little to no kindness.

Stage 3
There is a knowing that emerges from experience, that leads to understanding. The knowing and understanding that emerges is housed in and informed by kindness and honesty or its lack. This knowledge and understanding is framed in the principle of sharing. We share kindness and honesty or its lack. When we don't experience or express kindness, our knowing and understanding is about the lack of kindness. This may enable the absence of kindness in our practice, both toward ourselves and others.

The value and purpose of knowledge and understanding are held within the principle of sharing. It is here that a belief in kindness and sharing emerges that is different from mainstream. Kindness is not charity, is not welfare. Sharing strives for balance and harmony through Kind honesty. It is rooted in a belief that creation cares, is kind, and unconditionally sharing.

Knowledge and understanding are nation-building, community-building, individual-building responsibilities, informed by beliefs, values, experience, and relationships to self, others, and creation that embodies the principle of sharing.

Knowing and understanding is the challenging work,

[Banakonda, *continued*]
learning to be done by all of us. It is the work of relationship. We see ourselves and each other within relationship with each other. When we embrace and engage our values and principles they inform our application of practice. It facilitates our navigation of those painful life experiences that are in the way and informs the ways which we might move those obstacles aside. In this way, those very obstacles can become our teachers.

We each have a responsibility to learn from life. It is in this way that Indigenous learning and healing is framed. The focus is on wholistic ways of coming to see, value, and engage the learner in wellness, in self-development, and in personal and professional growth. An Indigenous practitioner must be informed by his or her culture to experience, express, and activate this in practice.

When doing self-reflection, struggle emerges when there is a lack of congruence between the kindness we want, the kindness we experience, and the kindness we express, in the way we carry and apply kind honesty.

Stage 4
Strength is kindness, honesty, and sharing. Strength is the culmination of all the principles of the Four Directions in application. It is a doing and a behaving that is informed by the principles. In other words, strength is the realizing and activating of the four principles in our personal and professional life.

The awareness and commitment to see, experience, know ourselves and each other allows us to not only accommodate human and cultural diversity, but also to facilitate the gifts that lie beneath the unrealized potential in all of us.

6 SOCIAL WORKERS: ON THE FRONT LINE

> I think my empathy level had gone. The continuous problem
> after problem after problem and seeing nothing done and it
> coming back to me. It was so repetitious you almost lose your
> feelings with it . . . which is really sad for me because I'm
> quite a compassionate person innately . . . and I hated that
> part of it.
> — a social worker in a Saskatchewan child welfare depart-
> ment, documented by Patti Cram, in her Master of Social
> Work thesis, University of Regina

Most social workers are employees of social agencies (also known as social services), funded and influenced directly or indirectly by government authorities. The practice of these agencies is an integral function of the overall system. In Canada, as in other rich countries, governments include a wide range of commissions, departments, and agencies supposedly organized for the purpose of enhancing the public's general welfare or our social and economic well-being. One way of promoting these goals is the deployment of social workers within social agencies, both within and outside government.

WHERE SOCIAL WORKERS WORK

Social workers are employed in a number of different social services in the public, non-profit or voluntary, and for-profit sectors. Undoubtedly the largest single area of social work is in government-run services or *public sector services*. Government services are often statutory; their tasks and outcomes are specified by government regulations and policies. An example is social assistance, better known as *welfare* – or *workfare*. These programs provide for the payment of limited amounts of money to people who have little or no financial resources. Social service workers assess the needs of applicants for assistance and decide whether they qualify based on the agency's regulations and policies. Increasingly automated and depersonalized, these programs allow less and less time for counselling or job-training projects. Instead, service users are encouraged to take any form of employment, regardless of wages or working conditions, to get them off the welfare caseloads.

Although social work has often been equated with public assistance, social workers are employed in numerous other agencies within the public sector. A partial list includes probation services within juvenile and adult correctional branches, alcohol detox centres, mental health clinics, and psychiatric services, outreach programs for homeless youth, and long-term care for people with (dis)Abilities. Social workers are also employed in the quasi-government or quasi-public sector, in settings such as hospitals, public health clinics, and public schools that have voluntary boards, but are funded and legislated by government to perform certain tasks.

In Ontario, examples of quasi-government agencies employing a large number of social workers are the Children's Aid Societies. Each Children's Aid Society has its own volunteer board of directors, responsible for ensuring that government legislation and policies are followed. These boards of directors also establish further policies and standards for social workers to follow. Most provinces maintain child welfare agencies within the public sector – that is, operated directly as part of the government, though some, like Nova Scotia and Ontario, operate child welfare agencies in both the voluntary and the public sector.

Many social workers are also employed in the *voluntary or nonprofit sector*, for agencies such as the YWCA/YMCA, Elizabeth Fry Society, or John Howard Society. The terms "voluntary sector" and "voluntary agency" are sometimes thought to mean that the services are provided by volunteers. But while volunteers do offer services in some of these agencies, the volunteers typically supplement the services that are delivered by paid social service workers. The agencies in this sector are governed by voluntary boards of directors made up of individuals who receive no direct remuneration for their activities on the boards. These boards in turn hire service providers, including social workers, to carry out their programs.

Sometimes the voluntary agencies are established by religious or cultural groups, which raise their own funds to finance, for example, the Ma Mawi Wi Chi Itata Centre, United Chinese Community Enrichment Services Society, Salvation Army, or Jamaican Canadian Association's Settlement Services for New Immigrants. Many of the agencies in the voluntary sector receive funding from donations collected through local charity appeals, such as the United Way. They also receive funding through government grants, and are increasingly shaped and constrained by government policies and forms of organization. From within this voluntary sector, during the early part of the twentieth century, social work evolved into a profession, which at the time received much of its activist, social justice, and participatory ethics. However, as public services are contracted out to the non-profit, voluntary sector, these social services have narrowed their focus to meet the goals of neoliberal governments rather than the needs of marginalized groups and communities.

In Quebec the voluntary sector is called the "social economy," which has been somewhat better protected from government reshaping. Yves Vaillancourt defines the social economy as "a vast array of enterprises and initiatives, mostly from the non-profit sector, including advocacy groups, voluntary organizations, other community-based organizations as well as cooperatives." These organizations are oriented toward innovations in networking and democratic practice, based on "values of solidarity, autonomy, reciprocity and self-determination" (Vaillancourt et al. 2004: 314, 315; Vaillancourt 2012).

Throughout Canada, a small but growing number of social workers also work in private practice, running their own offices much as lawyers do, with clients paying fees for service. Some of these workers have chosen to work in the private market because of the benefits they see in terms of being their own boss and running their office on their own terms. Others, such as feminist therapists, have ended up in private practice to avoid the restrictions set on their practice in public or non-profit agencies. And still others have been pushed into the role of private consultant to keep their employment with government agencies, who lay off their full-time staff and will only hire them back as private consultants. Many of these workers are not comfortable with being part of the private market but they have few other choices in today's tight labour market. Social workers also work in private agencies that provide social services for a fee, with the goal of turning a profit. Some social workers feel that profit-driven services are unethical, while others have no difficulty with this concept, and others accept it as an uncomfortable compromise.

It is not unusual for client populations to receive help from the public sector and the voluntary sectors at the same time. For instance,

> Social workers have been working with people with (dis)Abilities on numerous fronts, from community development to establishing advocacy groups, community living centres, and, overall, a place for (dis)Abled persons within society. They also help families secure the services and resources necessary to combat barriers associated with accessibility and accommodation, and engage in individual work recognizing the person with the (dis)Ability as the expert on his or her own life and abilities. (MacDonald and Friars 2010: 141–42)

Most social work textbooks present social work from an urban perspective – they assume that all service users are total strangers to the social service workers, and that numerous specialized services are in place within easy transportation, such as one might have in a large city. While most Canadians live in cities, social services are also provided in rural settings and where populations are small and support services are often sparse. In rural settings, there are often only one or two social workers in the entire community. Some social workers prefer living in a small community where they get to know people before they come for assistance. That often makes the relationships less formal than in urban settings. Contrary to the impression that rural settings have less food insecurity, rural poverty also takes its toll (Swift, Balmer, and Dineen 2010: 133–42; see also Daley 2015).

How People Become Social Service Users

The needs that bring someone to a social work agency – or bring an agency to someone – are many and complex. Problems can range from violence against women to poverty, child abuse to alcoholism, drug addiction to marital strife, or conflicts in the paid workplace or at school. We may find ourselves recovering from a serious illness that prevents us from returning to our job, and so might have to seek out a social agency to get financial help or advice. A person with AIDS in a hospital might be referred to the hospital's social worker, or a student having difficulty might be referred to the school district's social work counsellor. As parents, we could get a visit from a social worker if someone (a neighbour, teacher, or doctor, perhaps) suspects we have abused our child and reports us to a child welfare agency. If we have been convicted of a crime the court might order us to report to a probation officer, who may be a social worker. The *official* message to social service users is *we are here to help you* (Canadian Association of Social Workers 2016). The more subtle message is *we are here to help you with* your *personal or* your *interpersonal problem.* This implies that the problem arose entirely within oneself and has no connection to social conditions and systemic inequalities that affect everyone.

If a person is experiencing severe interpersonal problems (within their family, for instance), they might seek out social work counselling, which would usually put them in touch with a social service agency in the voluntary sector. Or they might find themselves going to a private practitioner's office. There is a marked contrast between someone voluntarily seeking help – say, with an addiction – and an involuntary situation in which a court sentences someone to receive social services. A rough guide is that involuntary social services are provided by government agencies, whereas the voluntary sector tends to offer services that clients are free to accept, reject, or approach on their own initiative. Thus the term "voluntary" applies to more than the social agency's board. It can also apply to the level of choice involved when someone accepts, or doesn't accept, the social worker's services. To the degree that a person's choice is reduced, government social services move in with their own definitions and solutions.

HIERARCHIES AND THE STRATIFICATION OF SOCIAL SERVICES

Social services are hierarchical or stratified in much the same ways as government and business bureaucracies. In other words, services are organized with some people and programs having power over others in a sort of pyramid structure, with the very few at the top having control over the many at the other levels of the organization. Among the reasons given for stratification are greater efficiency and accountability of professional social work services, where executive directors (in the voluntary sector) and senior social service managers (in the public sector) are seen as having primary responsibilities for the organization and its use of funds. This allocation of power and responsibilities operates on the assumption that those at the peak of the social agency's pyramid are the professionals who are the most qualified and competent. According to this theory, a measure of a person's competence in social work is the ability to rise up the career ladder. Social service workers are sometimes taught that the current structures of hierarchical authority are necessary and desirable, with little consideration of whether alternative, more democratic organizational structures might better serve service users and make agencies more pleasant places to work.

Bureaucratic hierarchies are sometimes defended by saying that someone has to be in charge. Such attitudes are deeply ingrained, resulting in some social workers feeling that their first responsibility is to their employer rather than to their clients. The loyalty to a hierarchy is offered as a "natural" condition, and the descriptions of the hierarchies tend to ignore their contested nature and downplay the aspect of social control embedded in these organizational structures. Similar social service hierarchies exist in the voluntary and government sectors; the main difference is that in the volunteer sector, social work managers or executive directors are accountable to voluntary boards of directors rather than to a government minister.

Another difference is size: a non-profit agency is usually smaller than a government agency. Voluntary boards, however, are influential in giving direction to social agencies and in promoting their credibility in the eyes of major funders. As in the public sector, social service executives strive to provide their operation with effective management. This includes financial management and supervision of either departments or front-line staff, depending on the size of the agency.

While social work executives in the voluntary sector are in strategic positions to speak out about the effects of unjust social conditions upon service users, they usually do not. It is not that they are told to keep quiet, though sometimes they are. There is a more subtle process at work as administrators learn that boards and government funders prefer a smooth operation, free from public controversy. In response to the ongoing funding crisis in social services, some non-profit agencies have deliberately recruited corporate leaders to their boards to assist in fundraising and make the agencies more appealing to corporate donors. The voluntary ethos of social justice and participation are unfamiliar to most members of the corporate world. Rather than adapt to the agency, corporate leaders exert pressure to make non-profit agencies look more like for-profit businesses.

In an example where this happened in a large, progressive, non-profit social service agency, workers note, "at some point management at our agency decided that they needed more people who are in business, more people who are powerful so they could pull in funding, and they got more of those board members in. Once they had them they realized that they came with a completely different world view and a completely different attitude and a completely different focus. Ever since then they've been trying to explain to them what the agency philosophy is." Another staff member added, "the board now is considerably more conservative than management is" (Baines et al., under review in 2016).

Boards are usually active in a monitoring role, and have a particular responsibility for the executive director, to evaluate performance, and including the power to hire and fire. In other words, boards not only have responsibility for the agency's financial position but also decide whether the executive director is suitable as the top manager of the agency.

The top-down flow of power in social service agencies can become, among other things, a channel for punitive actions against social service workers, leading to a profound sense of alienation. This was illustrated some years back in Alberta after the media reported on a number of foster parents abusing foster children. In response to these scandals, the provincial government decided that child protection workers must visit each foster child and each family on their caseloads once a month. Subsequently, one of the social workers said that at first glance it sounded like *"an improvement over just letting situations drift endlessly."* The worker added:

> *Now comes the catch: with 90 or 120 children on your caseload, plus all the paperwork, tell me how it's possible to carry out this policy? It can't work! It's impossible! Now if something blows and a child is harmed, the managers can say, "We have a policy, why aren't the workers carrying it out?" A classic case of blaming the victim! You answer, "But there aren't enough hours in the day," and they can't hear that. The managers will pass down the blame to the supervisors – why can't you manage your units? And the supervisors will yell at the line workers – why can't you manage your cases?*

If the constant demand for acquiescence does not wear us down, and if we retain our abhorrence of arbitrary power, gaining a promotion within hierarchical agencies can create other problems. For example, supervisors can easily become divorced from front-line colleagues and client realities as they shift their loyalties from the front line to management. A level of mistrust toward managers is not uncommon among front-line workers, and managers do not always react constructively to that mistrust. According to a supervisor in a welfare office: *"You find you now have two levels, your previous colleagues who are still line workers and your new colleagues who are also supervisors. You find yourself talking to other supervisors about 'they' at the line level, as if somehow 'they' were not quite as wise as you supervisors. 'They don't know.'"*

Gradually the separation becomes solidified. Supervisors attend certain meetings and have access to information and decisions – an access that the line staff does not have. Misunderstandings can easily develop, with line staff suspecting or knowing that supervisors are holding back information. Some supervisors try to be open with and supportive of front-line workers, and many succeed. But such openness occurs despite the agency hierarchy, not because of it. More often workers who move into management find themselves jumping to the defence of the system.

In class terms, just as the interests of managers in private business corporations become identified with the owners, managers of social agencies (and most of their consultants) tend to identify with the interests of those in control of the social service delivery system. In both cases, front-line employees end up subordinate and subservient to the power of the managerial group.

Racism and white supremacy have impacted Indigenous and racialized Black Canadians, and people of different ethno-racial backgrounds. These groups were the focus of a study by social work researchers Kevin Gosine and Gordon Pon (2010), who focused on the experiences of racialized child protection workers in the Toronto area. Many of the participants expressed concerns around systemic racial discrimination in the promotion and advancement of service providers within these agencies. In addition, based on the experience of the racialized child protection workers in this study, Gosine and Pon found that services to racialized service users were often impacted by negative stereotypes along with little understanding of cultural differences. These researchers noted that racialized workers in these agencies had to "contend with white-normed and middle class-oriented policies, tools, and practices which often prevented them from meeting the unique needs of racialized service users" (2010: Abstract, 1).

This kind of study clearly documents the gaps between the official mission statements of social service agencies, which usually emphasize inclusiveness, and the actual practices of agencies and some of their workers. In addition, within a government service, there can be talk among administrators and senior planners about respecting culture, but it fails to be implemented in practice. For example, in the child welfare system in Nunavut, there is much talk about providing a culturally relevant child welfare system that respects traditional Inuit knowledge, but as researcher Patricia Johnson points out, "this remains, unfortunately, just talk" (Johnson 2014: 282–83).

THE CHALLENGE OF SOCIAL WORK

Depending on the agency and the population they serve, most social workers help service users and communities to access financial and other resources, and provide various types of support, counselling, advocacy and, in some cases, community organizing and mobilization. Providing access to resources might include helping someone get access to subsidized housing, searching out a decent nursing home for a frail parent, or seeing that a child with a (dis)Ability is able to get to a good summer camp. One of the hallmarks of social work practice is the ability of workers to establish effective interpersonal relationships with clients. This requires that the worker attempt to enter the world view and psychic space of the client, to act on a sense of empathy and establish sufficient rapport to elicit a description of the problem as seen by the client. All of this, needless to say, is not an easy task. Certainly it can be argued that it is impossible for a social worker to ever fully understand the life or the world of the client.

Responses to oppressive narratives

As Black activists Wanda Thomas Bernard and Veronika Marsman point out, the Association of Black Social Workers was established to intervene in a social service system "that was not responsive to the problems and concerns of African Nova Scotians" (2010: 194). The association's participants became concerned when child welfare agencies said they could not find Black foster and adoption homes for Black and biracial children: "The experience of racism and cultural alienation was an everyday occurrence for most of these children at home, at school, and in the neighbourhood" (196). In response, the association worked to implement an Africentric set of principles based on "an African worldview that includes harmony, collectivity, and non-materialistic qualities of people; [and that] connects people culturally, historically, spiritually, and with community; and views the experiences of African people as key movers of their own liberation" (193). These principles, sometimes implicit, have guided the Association of Black Social Workers over its forty-year history.

During that time, it has pushed for the province to recruit and retain Black foster and adoption homes, and advocated for and succeeded in improving provincial family legislation. It has also run youth programs, including lessons in African Nova Scotian and world history and sessions in dealing with racism and handling conflict. This project is a case of social workers not limiting themselves to counselling, but becoming involved in public education, policy/program advocacy, and community development. This work continues today (Bernard-Thomas 2015; see also Association of Black Social Workers, Nova Scotia 2015).

People often feel ashamed or confused about the stressful situations that have prompted them to contact social services, whether it is alcoholism or unemployment or violence in the home. Social workers need to be skilled in asking the appropriate questions, in observing, listening to, and focusing on painful topics. In theory we try hard to be non-judgmental, to refrain from criticizing or blaming service users for their situations, and to support people to find hope that change can happen and their lives made better. In actual practice, we as social service workers too often focus primarily on our own views, our own preconceptions, our own definitions of problems, and our own sense of what is "normal."

For example, considerable heterosexism still exists among many social work educators, students, and professionals, who accept the prevailing systemic stereotypes that dehumanize lesbians, gays, bisexuals, trans, and other sexualities. In response, social work educator Brian O'Neill notes, "the first step in addressing the lack of attention to sexual orientation in mainstream social services is to acknowledge that LGB people are among the clients of the agency. Subsequently, queer people can be involved in the systematic review and development of policies to comprehensively address issues related to sexual orientation" (O'Neill 2012: 326).

Children may be concerned about their sexual and gender identities, or lesbian mothers may be seeking custody of their children. How will service providers treat people of all sexual orientations and identities with respect if social service agencies continue to privilege heterosexuality as "the normal" sexuality?

When gay and lesbian older adults go to counselling for issues such as misuse of alcohol, they may not get the help they need.

Furthermore, a study about long-term care in the Vancouver area found, "during the project, we heard repeatedly that the current generation of LGBTQ seniors is fearful that health authorities and residential care as well as assisted living facilities are not equipped to adequately meet even their most basic needs. They are concerned that the system is not designed to support them and that their case managers will not be able to ensure their health and wellbeing, and protect them from harassment, discrimination and abuse based on sexual orientation, gender expression and identity" (Aging Out 2015).

Attempts to "cure" people whose sexualities differ from heterosexuality have had a shameful history. It includes the Nazi Germany period, when gays, lesbians, and other Queer persons were arrested and forced into concentration camps, where they had to wear an identifying triangle sewn onto their clothes and were experimented upon by doctors who used various injections to search for a "cure" for their sexuality. Today in North America, though not at the point of the gun, "curing" is being pushed by religious fanatics who use fundamentalist dogma to pressure lesbian, gay, bisexual, and transgendered people to get into "treatment programs." Though at best well-meaning, such "treatment programs" represent a further level of insults and oppression under the guise of "help."

Though it is becoming more widespread, particularly in large urban areas, respect and support for Queer people can be found most consistently within agencies that are specifically oriented to the needs of Queer people and that adhere to Queer-positive values (O'Neill 2006). Although coming "out of the closet" is by no means an easy step in our society – it may alienate friends, family, workplace supervisors, and service providers alike – research has shown that being out has its advantages in relationships with health and social service providers.

A group of researchers based in Montreal, Toronto, and Halifax (Brotman et al. 2007) looked into the experiences that caregivers of gay and lesbian older adults had in health and social services. They found that caregivers who were themselves gay or lesbian – and were out – tended to have a sense of confidence in their own rights and as a result usually felt the most comfortable advocating for the rights of care receivers to full and equal access to services. These researchers stressed the importance of social work aimed at empowering Queer older adults and their caregivers, as well as the need to develop explicitly Queer friendly services or safe spaces for caregivers and care receivers who might still be "in the closet." Among other things, employees at all levels of social service agencies need to have proper training "so that they provide a warm and welcoming environment" (501; see also Furlotte et al. 2013).

Welcoming environments in health and social service organizations need to include bisexuals, transgendered, and other Queer people. They can face immense difficulties when coming out because of the conventional view of gender as being "either male or female," with attractions confined to "either male or female." In contrast to these binary prescriptions, the more fluid identities experienced – for example, by bisexual, pan sexual, non-binary Queer, or asexual people – are complex, and require social services that avoid "slotting people" into fixed categories. This categorization is reflected in this person's counselling experience:

> A person could be straight for a number of years and then live in the gay lifestyle for a while and then return to the straight lifestyle as I have. Would said person be bisexual or straight? I tend to value the romantic and spiritual connection that I have with someone, over the body parts they possess. I believe this is what makes me truly bisexual. If I like you I don't care what is in your pants. I will work with whatever is there. However, a counselor at my local GLBT community centre has diagnosed me as straight after asking me a bunch of questions about my likes/dislikes. (Madison 2009)

Service providers can be most helpful when they are open to the lived experiences of the people they are working with, but all too often such openness is undermined by a culture of prejudices against certain identities and a discomfort dealing with new, fluid understandings of identities. Considering the case of transgendered children, for example, Gerald Mallon cautions service providers: "Just as it is important that transgendered children are not mislabeled as gay or lesbian, although they frequently self-label as such prior to coming to a full understanding of their transgendered nature, it is also important that gay and lesbian children are not mislabeled as transgendered." He points out that in contrast to gay and lesbian children, who ultimately accept their gender while being attracted to others of that same gender, transgendered children have a consistent dissatisfaction with the gender they were born into; they find themselves identifying with a different gender (1999: 60, 59; see also Mallon 2015), and may be attracted to any number of other genders.

When trans adolescents defy gender expectations, they often face a backlash from family and peers, and especially at school. According to one analyst, this situation can lead to "intra-psychic problems and behaviour such as depression, low self-esteem, substance abuse/hormonal abuse and self-mutilation, compounded by additional factors such as running away from/being kicked out of one's home, homelessness, prostitution, dropping out of school and unemployment" (Burgess 1999: 58). Although this comment was made over fifteen years ago, the heterosexism that spawns mistreatment of Queer populations continues unabated, as suggested by a 2009 U.S. survey of transgendered students' experiences at school: "90% of transgender students heard negative remarks about someone's gender expression sometimes, often, or frequently in school . . . and also reported little intervention on the part of school personnel when such language was used" (Trans Youth Family Allies 2009: x). Also sobering, from 2015, "hate-motivated violence against transgender people rose 13 percent last year" (Ennis 2015).

Impact of underfunded social services

Negative attitudes and barriers affect various groups. An executive director of a Halifax employment project set up to aid prisoners from federal penitentiaries found herself working on a shoestring budget that had been cut back: *"If a prisoner isn't able to find a job after release from prison, what happens? He can go on welfare but many are too proud, so where can they get money to pay for food and rent? Crime becomes very tempting and the next thing you know, they're back in prison. Our society spends a lot on punishment, jails and the like but little on positive help."*

Workers in government welfare or workfare departments face particular challenges. They often carry caseloads of individuals and families that number in the hundreds, which leads to a different kind of struggle to survive. Ben, one of the co-authors, was told this by one of these workers:

> *From a service point of view, I don't even have time to listen to clients. In one recent month my total caseload was over 215 cases! I burnt out last August. During one hour then I had as many as five cases of evictions to deal with. It got to the point that emotionally I gave as little as I could to each client. Of course clients realize it and get resentful.*

Government social service workers have unique challenges in dealing with bureaucracy and regulations as their employers tend to establish rigid rules and policies. These rules in turn often place social workers at odds with service users. Supervisors are usually nearby to remind social workers about the agency's expectations, as shown in this experience of a social worker in a public assistance agency in British Columbia: *"As a social worker, you know it's impossible for a family to stay within the food budget. But you find your supervisor is putting pressure on you – to put pressure on the client to keep within the budget."*

Many service providers try to maintain a sense of personal accountability, of decency and respect for others, distinct from the requirements of the agency. At the same time, knowing that as a professional helper you are not really going to be helping clients get on their feet can produce a sense of demoralization – primarily among service users but also among social workers. After all their training, social workers often discover that while their social services do provide some help to clients, at best they can barely scratch the surface of the problem.

Rather than blame either the worker or the service user, we need to develop new models of organizing social services in ways that honour the dignity of both. These new models would require:

- sharing power between the worker and service user
- lowering caseloads to avoid long waits by service users
- loosening rigid rules and scripts to allow for flexibility in services
- inviting service users and communities into agencies as equal partners in supporting and caring for each other.

But instead of being part of the development of improved services, many social workers experience practice marked by time crunch, unreasonable supervisor demands, high caseloads, increasingly desperate services users, and inadequate resources. All these deepen the stress involved in providing and accessing social services.

The barriers faced by service users often originate in the dysfunctional ways in which social services are organized, as well as in the unhelpful policies that social workers are expected to follow. In agencies designed to protect children from abuse and neglect, government policies have been established with little or no input from social workers on the front lines. An example is the expectation that social workers will carry out certain types of risk assessment procedures when there is suspicion of child abuse or neglect. These procedures are rigid. They prescribe exactly when supervisors must be consulted and rely on extensive checklists and computer data entry.

Over a decade ago, Canada's national social work association took a courageous stand. It warned that child welfare services in many provinces are failing to implement the officially established purpose or mandate for which they receive government funds: "In many jurisdictions legal mandates are not being met, client needs are not being met, and social workers are not meeting the ethical requirements of their profession." The Canadian Association of Social Workers concluded that the service organizations were "more interested in saving money than [in] providing quality service to children and families." It saw "limited resources both within the agency and in the broader community . . . as a chronic impediment to good practice." As for the social service employees, "a lack of recognition and support" had left many of them "feeling victimized, helpless, isolated and disenchanted" (Canadian Association of Social Workers 2003: 10, 12; see also La Rose 2009: 234). Since then, underfunding has become worse, as evidenced by the recent Human Rights Tribunal on Indigenous Child Welfare finding. Cindy Blackstock, executive director of the First Nations Child and Family Caring Society and initiator of the complaint, discovered that Indigenous children and Indigenous child welfare is funded on average 22 per cent lower than non-Indigenous child welfare (First Nations Child and Family Caring Society of Canada 2014).

Banakonda

The conditions that Indigenous families confront with child welfare interventions are barely sustainable due to rigid policies and underfunding. Further, the challenging demands of excessive paper/computer work required, minimizes the time social workers have for front-line practice. This is aggravated by the fact that there are not enough social workers to serve the Indigenous population. These barriers are obstacles to serving the children, youth, and their families.

To be really helpful, many of these social workers need to be Indigenous and knowledgeable about colonial genocide past and present, and about Indigenous cultures and traditions.

It has never been helpful to remove children from family, home, and community.

The current practice of intervention does not address the problems that are there, or the ones that have resulted in children being removed, and it deepens the divide in the family structure. This is now intergenerational – undermining child, family, and community. The children and their relationships with themselves, their family, and their community are not addressed. Nothing has changed except the children become isolated and marginalized before and after returning, if they ever get to return.

The children then become "the problems," either way. The relationships are further harmed, communication even more difficult. The implementation of these interventions continues regardless of their overwhelming failure to achieve or contribute to the well-being of the child, the family, or the community. There have been no positive outcomes from the onset of these policies. The results cause me again to realize that these policies are about removal from our land.

Professor Cyndy Baskin, of Mi'kmaw and Irish descent, identifies a major problem with social service delivery to Indigenous people generally: "One of the main problems when non-Indigenous helpers work with Indigenous adults is that they overlook the Indigenous person's culturally held beliefs and values, instead using an approach to social work they assume to be universal" (2009: 136; see also Baskin 2016). Yet barriers to decolonization do not go away even when social services are delivered by First Nations people. As Mandell, Clouston Carlson, Fine, and Blackstock explain,

> Indigenous approaches to child welfare that emphasize the involvement of community, Elders, and extended family hold promise, but even in situations where Indigenous people have assumed authority for child welfare services, these services are delivered under the auspices of existing legislation resulting in "the lack of a cultural fit between child welfare, ideology, law, and services delivered." (Mandell et al, 2007, cited in Strega and Carriere 2009: 22)

Sometimes those barriers are broken down and innovative programs begin to help people (Mussell 2014; S. Johnson 2014; First Nations Child and Family Caring Society of Canada 2016a). But for both Indigenous people and non-Indigenous people, the innovations unravel due to funding cuts and the limited scope of social programs. A social worker in the Maritimes had established a program for school dropouts who were in conflict with their families and the law. The program consisted of building solid relationships with the youths and taking them out to work on fishing boats:

> After a couple of weeks the kid would return home and the mother would tell me – "My son looks great! I don't recognize him! He's got a tan, developed a bit of muscle, the lines under his eyes are gone, the tension is gone, he looks great!"
>
> *But it was all a mirage. Those changes meant nothing . . . nothing! Because these kids went right back into their old situations, there were no other choices. We had a temporary program and when it was gone, the kids were left with nothing, no jobs, just like before.*

THE BOTTOM LINE: MANAGERIALIZED SOCIAL SERVICES

Since the mid-1980s in Canada, social services have undergone waves of reorganization and restructuring (McDonald 2006). Most of this restructuring involves funding cuts, as governments move out of providing its own services to citizens and, instead, contract out these services to voluntary and for-profit agencies. If agencies want to receive funding from the government, as minimal as that often is, restructuring involves the adoption of private market-like management models that claim to improve efficiency and save money. Rather than empowering workers and improving performance, as they claim, these models routinize work, making it alienating and repetitive, and result in demoralizing working conditions and unsatisfactory services.

Examining data from over eighty front-line social service workers in Alberta, British Columbia, and Nova Scotia, Donna, one of the authors of this book, found "full-time, permanent, unionized jobs in the social services sector are being rapidly replaced by part-time, contract, on-call and other forms of temporary insecure work" (Baines 2007: 90). Intensified managerial control has meant not only that risk assessment comes under closer scrutiny, but also that "intake forms, case notes and even supervision are increasingly standardized, often taking the form of step-by-step 'best practice' flow sheets, computer case management packages and check box forms in which the interactions among layers in the social work endeavour are tightly scripted" (Baines 2011c: 33; see also, La Rose 2009). As she documented the flow of social service work being "sped up and readily assumed by part-time, temporary and contract employees," Baines notes that the result is a de-skilling of social work (2011c: 37).

As a result, "most workers felt that new forms of management have closed down ways in which employees used to have input into the priorities and organization of their agencies" (38). Baines (2011c) and others criticize these new forms of management for creating new barriers to social services, for lowering the quality of services that in turn increase the hardships experienced by social service users, and for eroding workplace democracy, where it existed.

The imbalance in power created by the top-down business management approach has much to do with these outcomes. As a service provider in an agency serving youth and families puts it, *"the person who supervises you clinically is the one who hires you, is the one who fires you, is the one who disciplines you, and is the one who overrules you."*

Given the squeeze on so many front-line service providers, it appears that the job of social work is being granted professional status only in a symbolic sense. In this context advocacy work is not an easy route to follow. For instance, Deena Ladd works with a Toronto worker advocacy centre for precarious workers – *"people who are in precarious jobs – they have low pay, no union, and incredible insecurity."* As of 2015, such oppressive terms of employment are continuing and accelerating (Mojtehedzadeh 2015a: A12).

Ladd, a social work graduate, also *"noticed that advocacy is a dirty word in most social agencies, not just in agencies working with employment programs."* A good part of the reason for this, she says, is "fear." The agencies receive funding from various levels of government, and their administrators are afraid that if they speak out they will lose their funding.

Although social work "professional colleges" can discipline their members for unethical conduct, these colleges have no clout when it comes to protecting social service workers who want to do advocacy work. The day-to-day control over practice is not exercised by the profession but rather by a combination of agency and social service managers, beholden to funders who today have their own neoliberal agenda.

PRIVATIZATION OF SOCIAL SERVICES

In many countries of the Western world, following the Second World War, many people gained increased social and human rights, due to an expansion of the social safety nets, alongside greater opportunities for democratic decision making at every level of life (Lightman 2003; Stanford 2015). However, this democratization and expansion of rights placed the interests of most people on a collision course with the corporate sector. In the mid-1970s corporate leaders, who had tolerated union and social rights in the first decades after the Second World War, decided things had gone too far and began demanding tax cuts.

Business leaders claimed that the growth in government spending due in part to the increase in social and human services, was causing "dangerous" government deficits and that without drastic action, these deficits would undermine the entire economy. Deficits are not generally a problem for large economies, like Canada's, as they can be paid down during periods of economic boom (Stanford 2015). However, corporate leaders used deficits as an excuse to attack social programs and to restructure society in ways that ensured no interruption or challenge to their profits (Stanford 2015). The corporate world also came up with a strategy to shrink government services, while simultaneously making profits from them: contracting out and privatization.

Privatization and contracting out are processes of providing funding to non-government agencies to provide services that the government used to provide. Governments do this to save money because the voluntary and for-profit sectors pay significantly lower wages and benefits than the public sector. Through the terms of the funding contracts, governments set the management mode of the agencies, namely the private market models mentioned earlier. Through insistence on outcome measures and targets, they reshape the everyday work of front-line staff by decreasing face-time with service users and increasing time spent keeping statistics and documenting outcomes (Cunningham and James 2011: 15–36; Davies 2011). This process also eliminates or reduces open-ended, social justice – based practices. Those practices, which include advocacy, policy analysis, community development, and social action, are not easy to slot into outcome measures, so they are largely ignored. By excluding such practices the voluntary sector gets reshaped and narrowed, though it still often prides itself on believing that it welcomes these kinds of practices (Baines 2011b).

The growth, in recent decades, of privatization and contracting out stems from business leaders, their think tanks, and their special interest groups lobbying government to move institutions such as prisons, hospitals, public schools, garbage collection, universities, and social services away from the public sector and into the private sector: once inside the privatized sector, private companies and corporations make considerable profit from government contracts (Davies 2011).

Governments have introduced competitive bidding for services not only operated by government but also for those operating outside of government in the non-profit or voluntary sector. The successful bidder gets awarded the contract to run the service, be it a prison or home care. It is expensive and time consuming to develop a viable, clear, and comprehensive contract bid, meaning that small non-profits often have a difficult time participating, and many have lost their funding or amalgamated with larger non-profit organizations.

Private corporations have a great advantage in competitive bids, as they typically calculate their costs based on a non-unionized, low-paid workforce. As a result, they can underbid the not-for-profit agencies, which pay salaries that are not particularly high but are generally higher than those paid by private corporations. In the case of some sectors, such as nursing home care, large international chains are often very successful. They can centralize administration, thus lowering their own costs and keeping profits high, whereas small non-profits find it almost impossible to meet government regulations and remain solvent. As international trade agreements between Canada, the United States, and other countries are being pushed aggressively by government and business leaders, it is likely that large for-profit chains will move further into service delivery, bringing with them dubious quality as well as poor wages and working conditions.

Where not-for-profit agencies, such as home-care services for frail senior adults, are required to engage in competitive bidding against business firms, the pressure mounts for all workers to adopt an impersonal factory model for social services. An administrator of a non-profit long-term care agency comments on the effects of privatization:

> For the client, there's no choice. A hospital will tell them, "You go home NOW: we'll give you home care at the level we decide." Clients come out quicker and sicker from hospitals, which increases the responsibilities of home-care workers. And by metering out maximum levels of service, staff is pressured, for example – when giving a bath to a client, to be in and out of the client's home in half an hour, little time for talk, little sense of humanity – off they rush to the next client. That, plus the government's

efforts to compress wages, leads to less job satisfaction, and will over time
lead to bigger job turnover – with less continuity of service for clients.
While all this is happening we see non-acute clients being squeezed out of
services they used to receive, and having to rely on the private market.

Though smaller private companies provide services, large, often American, private chains have expanded their service provision in Canada in the last decades, particularly in the areas of child care and nursing homes. Many charge their customers directly or receive a flat rate from the government – getting, for example, so many tax dollars per bed. Private companies promising to deliver services at lower cost are music to the ears of fiscally challenged governments. Furthermore, once these for-profit social services win government contracts, they have strong incentives to further cut their costs (usually in the form of reduced wages for workers and lower quality food and supplies for service users).

Austerity deepens
This shift to business management approaches has deepened in social services in the period after the global financial crisis of 2008. Following this massive banking crisis and deep recession in many countries, governments introduced policies referred to as "austerity," which involve deep cuts to remaining public sector services and cuts across the board to contracted-out services. Many authors note that the crisis was used as an excuse to restructure the economy to further favour corporations and private profit at the expense of poor and working people (Stanford 2015; Baines 2014; Teeple and McBride 2010). They point out that even the World Bank and the OECD (Organisation for Economic Co-operation and Development) have noted that these austerity policies have been harmful and not produced the economic recovery they promised.

For social services, austerity means making do with less and intensified scrutiny from the government over every penny provided in funding contracts. Scrutiny takes the form of outcome measurements and statistics mentioned earlier in this chapter. Through their involvement in these processes, social workers unintentionally become the long arm of the state, introducing austerity into the everyday lives of service users and communities. Though business approaches in social services began a number of years ago, austerity extends and deepens these approaches and is part of a worldwide restructuring led by global corporations. These private enterprises seem intent on shifting all services to the private market where profits can be made, regardless of the impact these shifts will have on those in need of care and support.

While alternatives to this business model do exist, they come from innovations where promising practices result in better services to long-term care residents (Baines and Armstrong 2015). But so far, these alternatives have been ignored. Business interests continue to have the ear of government as they push for contracting out and privatization, while also launching lobbying campaigns against unions. No surprise, then, that the percentage of workers in labour unions is dropping. At the same time Canadian legislation has removed collective bargaining from many sectors. The Canadian rate of unionization was 38 per cent in 1981, but slid down to 29 per cent in 2014 (Statistics Canada 2015). Currently, the overwhelming majority of workers in Canada remain outside of collective bargaining.

Roy Adams notes that in 2007 a Supreme Court of Canada case involving B.C. Health Services, affirmed that collective bargaining by workers is a human right. He concludes that we cannot have real democracy when a huge majority of working citizens do not "have the right to negotiate their pay and working conditions with their employers." On the contrary, he says, "they are effectively serfs of unaccountable industrial barons in workplaces that blatantly defile the basic principles of equality, dignity, respect, freedom, and democracy" (2009: 45; see also Heron 2012).

Real democracy must include an expanded membership base of organized labour. Progressive social workers need to intensify support for labour unions as they push for more inclusion of who has the right to full collective bargaining and for a voice in their workplaces. We believe that a larger, stronger unionized workforce constitutes a vital element in reversing the cuts and deterioration in social services that accompany privatization and contracting out.

To reverse these negative trends means that for our identity as social *workers*, and social service *workers*, we will need to correct the balance by recognizing we are also *workers*, with rights and responsibilities. By understanding ourselves as workers, it becomes easier to recognize what we have in common with other workers, who also experience alienation, frustration, and powerlessness at their work-places. Such enlightened consciousness may also facilitate our taking action in solidarity with other workers to support all of our efforts at improving working conditions. In this process, we are interrupting the prevailing individualism that sees each of us as separate, isolated individuals, with the illusion of having total control of our destiny. We nevertheless support individuality, which respects the unique dignity and potential of each person, while at the same time we are committed to developing our connections with community; we are seeking to take action to enhance our collective well-being. We are reaching for a better direction.

In reaching for a better direction, it will also be important for social service providers to engage in a decolonizing process that addresses all social services, ranging from financial aid (social assistance) to child welfare services.

A CHALLENGE: THIS STORY MUST CHANGE

Banakonda

It is critical to consider the impact child welfare services have had on Indigenous communities, families, and individuals. The attitudes and policies that authorize the removal of Indigenous children from their homes and communities, into residential school, into group homes and foster care, continue to harm the health and welfare of Indigenous children, families, and communities. It is social workers who are removing Indigenous children.

Throughout the closures of residential schools and to the present time, so many Indigenous children have been removed from their homes in such dramatically increasing numbers that they now far outnumber those children removed into residential schools.

In bringing the federal government to the Canadian Human Rights Tribunal, Cindy Blackstock highlighted systemic discrimination against Indigenous children. In 2015 the Canadian Human Rights Tribunal agreed with Black-

[Banakonda, *continued*]

stock and found the federal government's funding decisions had indeed discriminated against First Nations families on reserves. This provided a window into the systemic economic discrimination against Indigenous children, their families, and their communities.

This decision by the Human Rights Tribunal addressed only the economic discrimination, but it is fundamentally the systemic violations of human rights and of the Treaties that remain the underlying challenge to redress. The "Two Road Wampum Belt Covenant" is a Treaty and outlines the agreement between First Nations and the Crown to protect Indigenous land, water, culture, language, and trade.

Violations of the Treaties and of human rights, along with current austerity policies, have further aggravated the chronic underfunding that has long resulted in insufficient social programs, education, and housing for Indigenous people. The systematic underfunding of child welfare, social services, welfare assistance, and educational programs results in a severe absence of community resources, family resources, and individual child resources to meet the needs for whole wellness.

Our people deserve equity, opportunity, and justice.

Our children need health in their spirit. They need to belong, be valued, to hope, to see and believe in a good life.

Our children need to experience heart, experience good feelings, and experience safety, and to engage and express good feelings.

Our children need to have good thoughts, come to know and understand themselves and others in a good and kind way.

Our children need healthy bodies, to house their spirits, hearts, and minds, to do good and live a good life.

It is these that create a healthy community, healthy families, and vibrant contributing human beings.

Governments deliver recreation, education, and health

services, but to Indigenous communities, these are dramatically fewer in quantity and inferior in quality. So much so that it causes Indigenous people to live on the edge of survival, further aggravated by the stigmatization that poverty itself causes. For those in poverty are always blamed for that poverty. This unwillingness to provide equity in services is evidence of another agenda. That agenda has consistently undermined good social work and community work, making impossible the application into practice of the four principles, kindness, honesty, sharing, and strength into practice. Indigenous people have been consistently unable to access these government services in any operable way within our communities. When we move to urban centres, we can access more, although still not equitable. Herein lies that hidden intention of government. We are supposed to leave our land. This is the purpose of inadequate services in our territories.

Governments and all Canadians must be held accountable. Canada and the Americas as a whole must reconcile with long-standing practice of dispossessing Indigenous people, including life-taking, life-demeaning methods of acquiring land. To embark on a new narrative, "Oh Canada, Our Home on Native Land" would be a good beginning. However, this needs to reach the streets, into the homes of every Canadian, and into the decision making and implementation of government and business institutions and structures.

Intentional harmful discrimination as a way of acquiring the land for mining, oil, timber, and mineral extraction is exploitation and subjugation, and operates from a belief in settler-entitlement. In the end such discrimination will cause indiscriminate suffering at a level of "equality" we have never known. Settlers continuing to turn their heads away from recognizing our rights, will be at all our peril. For ravishing the land, the water, the air, for materializing life will truly be at the peril of all humanity. They are connected: what is happening to Indigenous men, woman,

[Banakonda, *continued*]
and children, to people of colour, to people living in poverty, and to the dispossessed generally, will in the process, impoverish and compromise the very survival of all humanity.

For reciprocity is the blueprint of life – imbalance always leads to harm if it is not addressed.

Restoration must assure the delivery of true justice, the forever reaching for harmony and balance. This needs to be an operational principle, meeting the needs for life-affirming Indigenous services that respect Indigenous culture and traditions.

As well as the need for good healing practices, Indigenous communities must be allowed to create and practice their own economic development plans, using community-sustaining models grounded in Indigenous culture and values, in respectful relations with land, air, water, and the life that inhabit this earth. Benefit from Indigenous land needs to fundamentally benefit Indigenous communities.

The current practice of extraction for the benefit of mainstream to the detriment of community and environment, continues to cause severe illness, loss of life, health, and well-being. I refer to mercury poisoning in Grassy Narrows, long standing and continuing, without action, forced relocation into areas where flooding happens every spring, and communities without drinking water, James Bay. No drinking water, in Shoal Lake. These examples go on and on across Canada, and not just in the North, long standing and unattended. And what is the response, the call for . . . "the Indigenous people should be moved again." Why is the cause of poisoned water, ground, and air – mining, deforestation, hydro plants – continuously ignored? This story must change.

7 REALITY CHECK: SERVICE USERS' EXPERIENCE

> The way they look at the dollars – it's like they just ring up their figures on a cash register. You're worth so much for this, so much for that – they make you feel like an animal.
> — A woman on welfare in British Columbia

"**W**hy are we not heard?" This is a question often asked by people who experience oppression. Social services that provide assistance to disadvantaged populations are typically focused on their mandates, rules, sense of what is best for others. In contrast, in this chapter we present the experience and voices of service users. As anti-oppressive social workers, a pivotal aspect of our work is learning to listen deeply and non-judgmentally to service users, as well as fostering opportunities for them to have a full voice on decisions affecting their lives and communities.

Jean Swanson, who knows firsthand about being poor and on welfare, offers this advice in her classic book, *Poor-Bashing*:

> People who aren't poor will need to do a lot of listening, be willing to learn, leave space for others, and actively work to end poverty. If we can do this with respect, it could bring together a lot of people who have been separated in the larger struggle for worldwide justice. (2001: 188)

If we do a lot of listening, and are willing to learn, we may recognize another person's pain and hear their implicit call for justice. As we listen, however, what we are able to hear will be screened through our own understanding of poverty. We are likely to be influenced by deeply entrenched attitudes and ideas that predispose us toward devaluing people who are poor. In our everyday conversations, and in the media, we frequently hear judgments about one person or another having "poor" health, "poor" judgment, "poor" hearing, a "poor" self-image, or a "poor" driving record. We typically use the word "poor" as an adjective to describe deficiency, failure, or inadequacy. In these ways our habits of language equate "poor" with defective qualities. We can all too easily slip into applying such negativity to individuals and families who lack adequate income and hence, are poor.

This stereotyping can also easily reinforce baseless prejudices against poor people as being lazy and irresponsible. These dynamics may explain why it is easy for slick politicians and demagogues to engage in welfare bashing. Attacks against people who need welfare often reinforce their feelings of being failures. When we disparage social service users, we feed into self-righteous campaigns for further cuts of "government waste" in public services and calls for more austerity.

These negative attitudes, narratives, and prejudices undergird institutional practices that further harm people who already experience oppressive social conditions. Such harm from poor-bashing is aggravated by other oppressive practices and prejudices, such as racism and colonialism. Such harmful narratives and practices continue to undermine the well-being of Indigenous children, as many as 40 per cent of whom are living in poverty (Campaign 2000: End Child and Family Poverty 2015: 6).

Indigenous children in residential schools not only experienced harsh and austere conditions, they were also deprived of love and affection. A survivor of the Indian residential school system in Canada recalls her experience:

> We were basically never nurtured. We were emotionally deprived by invalidating our emotions. And if you did cry nobody acknowledged it. Nobody came over to ask. "What is wrong Lucy?" You just had to lay in your bed at night and just cry. (Truth and Reconciliation Commission of Canada 2013b)

Another survivor talks about her emotions:

Anger was my number one emotion I ever felt, and loneliness, a deep-rooted loneliness. But I never expressed it. I never let people know about it, which led me to depression. So I suffered from depression, loneliness and rage. (Truth and Reconciliation Commission of Canada 2013b)

Today, these and other accounts of these "schools" have become a matter of public record. But there is less documentation about the intergenerational impact upon the children of the survivors from residential schools. The impact is not only emotional. Kathy Absolon explains:

I began to connect my aching back with my own history . . . The aches and pains of being dismembered as a people and being severed from our families of origin, as was the case in my family with residential schools and the reservation system, runs deep. I missed having aunts, uncles, grandparents and cousins around me. We were severed from them and their ability to transfer their knowledge to us. . . . Oh how thirsty I was to learn about what happened to our people. It was like I was born into a time where the cyclone had hit and the people were still walking around in states of trauma. No one could explain to me what happened. No one could connect the dots between my personal chaos and the political, institutional and cultural attacks against Indigenous peoples in Canada. No one could explain because everyone was reeling from the colonial aftermath. (Absolon Minogiizhigokwe 2011: 15, 18)

No wonder children today suffer too. Today, there are large numbers of Aboriginal children in the child welfare system: even more than in residential schools at any one time. (Brittain and Blackstock 2015: 70–75) Rather than improving, the situation in Canada generally seems to be getting worse. Peter Menzies is a social worker and member of the Sagamok Anishnawbek First Nation. Using 2013 statistics, he was disheartened to report that "of the roughly 30,000 children aged 14 years and under who were in foster care, 48.1 per cent were Aboriginal" (Menzies 2014: 53).

For every child who comes under the authority of the child welfare system, there is a story about the child, but there is also a story about the parents and family. Here is an example of a mother whose children were removed from her care. Did the social worker have any idea what this mother had experienced when she was a child? At the age of five she was taken to residential school against her will, and against the will of her family. She recalls what it was like on the first morning:

> I was served oatmeal, crusty and brown. I was upset and for the first time, I really felt I was alone. Everything was strange to me with no time to adapt. I had trouble swallowing, being a slow eater. I did not like the bitter taste, which caused me to gag. I could not help but cry. The nun ordered me to hurry up, slapped me on the back of my head and angrily told me to shut up and eat. I puked in my bowl and I was forced to eat my own vomit. I never forgot that or the many other physical abuses I received as punishments. . . . [During my first year of the education routine] I received verbal abuse by name calling when I got the answer wrong. I was called "a stupid savage," and "a dumb little Indian," I was told I would never amount to anything, and that was told to me in front of others. At times I witnessed others being belittled. All of those insults took the joy out of learning. . . . All this affected my performances during later school years. It damaged my self-esteem and attitude. It affected my social skills by twisting them into negative perceptions and behaviour in relationships, which developed from what I observed. I disliked school. Later, I became another drop-out statistic because of what Residential School did to me. . . .
>
> Their religion developed a fear in me towards the nuns and priest and their vengeful God. It developed into feelings of my being ashamed and guilty being an Indian child. My Spirit was deeply wounded. It was confusing because it made no sense. I was told and threatened that if I did not listen to them, God would send me to hell. . . . I will not go into much details with my sexual abuse experiences but during those times, I always felt confined, and each sexual abuse incident unbearable. There was an adult male perpetrator who abused me – a priest with grey hair, stinky breath who dressed in a black robe with his rosaries. At such times, he would tell me, it was God's will. This confused me because he was the man of God. I felt so much shame and guilt. As a result, I disliked my body. Later, I became anorexic because I wanted to disappear. Sometimes during the night, footsteps were heard coming into our dorm, choosing his victim and taking that child away. I was one of them. (Timmins 2015: 92–93, 94)

The impact of these abusive experiences was monumental:

> As such, those horrific memories haunted me in my nightmares and polluted my mind with self-loathing, fear, shame and guilt. I succumbed into emotional turmoil; depression, suicidal attempts, feeling misplaced, worthless and useless. I drifted into the world of alcohol and drugs to escape the memories and to numb the pain. My life spiralled downwards. (95)

Fortunately, she did manage to stop the downward spiral. She went back to her culture, and was helped by Indigenous Elders and Knowledge Keepers who made a big difference.

In light of the harm done to Indigenous people by colonialism generally, and residential schools specifically, it is not surprising that there would also be overrepresentation of Indigenous people among the homeless population. In addition to this overrepresentation, there is another, related issue: Why in a rich country like Canada are there so many Indigenous and non-Indigenous people who are homeless, anyway? Why is inequality growing worse among mainstream Canadians? Why are social problems getting worse? Why are more people hungry and homeless than ever before? Many people believe that because Canada still has some social services and supports there is no reason to worry: those who need help can get it. This assumption merits a closer look.

A former welfare client who is a single mother describes her struggle to stay off welfare.

> *By November of last year I went off welfare. I was holding down two jobs, one with the Y, the other with a day care, but the salaries were terribly low. I was bringing in $100 less than when I was on welfare. So I got a third job, at another day care. All these jobs were for different times of the day, different days of the week, but it ended up I was working from 8:30 a.m. till 6 p.m. for five days a week, juggling these three jobs. It was hard but I just never wanted to go back to welfare. I felt I was better than dirt.*

Why does receiving assistance make someone feel like dirt? People internalize the stigma against welfare for many reasons. One woman on welfare said that it was not much different from her experience of having a bad marriage – either way you get *"put down all the time – that's pretty hard for the head to take!"*

Another welfare client put it this way: *"As a single parent on welfare, you feel so vulnerable, so unprotected. You're game for the weirdo's on the streets. I've got a double lock on my door, but that doesn't stop the strain – the strain is financial and emotional and it can get to your health too."*

Service users are reminded again and again, sometimes subtly and sometimes not so subtly, that they come from a certain culture, class, gender, racialized group, or other groups who are deemed "inferior." People who are gay, lesbian, bisexual, trans, "deviant from the norm," have a (dis)Ability, or are a "senior citizen" often report that within the social service system they receive the message that they have less right to dignity than others. For women, being on welfare can lead to other problems.

> *I did a favour to this neighbour, she was going into hospital to have a baby, so I offered to babysit her two children. Fine? Her husband comes to my place and you know what he wants? He wants to go to bed with me! I refuse and he says, you'll be sorry. He figures I'm on welfare, I'm a single parent. I'm fair game. I told him where to go.*

That kind of treatment month after month demoralizes service users and over time can have a devastating impact.

Given that the amount that welfare departments allow for rent is typically much lower than the actual rent charged, recipients end up having to make up the difference out of their food budgets. Canada has over one million people on welfare (Stapleton with Bednar 2011: 7). The dynamics lead to clients feeling trapped. Even when, as happens occasionally, the welfare rates are raised, the trap remains. *"Sometimes welfare gives us a raise – at last. We won't be eating macaroni. But nothing changes. Because then the rent goes up and wipes out the raise."* The irony here is that the woman quoted above was living in public housing and the rent was raised by the public housing authority, an organization that is supposed to be committed to accessible and affordable housing regardless of income. What one branch of government is giving with one hand, another branch is quite consciously taking away with another.

Numerous reports confirm that a sense of fear permeates social assistance, as a service user in the Maritimes describes:

When I applied for welfare, I even knew the amount I was entitled to. It was higher than what my social worker said – but I was afraid to push for it. I was reluctant because of fear – I might lose all of it. I can now see how you become too dependent on the worker – how women's passive roles are reinforced by welfare."

How can these and so many other examples of mistreatment happen in Canada, a country with a Charter of Rights and a reputation for being a good place to live for all? Service users, social workers, social critics, and government officials have known for years that not all was well with social services, and yet these problems are tolerated rather than resolved.

WELFARE "REFORM": SMOKE AND MIRRORS

Over four decades ago the Special Senate Committee on Poverty criticized welfare offices for what it saw as a system that "repelled" both service user and service provider (Special Senate Committee on Poverty 1971: 83).

Over two decades later, Senator Erminie Joy Cohen presented her report, *Sounding the Alarm: Poverty in Canada,* in which she concludes, "the government of Canada has made many promises to the international community to protect the lives and livelihoods of its most vulnerable citizens. Yet to date, it has made no progress in this area" (1997: 44). By 2013, not much had changed in reducing poverty. If anything, systemic inequality is getting worse (Citizens for Public Justice 2013a, 2013b, 2015). This slide backward toward less equity is further documented with reference to the United Nations' Covenant on Economic, Social and Cultural Rights that calls upon the participating states to recognize the right of everyone to an adequate standard of living, including adequate food, clothing, and housing. While Canada signed this covenant in 1966 and ratified it in 1976, by 2015 the federal government still has no national strategy to eliminate poverty (Schmidt 2012; Blatchford 2015).

There is no strategy in place at the national level to address the needs of *one in seven* people in Canada who live in poverty. . . . The experiences of poverty – hunger and inadequate nutrition, substandard housing, preventable illness and disease, precarious employment, huge levels of family stress and social isolation, feelings of inadequacy, diminished opportunities to develop and learn, and discrimination and stigmatization – exact a heavy toll on individuals and families living on Canada's economic margins. . . . A Hamilton study found a 21-year difference in average age at death between neighbourhoods at the top and the bottom of the income scale, an appalling gap in a country that prides itself on universal health care and that has the resources to address poverty. (Canada Without Poverty 2015: 3, 11)

Meanwhile, Food Banks Canada documents that over 800,000 people were helped by food banks across this country. This is a 26 per cent increase from 2008 (Food Bank Canada 2015: 1). In 2015, Campaign Two-Thousand's Report Card on Child and Family Poverty gave government a failing grade. "Child poverty continues to deprive over 1.34 million children of their only childhood. Choosing to allow child poverty to continue forces children to endure hunger, deprivation and exclusion, and compromises their health and life chances" (Campaign 2000 2015:1).

These hardships, which trigger anxiety and emotional pain, are given voice by a single mother:

We have to make tough choices between rent and food and all that stuff, so it cause a lot of depression too. . . . stressful, stressful you feel like you're hopeless you feel like it shouldn't be like that and sometimes it makes me very angry and it seems like nobody cares because you tell them, you know what, I'm hungry I need. . . . a hot meal and no one cares. People care but you know it's like you're at the point when you need the help [but] you don't find the help. It makes me angry, just make you very angry; sometimes it's stressful. Sometimes you feel like don't even want to live no more. (George, Munawar, and Atcha. 2013: 39)

Independent research into government welfare departments tends to confirm the harsh experience by social service users. Marjorie Griffin Cohen reviewed welfare policies in British Columbia with this conclusion:

The process of seeking income assistance has become so restrictive, and so complicated to navigate that it is systematically excluding from assistance many of the very people most in need of help. The result is a very rapid spike in homelessness and increased hardship in B.C. Our long-term study with people on social assistance indicated that a large number were denied assistance. To survive, they returned to abusive relationships, or relied on panhandling, illegal activities, or the sex trade. Some are living on virtually no income on the streets. (2009: 22)

Viewed as an irritant because of its anti-poverty advocacy, the National Council of Welfare had its entire funding cut by the federal government in 2012. During its forty-three years of operation, this Council had been an effective forum, giving voice to the experience of low-income people in Canada. But this voice was more than embarrassing to all levels of government, particularly federal. The voice of people living in poverty proved to be an indictment of the failure of government policy favouring tax cuts and cuts to social programs. The voice of impoverished people reminded the country that government policies were causing pain and suffering for many, contrary to the glowing promises of well-being for all, made by Canada's economic and political elites.

Despite various attempts to stifle public debate, there are independent, persistent, and courageous voices that continue to put a public spotlight on the need for enlightened social policies, social programs, and social services (Brittain and Blackstock 2015; Citizens for Public Justice Ontario 2015; Ontario Advocate for Children and Youth 2014). These voices continue to call for social and economic justice despite funding cuts. Among other issues, they criticize Canada's decision makers for allowing homelessness in Canada to be as high as 235,000 people in a given year (Gaetz, Gulliver, and Richter 2014). At its core, these issues are about whether our nation's wealth will be distributed according to principles of fairness and equity, or whether a relatively small group of people, with their disproportionate and unfair privileges, will block progress toward social justice.

Rather than say we don't care about social problems and don't want to spend money on them, most politicians and business leaders have become adept at spouting soothing, bland words, which are extremely deceptive. For example, to justify tax cuts and current neoliberal trends, Larry Elliott, a writer for the *Guardian Weekly*, decodes their actual meaning, which he supplies in brackets in a classic translation:

> We must become more flexible [accept lower pay] and dynamic [enjoy fewer work benefits]. Rigidities [trade unions and social programs] must be eliminated so that we can be more competitive [companies can make bigger profits and pay less tax] when facing the new global challenge. [If you don't like it, Buster, there are plenty of people in low-wage countries willing to take your job.] (Elliott 2004: 17)

In January of 2015, Canada's official unemployment rate was just below 7 per cent (Canadian Broadcasting Corporation 2015). This rate is supposed to measure how many more people are looking for jobs than there are jobs available. But the official unemployment rate does not include workers who have stopped looking because so few jobs are available. When the official unemployment rates are announced, they are often accompanied by reports of the number of new jobs created, but these reports make no comment about how many of these new jobs are precarious, that is, part-time, short term, non-unionized, in unsafe working conditions. Neither does it take into account women's unpaid work in and out of the home. So the real unemployment rate may be the official rate multiplied by two or more. Furthermore, the official unemployment figures do not address jobs that pay under the poverty line. Dianah Smith describes her sister working at a low-paying job where there was no union:

> After my sister's long-term relationship dissolved she took on a weekend part-time job. This was in addition to her full-time job during the week. It meant she would be working seven days a week in order to "make ends meet." The weekend job consisted of folding hundreds of pieces of linens and towels. The workers, mostly older immigrant women recently arrived from Eastern Europe, Africa and the Caribbean, were stationed on an assembly line: a massive pile of towels and linens would drop from a cage that moved along a wire above these stations. The job was to fold all of this linen in record time and to bring these piles to another station. The cage would come by frequently, dropping pile after pile of freshly laundered towels and linens

in front of each workstation. There were daily quotas, and if you were unable to meet it you would be let go.

My sister worked at this job for three years. She now says that her back, knees and feet are messed up because of the many hours of standing she did during each shift. (Smith 2015: 29–30)

As a result of the October 2008 financial crash in the United States, many full-time jobs were lost in Canada. Yet even before this steep economic downturn, the rules for who has the right to receive unemployment insurance were constantly changing to make fewer and fewer unemployed people eligible for this social insurance program. The Canadian Labour Congress in 2014 noted only 37 per cent of unemployed Canadians are eligible for Canada's employment insurance (Canadian Labour Congress 2014: 1).

At the same time as Canada's social safety net is being shredded, the failure of our economy to create enough decent jobs has meant that crime can appeal as an option, which in turn closes more doors. A young Black Maritimer gives a graphic account of the impact of racism and a "clouded" personal history when a job referral agency sent him out for an interview:

> So I called and made an appointment. When I went up to the office, there were two women sitting in the waiting room. I sat down and waited too. This fella comes out of the office and calls out my name. I said "Yes, I'm here" and I stand up. The fella looks up from his file, sees my face and freezes. Why he practically pushed me down on the chair! I knew I had no chance at a job there. And anyhow, whenever I apply for a job right on the application form there's a section that says, do you have a criminal record? When you put down "yes" that finishes your chance for a job.

High unemployment not only hurts the most vulnerable in the workforce – women, people of colour, and youth – but also undermines the labour movement's victories from an earlier era, victories that promised a secure income to anyone willing to become employed. When unemployment insurance benefits run out, or if an applicant does not qualify, the source of support shifts away from the federal government to provincial and municipal public assistance (or welfare) programs.

DIFFERENT SHADES OF SOCIAL COERCION

High unemployment and inadequate unemployment insurance and ineffective social services often result in people being forced to take dead-end jobs at low pay. And policies like workfare (or working for social benefits) mean that people can be cut off welfare if they refuse to take even an unsafe, poorly paid, dead-end job. This form of social coercion moves many people into the low-wage, insecure labour market where they remain poor, exploited, and frequently unemployed, as employers relocate to new jurisdictions (or lose contracts) and lay workers off. This can contribute to family tensions where children may suffer the brunt of adult disappointments, frustrations, anger, and despair. That in turn, may result in a child protection worker assessing that, for a child's protection, the child needs to be removed from the parents; if the abuse or neglect is severe enough, the child protection worker may recommend to a judge that the child be placed in a foster home. See chapter 6, where Banakonda elaborates on how this approach further harms the child.

When there is child abuse, the coercion is personal and direct, sometimes based on a combination of ageism against young people, and illegitimate patriarchal privilege that enables a father to feel entitled to abuse his children:

> *The incest usually happened when my dad came home from the bar. He'd be drunk and he'd come into the room and like we'd be in bed most of the time when he came home, because we knew he'd be drunk. So we'd go to bed and he'd come into the room and he'd sit on my bed and he'd put his hands on my breasts and my privates and I'd just – I'd wake up and I'd be really scared. And upset about it. And I'd wonder, well, what's going to happen? I don't want this to happen – and then he'd climb under the covers and start committing the incest and I'd tell him to stop – that it hurt – leave me alone – that I didn't like it – but he just wouldn't go away.*

Though they are supposed to protect children from abuse or neglect, child welfare agencies can have indirect coercive effects on children. From a young child's point of view, separation from home can be a frightening and bewildering experience. While the social work professional has an adult view of how it all fits together, the child's experience is usually one of powerlessness and confusion.

Social workers, emergency shelters, courts, police, foster parents, group homes, and other institutions – they form a maze that adds to the anxiety. One child compared his experience to being a ball in a pinball machine, with the buttons being pushed by the child welfare system and the child bouncing from one hard place to another. This "bouncing" is quite disconcerting when traumatized children are taken into care, only to be re-victimized.

All too often when children come into the care of social services, they are sent to group homes where they don't receive good care – which results in some children acting out in aggressive ways. In response the group facility calls the police or security, and the children end up being criminally charged under the Young Offenders Act. Before they know it, they get locked up in detention centres for youth. The correctional system is highly coercive, either for people awaiting trial or for people convicted of crimes, as it includes police, judges, and prisons. Within the correctional system, social services may attempt to rehabilitate offenders. A prisoner from the Maritimes had this to say about whether the criminal justice system helps people change the course of their lives:

> Rehabilitation? I get a laugh when a judge says he's giving you a jail sentence so you can get "rehabilitated." What rehabilitation? It's a big farce. There's only rehabilitation in the imagination of the judge. When you get sent to prison, there's a piece of paper and it tells them to take you from point A to point B. Point B is prison. The prison gets the piece of paper and the only thing they do, they try to keep you there.

For years, it's been known that prisons do more than just "try to keep you there." Not rehabilitation, though, as a young girl in the Burnaby Youth Secure Custody Centre notes: "So where was my rehabilitation when I watched my friends get the shit kicked out of them by uniformed guards?" (Justice for Girls 2003). In 2014, Anna Mehler Paperny from Global News reports that a federal prison watchdog report found "despite ample evidence of the harm it causes, Corrections Canada keeps putting inmates with mental illness in solitary confinement. 'Nearly all' inmates who'd killed themselves while in segregation had known [to prison authorities] significant mental health issues." What's more, "the majority of segregated inmates had a history of previous suicide attempt(s), suicidal ideation and/or self-harming behaviour" (Mehler Paperny 2014).

The revolving door syndrome, common within prisons and mental health services, means that often service providers fail in their rehabilitation efforts – and it is the punitive nature of the institutions that prevails: *"You get hardened. So if I'm walking down a cell block and someone is stabbed, I keep walking. I don't see nothin' and I don't say nothin'. You keep your mouth shut for your own good."*

Jonathan Rudin, program director of Aboriginal Legal Services of Toronto, points out that Indigenous people, while being less than 4 per cent of the population, are 27 per cent of inmates in provincial and territorial prisons, Indigenous women make up 32 per cent of women in federal prisons; 35 per cent of youth in custody are Indigenous. He adds, "the percentages of Aboriginal inmates have been on the rise for years for both adults and youth: we now have the highest levels of Aboriginal overrepresentation ever recorded" (Rudin 2014: 344).

While at times, the future looks bleak, we need to remember that progressive change is rarely led by political and business leaders. Instead, the building blocks for social change usually come from individuals within local communities who illustrate a resilience to overcome oppressive conditions. The following is an account by a young Indigenous adult:

> By the time I was 14, I was selling and doing drugs. . . . My life has been full of mental, sexual, physical and emotional abuse. I was molested as a child, raped at 17 and again at 20 . . . I was so beaten down that I had no love for myself, and it was very hard to love another. One day, after being high for days on end, I needed an escape. I realized I could no longer live this way or I would die. I didn't love myself enough to stop using, but I thought if I had something else to live for, to love, I would find the strength to get clean. My boyfriend and I decided to have a baby. My incentive for living was clear as day. I got pregnant and enrolled in school. I made it my goal to get clean and provide my son with everything he needed to lead a happy, healthy life. It was no longer about me anymore. I had to be responsible and provide for my child. I am proud to say that I have been clean since 2008. I have graduated from college and am working

full time as a child and youth worker. My son is beautiful, healthy and happy. He is the best thing that ever happened to me. If it weren't for him, I would be dead by now. He will always be my motivation and my light. (Menzies and Lavallée 2014: 117–18)

For this woman, the lesson is "everyone has the capacity to overcome addiction – they just need to find the incentive that will give them the strength to carry them through" (118). Resilience and personal growth, experienced by survivors of oppressive conditions can become springboards to reach for personal and political liberation.

Caring Social Services: Take a Deep Bow

Although service users can experience indifference, disrespect, coercion, or other forms of mistreatment within social services, not all service users have negative experiences. For example, a young service user speaks about his experience with the Canadian Mental Health Association:

> I feel happy and proud because I've overcome my mental illness in some ways. I have learned coping mechanisms that have helped me a lot from my very helpful social workers and myself. These coping mechanisms have helped me stay stable so I haven't been in hospital for two years. My relationship with my father is improved from before. I've worked in different jobs and have kept a job for a year. (Gauci, Bartlett, and Grey 2004: 5)

Another service user notes the following in regard to the care she received:

> Since I came to this agency I see a hundred percent change in myself. When I came here, I was terrified, was not capable of doing anything. I was thinking that death was my solution. Now, I have my goals in life . . . It seems like a dream to me for who I am now. Often I ask "Am I the same person?" (George et al. 2007: 17)

These examples of good practice and satisfied service users are just a small sample of the constructive help being delivered by social services across Canada. Yet these instances of positive experiences are just tiny pockets within a much larger reality: a sea of oppressive experiences that many service users endure in welfare offices, child protection agencies, correctional institutions, and other social services across the country. These examples of constructive practice provide hope for social service practitioners and service users alike. They demonstrate what is possible for all social services to accomplish – if certain changes are made. This brings us to consider ways of challenging the feelings of hopelessness that are often experienced by social service users, social workers, and other social service providers.

8 CHALLENGING FEELING HOPELESS

May the stars carry your sadness away,
May the flowers fill your heart with beauty,
May hope forever wipe away your tears.
And above all, may silence make you strong.

— Chief Dan George

Understandably, both social workers and service users can experience a sense of hopelessness in light of the huge barriers, abuses, and harmful social conditions. At the same time, when people come together to focus on these personal and systemic abuses, and when they become aware of the injustice of these barriers, abuses, and conditions, they may reach for their inner resilience and say, "Enough – we will not accept this any longer." When they organize themselves over a period of time to demand social justice, they may become a social movement. In Canada, a multitude of different people have come together in progressive social movements at different points in time: Indigenous peoples, organized labour, lesbians, gays, bisexual and transgendered people, older adults, women, people with (dis)Abilities, racialized people, anti-poverty networks, human rights activists, and members of diverse cultures.

SOCIAL JUSTICE MOVEMENTS

Resistance by Indigenous people have resulted in anti-colonial approaches (see Kinewesquao 2009; Assembly of First Nations 2016; Métis National Council 2016; *Canadian Encyclopedia*, Inuit Tapiriit Kanatami 2015; Absolon Minogiizhigokwe 2011: 91; Henry 2015,

Hart 2015; Brittain and Blackstock 2015). Michael Anthony Hart (Kaskitemahikan) gives his view of that process:

> Anti-colonialism includes actions such as social and political mobilization to de-legitimate and stop the colonial attacks on Indigenous knowledge and peoples. It seeks to affirm Indigenous knowledge and culture, establish Indigenous control over Indigenous national territories, protect Indigenous lands from environmental destruction and develop education opportunities that are anti-colonial in their political orientation and firmly rooted in traditions of Indigenous nations. (2009a: 32)

The Idle No More movement, which began in late 2012, is an example of an anti-colonial social movement. Idle No More was founded by four women in Saskatchewan who were seeking to counter legislation that affected Indigenous lands and Treaty rights. Founded on non-violent principles as well as Indigenous ways of knowing, and rooted in Indigenous sovereignty, the movement emerged out of a desire to actively protect water, air, land, and all creation for future generations. More specifically, Pamela Palmater, who is a Mi'kmaw citizen and member of the Eel River Bar First Nation in New Brunswick, explains:

> The creation of Canada was only possible through the negotiation of treaties between the Crown and Indigenous nations. While the wording of the treaties varies from the peace and friendship treaties in the east to the numbered treaties in the west, most are based on the core treaty promise that we would all live together peacefully and share the wealth of this land. The problem is that only one treaty partner has seen any prosperity. (Palmater 2014: 37)

Palmater notes the contrast to the prosperity of mainstream Canadians:

> First Nations have been subjected to purposeful, chronic underfunding of all their basic human services like water, sanitation, housing, and education. This has led to the many First Nations being subjected to multiple, overlapping crises like the housing crisis in Attawapiskat, the water crisis in Kashechewan, and the suicide crisis in Pikangikum. (Palmater 2014: 39)

Palmater notes that Idle No More grew rapidly as the women who founded it were joined by grass roots Indigenous leaders and their supporters:

It originally started as a way to oppose Bill C-45, the omnibus legislation impacting water rights and land rights under the Indian Act; it grew to include all the legislation and the corresponding funding cuts to First Nations political organizations meant to silence our advocacy voice. (Palmater 2014: 38, 39)

While Idle No More energized Indigenous people as they held rallies, educational workshops, drumming flash singers in shopping malls, ceremonies, peaceful blockades, hunger strikes, and various other forms of activism, it also generated support from the wider community. For example, Academics in Solidarity gathered over 2,000 signatures to their letter, which included this statement of support:

We, as academics teaching in universities. . . . call on our government to address the urgent situation in Aboriginal communities across this country. . . . We stand in solidarity with Chief Spence's attempts to change the abusive manner in which the Canadian Government has ignored, threatened, and bullied Indigenous peoples. (Academics in Solidarity with Chief Spence and Idle No More 2014: 230, 231; see also Porter 2015)

Like all social justice movements, Idle No More had a strong educational impact on its own communities, and reminded everyone else about the legitimacy of their quest for justice. As part of pressing for human rights, some Indigenous leaders focus on economic rights, especially for recognition of land titles of their territories, despite the objections of governments. Since the federal and provincial governments have refused to recognize such Indigenous title to their land, Arthur Manuel went above their heads to a company called Standard and Poor's. This company provides independent credit ratings of various regions of the world, including Canada and its provinces. A wealthy company in its own right, with assets of more that 1.5 trillion, Standard and Poor's credit rating services are taken very seriously by our politicians. Investors the world over use this credit rating to decide whether it is worth investing in our regions. Therefore, federal and provincial politicians are very eager to receive good credit ratings.

Indigenous leader Arthur Manuel met in New York with company officials at the head office of Standard and Poor's. Using the government's own report, Manuel indicated that Standard and Poor's credit ratings were based on incomplete information supplied by government. He showed that such reports did not disclose the information required by internationally recognized accounting standards. This was because such reports did not "account for all of the timber, mineral, oil and gas, and other resources that have been taken off our Aboriginal title lands" (Manuel and Derrickson 2015: 159).

Manuel goes on to ask, "If Canada had this outstanding debt to First Nations on Aboriginal title lands, something that the World Trade Organization has recognized, where was it in Canada's books?" (156). The point being that by not showing it in its financial reporting as a "contingent liability," Canadian governments were misleading investors by hiding the debt owed to First Nations for the resources extracted without the consent of Indigenous people in those territories. The point is that the taking of timber, minerals and other parts of nature without the consent of Indigenous people is tantamount to theft, the extent of which can be calculated, and which presents a warning about liability that any potential investor must be cautioned about.

This is not just a negotiating tactic by Indigenous leaders: it goes to the root of Indigenous insistence that decisions by business and political leaders recognize Indigenous title to their traditional territories.

Each social movement expresses its own meaning for its goals by drawing on its own lived experience to shape its social analysis. Each social movement experiences an ebb and flow of lesser or greater influence, depending on factors such as leadership, geographic region, forces arrayed against it, and shifts in public opinion. Each of the "isms" (racism, sexism, colonialism, heterosexism, capitalism, ableism, ageism, etc.) has resulted in social movements that push back against the injustices caused by the particular "ism." Each social movement helps to reduce the isolation often felt by people who may believe they are the only ones suffering, until they meet "others in the same boat." Often the movements will work separately on their respective concerns. At other times some of the different social movements will join together to press for change. Examples of several movements coming together to produce sizable public support include campaigns focusing on environmental contamination and international corporate power abuses (Gregoire 2016; Suzuki and Moola 2016; Klein 2015; Dreier 2015; Choudry 2015, McQuaig 2016a, 2016b).

Sometimes social activists will start new community networks. One such activist, Deena Ladd, a co-ordinator of Toronto's Workers' Action Centre, describes such a situation:

> We're starting a new movement of workers who are not unionized because they work on short-term contracts through temp agencies, often working part-time at very low wages. On a personal level, these workers are often quite depressed because they can't get good jobs, and they're often exhausted from working long hours. We work directly with them, giving personal and political support. We show it's possible to fight back.
>
> When a worker doesn't get paid, we go to the employer. That happened this month with a restaurant employer. Three of us, including the worker, went at the restaurant's most busy time and tactfully but firmly demanded payment. The employer paid part of what was owing, with a promise for the rest next week. We let him know: if he breaks his promise to us, we'll return to leaflet his restaurant customers. And we'll do it if he breaks his promise. Through our work, we break the isolation experienced by these workers. We also do skill development and leadership training. How to use the media? What's policy? Why do employers have so much power? Are you being used? We have food at our meetings and have fun along the way. We're building relationships and we're also building a membership base.

In 2009 Ladd, working with social policy advocate Trish Hennessy, reports on the progress of this new movement. It succeeded in convincing the Ontario government to enact legislation giving new legal protections for temporary agency workers, and to provide a multi-million-dollar budget for hiring new enforcement officers to keep employers in line with the law. Ladd and Hennessy note that these small but important steps are the result of workers empowering themselves, due to the approach used by the Workers' Action Centre when workers phone for support and advice:

> We start from the position that we're not the experts – they are – and we invite them to get involved by working with others for long-term change. Our workers' hotline delivers support in six languages and becomes a first step for new workers to become involved in our campaign. Every week, we hold sessions for new members, in which we give an overview of basic rights in Ontario and create a safe space to ask questions, share experiences and break the isolation that non-unionized workers face. Something important happens: a group of people who have never met each other begin talking about realities facing them on the job and what's happening in their lives; they start agreeing that what's happening isn't right and that they have a role in doing something about it. Together. Everything we do follows this basic principle: Nothing about us without us. (Ladd and Hennessy 2009: IN5)

Today, the Workers Action Centre continues to be an effective advocacy organization, true to the principles it espouses (Mojtehedzadeh 2015b: A1). It is reducing the isolation of its members and pushing back the sense of hopelessness that accompanies the barriers, until there is a group to challenge these unjust conditions. As movements get stronger and form coalitions and alliances with each other, they often raise the political and personal consciousness of each other and the public. Examples are found in the websites of the Council of Canadians, the Real News Network, rabble.ca, and many others. Sometimes social activists take to the streets. More often they work within institutions where members are employed or have other attachments, creating spaces for new non-oppressive social relations, locally and globally (Smith 2008; Bantjes 2007; Rebick 2009; Vancouver Media Co-op 2011; Hadden 2015).

These movements sometimes also include social agencies that push for wider changes, while at the same time providing counselling to service users. For example, SOS (Surpassing Our Survival), a sexual assault agency in the interior of British Columbia, helps women and children who have been sexually abused. Dawn Hemingway, Clarie Johnson, and Brenda Roland tapped into their activism with the women's movement as they documented their experience with this social agency's commitment to "unrelenting public education work linked to collective action" (2010: 80).

The combination of education and action is reflected in letters to the editor that sos sends to newspapers in response to sexist media stories. This combination is present in its practice of using art creatively – such as quilting to express not only the trauma of sexual violence but also visions of a respectful world. The agency's community work includes providing leadership in Prince George in organizing Take Back the Night, "an internationally recognized event in which women and children march through the streets to highlight their right to live without fear of violence, harassment and sexual assault" (Hemingway et al. 2010: 80; sos Society 2013; Mallam 2014). SOS also joined with First Nations and community organizations across the North to march, dance, and drum on Highway 16, to demand action by politicians and the police concerning women, mostly Indigenous, who are murdered or missing from this road that runs from Prince Rupert to the Alberta border.

In counselling mothers of sexually abused children, sos relies on research showing that in the vast majority of cases the perpetrator's secretive methods prevent mothers from knowing about the abuse. That is why, in its counselling, the agency works to counter the rampant mother-blaming by professionals, including by child protection workers, doctors, teachers, and police. In addition, this social service agency has programs for male youth and adult men who have been sexually mistreated as children or as adults, and also works with other community agencies that help offenders take responsibility for their actions and work for personal change. Hemingway, Johnson, and Roland remind us, "sexual assault is a gendered crime. The reality is not that men are not victims of sexual violence; it is that they are almost always the perpetrators of sexual violence against both women and men" (2010: 88).

Hemingway, Johnson, and Roland are asked why sos does not focus only on its clinical counselling:

> We fully understand the importance of day-to-day work that addresses critical, immediate needs. It must be done. But, ultimately, meeting these immediate needs is not very meaningful if not carried out in the

context of fighting for longer-term fundamental changes that will eradicate sexual violence. In practice and of necessity, these potentially contradictory approaches are, in fact, concurrent and complementary undertakings. Our belief, borne out by nearly 25 years of practice, is that you cannot successfully do one without the other. (2010: 90)

That is why it is important for us in the social services, along with other professionals, to align ourselves with progressive social movements. Without the pressure from social movements, there would be no progress toward equity. People who are benefiting from the "isms" will typically use their power and privileges to block change. An example is the way police attitudes and behaviour have the effect of entrenching racism against Black people and other racialized groups in North America. The shooting and killing of unarmed Black men by White police officers is an all-too-familiar scene. But rather than submit to these abuses of authority, Black communities have been forceful in their protests. Black Lives Matter is a social movement that has arisen out of the rage of Black people, especially Black youth, saying they will no longer put up with white domination and violence against their communities (Tomlinson 2016; Black Lives Matter 2016).

As with all progressive movements, the actions of activists in Black Lives Matter take different forms depending on local and regional leaders, and on potential alliances with other social movements and progressive networks. Black Lives Matter, similar to other social movements, is the engine that mobilizes non-violent power from the grassroots outward and upward. In the process, hopelessness may be reduced, contributing to a new surge of energy in the struggle for justice.

Under certain conditions, and with the help of allies inside various institutions, social movement participants can develop enough public pressure to bring about social change. When this happens, though, typically, there is backlash against social activists. This calls on our inner strength and courage as we navigate the turmoil of moving forward (Vincent 2016; Heschel 1996). In her role as whistleblower, child advocate Cindy Blackstock suffered the indignities of harassment that accompany backlash, prompting her to take the federal government to the Canadian Human Rights Tribunal. We are thrilled that she won in that Tribunal, on behalf not only of herself, but also of Indigenous children living on reserves (Harper 2016; Diebel 2016; First Nations Child & Family Caring Society of Canada et al. v. Attorney General of Canada for the Minister of Indian and Northern Affairs Canada. 2016b and 2016c).

While Canadians still have a huge distance to travel to achieve a full measure of social justice, nevertheless we have seen modest changes in some areas. As just one example, Marilyn Callahan reminds us that sometimes we lose sight of progress made due to the women's liberation movement:

> When I began to participate in feminist groups in the 1960s, the world was a very different place for women. There were few women in any of the well-paid professions such as law and medicine; divorcing women had no claim to the matrimonial property; First Nations women lost their status if they married non-status men; sexual assault was often blamed on women; and most young women did not expect to have a career and marriage at the same time. Dramatic changes have occurred since then and feminist groups can take credit for many of these, working outside and within policy-making structures. (Callahan 2004: 139; see also Catherine Porter 2016)

Today, while the push continues for changes toward full equity, backlash from the super-privileged is increasing, threatening to roll back previous progress.

LABOUR UNIONS AND SOCIAL WORK

Unions hold a unique position in society, because they fight for working people and the larger community, which is really all of us. Plus, they are one of the few social movements that have special legislation that dictates what they can and cannot do. For example, they can organize workplaces and negotiate with management over wages and conditions but they cannot take over as management or negotiate how management will manage a work place. Unions have long been of interest to social service workers because of their capacity to draw large segments of society together to fight for better services, stronger communities, and social justice for all.

Labour unions are formed not just because workers need better pay and need to overcome difficult working conditions. They are also formed because workers are fed up with arbitrary, dictatorial managers – and this is as true in non-profit social services as it is in the private, for-profit corporations. Even though the playing field remains highly uneven because of the larger legal, political, and economic authority vested in management, unions give voice and some protections to people who otherwise would be worse off. They represent a practical way of contesting the one-way flow of power from above and, by bargaining for better wages, they help to redistribute wealth from rich employers to working people. They challenge hopelessness by motivating their members to join others in working for progressive change (Ng 2015: 491–96; Heron 2012).

Another advantage of being part of a larger union is that members benefit from the strength of the larger group and its collective agreements. Unionization, especially in the public sector, raises salaries for social service workers, although the government often rolls back these gains through contracting out or by demanding wage concessions. Unions also protect workers against arbitrary actions from employers, as social worker and union leader Karen McNama notes:

> Unions are important for front-line social workers because they serve as a protection against abuses by managers. By "abuses" I mean the long hours we are made to work; the heaviness of the caseload and I don't just mean numbers. Unions allow us an opportunity to have a voice, to disagree with management without getting hit with "insubordination."

It is well known that, historically, labour unions struggle for better working conditions and pay. Perhaps less well known are the efforts by the labour movement to urge governments to introduce and then strengthen social programs such as old age pensions, unemployment insurance, and medicare. These social programs would not have been established if organized labour had not pressed for them through the political arena (Lundy 2011). During periods when these programs come under attack it is often the labour movement, working with others, who organizes opposition to cutbacks. In previous decades, most social service providers were employed at workplaces that were unionized, but more recently unionized services are decreasing due to privatization and the fact that some social agencies have closed their doors because of lack of funding.

Despite huge stress among people seeking help, along with the tough challenges of working in the context of cuts to social programs and privatization, as social workers, social service workers, and other human service professionals delivering social programs, we can still manage to gain some satisfaction in our jobs by contributing to personal care and social change. As one worker said, referring to why she worked through her union to build equity and fairness in her workplace, "if you haven't got meaning on these jobs, what have you got?" (Baines et al. 2012: 367) As social service agencies have become increasingly managerialized, hierarchical, and focused on cutting costs, many social workers feel that there are few opportunities to express social justice values at work, and they feel that they have lost their voice in the workplace (Baines et al. 2013: 24–42). Unions have provided an alternative space for workers to support each other, join with other unionized social service workers in important causes, challenge cut backs and uncaring practices within and outside the workplace, and regain their voice (Baines et al. 2012; see also Canadian Union of Public Employees 2016).

Unions have also worked to improve the workplace and find resources needed by clients. An experienced social worker, Pam Chapman, noted about her work at an emergency shelter in a dilapidated, stuffy building that was understaffed and overcrowded, full of babies crying, and mothers yelling. Staff had been continuously asking management to address the building's conditions, but nothing had changed.

> Fortunately, the union did make a difference. The union steward got all the staff together and invited us to document the problems as well as our suggestions for solving these problems. Besides the overcrowding issue, we wanted a children's program in the shelter. The union called a meeting with the shelter's management and demanded action. Soon after, the children's program was established and other conditions improved as well.

For students, educators, and workers, the labour movement's emphasis on solidarity and collective action in general casts the role of social workers into a broader emancipatory context. It encourages both reflection and analysis of wider issues and the formation of important links with other movements and other workers.

DEALING WITH CHALLENGES: TINY MIRACLES

The challenges facing social service providers are enormous and growing. They include the consequences of annual cuts in many social programs such as social housing, child-care programs, income supports, and various social services. These program cuts, as a result of tax cuts demanded by Canada's privileged elites, restrict the capacity of social workers to provide effective help. While some people quit their jobs in the social services, surprisingly, most social workers and social service workers remain. In light of the incredible challenges, what on earth would motivate anyone to stay within such a beleaguered environment?

From our years of experience and from listening to many seasoned social workers, we believe the answers have to do with holding certain values about life. We are not sure if we as human beings are "hard-wired" by a need to see people treated decently, or whether we are nurtured into these values at an early age by caring people, or whether there exists some combination of these two or other factors. But we do know that these values run deep within many, if not most people. From observed behaviour we can also clearly see that these caring values are stronger in some people and weaker in others. Our observations point to this human quality of caring about others being present across different cultures, different nations, and different time spans. Granted, too often this quality is suppressed or otherwise blocked. Nevertheless, caring about others seems to be a universal quality that is persistently present, though expressed differently by people from different cultures, different parts of our planet, and different time periods.

This core value of caring provides the resilience to "hang in there" to deliver good social services, even under the most adverse conditions. We also observe that experienced helpers are not naïve. We experience the constraints and the frustrations of the work. Yet we refuse to resign ourselves to hopelessness. We recognize that even when our social services successfully help service users, we still live in a society infused by harmful expectations, behaviours, and attitudes that flow from systemic forms of privilege and oppression. Neither the helpers nor the people being helped escape the constant barrage of commercials and other mainstream messages that encourage us to leap into consumerism and become preoccupied with its self-indulgent satisfactions.

Yet these negative pulls fail to dissuade most of us from delivering the best social services possible under the circumstances. Social services enable us to "stand with" people who experience exclusion and to oppose unjust structures. As we stand in solidarity with individuals, families, and communities that have experienced systemic disempowerment, we try along with many others to make a difference. Sometimes the results are small "miracles."

At times and despite all odds, social services offer opportunities for good practice, along with dedicated workers who deliver it. Sandra, a mental health social worker in Alberta is an example:

When I first met Melissa (not her name) she kept her head down so far I couldn't even see her eyes. I could hardly hear her voice, she was so extremely soft-spoken. She had been severely abused as a child. When we first met, she was living in a shack with her son – no running water, no conveniences, and the roof leaked.

In developing a therapeutic relationship with her, I remember giving her many choices. I suggested she could write down some of her experiences of abuse. I said she could burn what she had written and I'd never see it. Or she could write about her experience, then give it to me, and I could read it in her presence. Or she could write it up, leave it with me, and I'd read it before our next meeting when I'd give her feedback. She decided on the last option. So that's what we did. She wrote, left it with me, I read it. Then we met for me to give her feedback. We did this for three months.

When we talked, I validated her pain, helped her to identify her inner strengths, and affirmed these strengths. I started to see progress. I pointed it out to her. She needed encouragement, which I gave her. She started to take charge of her life. We worked on her goals, such as finding better housing. At the end of three months I felt she was on her way to developing the confidence she needed.

About four or five years later, Melissa came in to talk again. She was

*now talking face to face. I could see her eyes easily. She was much more
confident. She was excited to tell me that she'd gone back to school –
upgrading – and was now a university student working on her degree.
She was living in her own place, a decent place. I could tell she was on
her way! That was very satisfying for me. I felt I'd helped her turn things
around. I'm Aboriginal like she is. Our communities have such problems:
it felt good to help someone from our communities. My husband is Aboriginal too, and I couldn't do this work without his support.*

ALTERNATIVE SOCIAL SERVICES

For Indigenous people, alternative services mean an alternative to
mainstream social services that are often still enmeshed in neoliberal, colonial practices. As part of the political mobilization by First
Nations, Métis, and Inuit peoples for autonomy and self-government,
the transfer of social services to Indigenous communities across the
country is underway. Aside from being grossly underfunded, these
services face an additional challenge: the implementation of services
that genuinely reflect Indigenous cultural traditions and aspirations
rather than merely reproducing Anglo-centric and Franco-centric
social service hierarchies run by Indigenous people.

Despite these barriers, Kathy Absolon is able to write about "surviving and thriving in the landscape of practice." She points to the
emergence of a sense of solidarity and nation building among Indigenous peoples, despite the "government's attempts to divide and pit
Indigenous people against one another."

> We have survived the militant attacks and numerous attempts to cre-
> ate divisions in our nations, communities, families, lives and ourselves.
> Yes, there are many casualties, but today we are still here surviving
> and, in some cases thriving. We talk to one another and show care. We
> have the power to dialogue. The voices that we have and the distinct
> way that we have of telling our story provide us with doorways to free
> our minds, hearts, spirits and bodies from colonial shackles. Singing,
> story-telling, dancing, smudging, chanting and talking with one
> another are healing practices resonating with the sound of our voices
> and use of our bodies. (2009: 194–95)

Indigenous approaches to building upon cultural traditions are not restricted to a particular agency in a specific region, but rather reflect the construction of alternatives to the continuing, pervasive, colonial domination that exists in Canada. When alternative social services are based on Indigenous knowledges they become important supports to the movement toward self-determination by Indigenous people.

Alternative arrangements sometimes happen within educational institutions. For example, the School of Social Work at Ryerson University developed a partnership with an Indigenous organization to oversee a social work degree program for Indigenous students. While the same courses are offered, they are also Indigenized by inviting Indigenous Elders and Knowledge Keepers as instructors. For the past ten years, over eighty students have graduated with their social work degree from this program. They have gained social work knowledge, but also a sense of confidence about their Indigenous identity, an affirmation about the value of their beliefs, ceremonies, and pride in their cultural legacy.

Programs that are alternatives to disrespectful or disempowering social services usually spring from the work of a specific oppressed community or movement: First Nations people, labour union organizations, women, people with (dis)Abilities, racialized and ethnic communities, Queer people, local tenants' groups – with women being worse off in each of these groups, which is why women are the majority users of social services. Alternative services emphasize the principle of control by service users over professional services. Examples of alternative social services within the mainstream include establishing a shelter for battered women, a crisis phone line, or a drop-in and information centre.

The women's movement is especially influential in developing less hierarchical approaches to organizing and delivering feminist services. Many of the original feminist services are organized as co-ops or collectives, so that staff co-operatively make major decisions, often with considerable input from the users of the service. Front-line staff and sometimes users – not only management – have major say in hiring. The services are often staffed and co-ordinated by people rooted in the particular community being served, people who are personally committed to the reduction or elimination of structural inequalities. Despite the inevitable differences and diversity, participants tend to have a shared analysis of the basic causes of problems and what creates the need for their services, as Helen Levine shares in her observations:

> It was no accident that consciousness-raising in small groups sparked the widespread beginnings of the contemporary women's movement. It offered safe space for women to tell the "real stories" of our lives, to listen to one another without judgment and blame, to grasp the commonalities among us. It was a woman-centred base, grounded in internal and external realities that led to opening up, sharing, analysis and action. I see this as a continuous and essential base in any social change movement.

In another area of social work, Jennifer Ann Pritchard contrasts her eight years of experience working in bureaucratic group homes with her student experience in social work of working for an organization run by people with disabilities:

> *Group homes give services which are highly individualized, so people with disabilities are kept separate from each other – there's no such thing as meetings just among people with disabilities. But in self-help groups there's more of a collective sense of potential, hope, possibility, and risk-taking . . . and I found that people with disabilities had a type of camaraderie and humour with each other that's rare in group homes. In the group-home system there's a tendency to deny the disability, to render the person with disability as much like a non-disabled person as possible. By contrast, in self-help groups people embrace their disability, saying, "This is who I am, dammit. I am as valuable as anyone." There's a strong sense of validating each other's experience with disability. In this way, people with disabilities are turning the tables on the conventional perception of disabilities as being ugly, not valuable, and a lesser form of life.*

Negative attitudes and practices in social services have also had implications for people with diverse experience related to sexual orientation and gender identity. Heterosexism and related negative attitudes and practices among social service providers have resulted in a reluctance on the part of many gay, lesbian, bisexual, and transgendered people to ask for help. In response, Queer communities have begun to initiate Queer-positive social services. One example of a Queer-positive service, in the Maritimes, is the Youth Project. The mission of this non-profit organization is to "make Nova Scotia a safer, healthier, and happier place for lesbians, gay, bisexual and transgender youth through support, education, resource expansion and community development." At least two characteristics point to its "alternative" components. First, in its service delivery, "the staff and volunteers present and embody an alternative vision: a place where experiences of hatred and domination are absent, and support education and social opportunities are offered" (Brown, Richard, and Wichman 2010: 163). Second, the organization's decision making provides a strong voice to youth.

> The Youth Board represents a structural level of governance that institutionalizes the commitment to an inverted hierarchy, where young people are responsible for and resourceful in contributing to the design and implementation of services to meet their needs. Youth Board membership requires that all participants are under the age of 26 years and represent the diversity of experiences and identities surrounding sexual orientation and gender identity. (162)

Another youth-focused organization, Grassroots Youth Collaborative (GYC), specifically calls for a high percentage of its staff and volunteers to be youth:

> The agency should primarily serve youth and be youth-driven, meaning that youth between ages of 13 and 29 years should be fully represented in all areas of the agency and account for over 50 percent of all their volunteers and staff. Youth should also be significantly represented within the board of directors. (Wright et al. 2010: 176).

The agency also is set up so that it must be non-profit and it is committed to anti-oppression and anti-racism.

These kinds of alternatives, often supported by progressive social movements and based on the authentic needs of service users and their respective communities, constitute a form of resistance to the mainstream ideologies, narratives, and practices that are often oppressive and are reinforced by conventional agency structures. Social movements offer a different view of personal problems. They see unequal power relations and unequal material resources as major sources of a particular problem or set of problems. Consequently, social movements frequently point to visionary ways of reorganizing society based on principles of equity and democratic accountability. For example, some people in the labour movement are now supporting a redesign of the workplace that challenges the typically obscene gap in levels of compensation between executives compared to other employees (Davidson 2010).

Alternative services represent a hopeful potential. They invite questioning of top-down structures, and point to a better model of how social programs could be delivered (Baines and Armstrong 2015). But changes to democratize social services, while necessary, are not enough to improve service delivery. Generous funding is also necessary.

AN ACTIVIST AGENDA BY PROGRESSIVE SOCIAL WORKERS

As progressive social workers we do have some influence. As much as it is possible for each of us, our active engagement in promoting universal, generous, publicly owned and fully tax-supported social programs will make a difference. We recommend engaging in social activism to vastly expand universal social programs as a key to social progress.

In this process, it is very important for the voices of service users to be heard and respected at the decision-making levels of social agencies; and the voices of service providers and their labour unions are equally indispensable. Better, more effective services are far more likely when staff, front-line workers, supervisors, managers, and funders participate in continuous staff development programs that focus on countering systemic barriers that stand in the way of effective help. Indeed, if such service innovations were in place the need for alternative social services would be greatly reduced.

In other words, there are good models available for more effective social services, but these will remain on the drawing board so long as the grossly inadequate funding continues. For a variety of reasons, as social service providers and educators, we have known for some time about inadequate funding, but have not unified ourselves to speak out against it. We must speak out on it now, or before long social services will be gone.

In preparing to speak out against the grossly inadequate funding of social program, we must learn from history. Before the 1920s, parents in Canada had to pay a fee if they wanted their son or daughter to go to high school. Progressive reformers advocated for free high schools to be paid for by taxes. Nay-sayers at the time, often affluent families who did not want to pay for others, argued "if you raise taxes, that will wreck the economy." Nevertheless, the advocacy of progressive reformers won the day. High schools became available to all, paid for by taxes, and remain so today.

In the 1950s and 1960s, progressive reformers advocated for a universal program of access to medical care. Rich people who could afford to pay for a private doctor did not want to be taxed to pay for others. They argued, "you can't raise taxes now: it will wreck the economy." Many doctors at the time joined the nay-sayers. During the 1960s progressive reformers won. Universal health care insurance, sometimes referred to as medicare, was legislated and is paid for by our taxes.

And now in the twenty-first century, the time is overdue for us to take a giant leap for social progress. We need to join with others in strong advocacy to greatly expand universal access to social programs, modelled upon medicare, in areas ranging from child care to long-term care, from social housing to food security, from dental care to pharma care, and from mental health services to costs of university education. and a host of other areas neglected up until now. For this to succeed, we need to dramatically strengthen the revenue base, which means achieving a reformed tax system, including effective tax collection from off-shore tax havens, to make a deep inroad against the inequality of wealth and incomes in Canada.

We can predict that nay-sayers will again argue "If you raise taxes now, it will wreck the economy." As in the past, we will need to mobilize public opinion to defeat the nay-sayers. To succeed, we will need to replace the regressive taxes that are in place today; a switch to a progressive tax system would collect far more taxes from the very affluent and from corporations who can well afford it.

Any progressive agenda must also include, in direct consultation with Indigenous leaders, ways to respectfully join Indigenous leaders and their organizations in pressing for the implementation of Treaties and related human rights issues, including generous funding in areas such as Indigenous governance over education, health, social services, and economic development.

We can expect strong opposition. That is why we must support and join social movements and people organizing themselves through advocacy and activism. As we reach for social justice, we must not leave out key cornerstones for an equitable future. We need to deepen our understanding of the unequal power exercised by privileged individuals and organizations. In this process, we must face the imbalances and distortions created by Canada's colonial, racist, capitalist past and present. We need this understanding to develop approaches to correct these imbalances and distortions.

One approach is to seek out voices of community groups and persons affected by social and economic policies and programs. The point is to change the top-down, patriarchal decision making prevalent today. The following voices (of groups in overlapping categories) must be heard and no longer excluded in decision making:

- Indigenous people
- people living in poverty
- social service users
- women
- labour unions
- racialized groups
- Queer people
- people with visible and invisible disabilities
- older adults
- youth
- workers in precarious employment
- other equity-seeking organizations and other human rights groups who experience marginalization.

We must reach out to them as not only part of decision making for program development, but also for tax reforms and allocation of funds at all levels of government. Because of past and present colonization, it will be vital to reach out to Indigenous nations, their communities and leaders. This would build our capacity for a new relationship based on respect and dignity, including respect for the land, the water, the air, and for our ecological interdependence. In the process of reaching for this, we will enter into a new chapter of learning ways to protect the wellness of ourselves and of future generations. Ultimately this means working for basic change, that is, for fundamental transformation to bring about economic, political, and social justice. This is also known as liberation.

9 TOWARD LIBERATION

> Remember this: We be many, and they be few. They need us more than we need them. Another world is not only possible, she is on her way. On a quiet day, I can hear her breathing.
> — Arundhati Roy, World Social Forum, Porto Alegro, Brazil

Donna: As social workers who are oriented toward progressive change, we are not alone. We have allies everywhere in the movement for social justice, both locally and globally – clients, anti-poverty activists, unions, the women's movement, anti-racist groups, Indigenous organizations, and anti-globalization activists. We have professional allies among people in other occupations, people who face similar conditions – nurses, teachers, and academics, for instance. But that is not all. Policy analysts, community development workers, public officials, and those working in progressive think tanks and research institutes also share common ground in this struggle to shift social priorities and resources to those at the margins in society.

CHALLENGING MULTIPLE OPPRESSIONS

The suffix "ism" provides a short-form way of referring to the multiple oppressions stemming from colonialism, racism, sexism/male dominance, capitalism, heterosexism, ageism, ableism, and other types of power over others that have embedded themselves into our lives. In addressing these "isms," and how they differ from and interact with one another, we need to also consider how they operate in our own individual lives – including how they influence our attitudes

– in our efforts to find ways of providing respectful, effective help to social service users.

As we reflect on the multiple identities that make up our social location, we need to avoid classifying ourselves or others into stereotypes. For example, all women are this; all men are that. In contrast to those kinds of generalizations, we need to understand that other people who share our identity possess a variety of differences in behaviour, attitudes, and expectations. Additional dimensions of difference – for example, among women – may be due to different cultural backgrounds, or different class positions, shades of skin colour, sexual orientations, gender identification, ethnicities, ages, physical or mental abilities/(dis)Abilities, or other differences due to other intersecting dynamics of privilege and oppression.

Systemic differences – systemic because they are built into our social structures – have their own impact on people of privilege. Men, for example, continue to be privileged by receiving sexist benefits due to systems of male dominance. But the *intersecting* dynamics of privilege and oppression make this experience of privilege quite different for, say, two men, both lawyers, one White and one Indigenous.

Depending on the person, our identities may provide us with privilege, and at the same time other identities we possess may create disadvantages. For example, an African Canadian woman may experience vulnerabilities due to her gender and skin colour, yet she also gains a certain privilege from being non-Indigenous. Akua Benjamin, a Black social work educator and activist at Ryerson University, recalls experiencing this phenomenon, during a conversation with an Indigenous friend:

> *She turned to me and asked, did I realize I was part of the oppression of her people? I was shocked; totally speechless. Me? An oppressor? My ancestors were forced as slaves to come from Africa. We were forced onto ships which brought us to the Americas – to labour in horribly cruel conditions. While First Nations were being exterminated, we were slaves – so how could I be an oppressor?*
>
> *Then I stopped myself and reflected. I listened again to what she had said, but this time I heard her as an ally, as if by a second ear. It was a rude awakening. I'm in Canada now – and benefiting from what the Euro-*

peans had done. Now I'm making my life here without any acknowledgement that this was indeed the First Nations' home, not just their land. This is the unsightliness of privilege. We must meet it through a double consciousness. By double I mean for us to develop a critical awareness of – our past and present realities of our oppression – and simultaneously of our power and privilege. I should add, as a matter of historical record, many slaves survived as a result of the assistance of First Nations peoples.

Those of us who are non-Indigenous do not escape the benefits of colonialism, even if we experience disadvantage from other parts of our social location. Moreover, even if we dedicate our efforts to building a world free from all oppression, colonial benefits still flow to us. By living in urban or rural environments on land that was stolen from Indigenous people, we are benefiting from the displacement of Canada's first inhabitants.

Does this mean that our personal beliefs, attitudes, and values make no difference? No: they do matter. Our subjective responses to our own social location and to the location of others make a critical difference. They are highly relevant to whether we will conform to certain unjust social relations or whether we will oppose them. To put it another way, being mindful of our continuously evolving critical consciousness strengthens our capacity to become social justice activists working for progressive change.

THEMES FOR LIBERATION IN SOCIAL WORK PRACTICE

Social workers who put priority on social justice usually apply practice frameworks known as "anti-oppressive" or "structural social work" or "critical" or "progressive" social work. These are also umbrella terms that cover a wide range of more specific practices ranging from feminist to anti-racist and decolonizing approaches. When social service providers apply an anti-oppressive, structural-social-justice analysis, what does social work practice look like?

Steven Hick et al. (2010) invited numerous social work educators and practitioners to answer an important question. Is it possible to actually practise structural social work, or is it just a theory? The findings show that, yes, it is possible:

It is happening. It is not just a theoretical proposition; it is not romantic idealism. We are engaged in structural social work practice and the chapters in this book [*Structural social work in action*] are a testament to the fact that it is working. We are making a difference in the lives of clients and in our lives, and we are making changes in societal structures. (2010: 236–237)

One of the chapters of Hick's book is co-authored by social worker Vivian Del Valle and Ben (one of the authors of this book). It relates how Vivian provides counselling to a woman who was sexually and emotionally abused (Carniol and Del Valle 2010: 121–37). The service user, Carolina (not her real name), comes from Latin America to live in Canada with her family. In Canada, her son-in-law works in construction during the day, and his wife works at cleaning office buildings at night. Carolina looks after their children. Over a period of several years, while his wife is at work, the husband sexually abuses his mother-in-law – repeatedly and violently raping her. He threatens to harm her grandchildren if she ever tells anyone. When his wife finds out about the abuse, she calls the police, who investigate, arrest her husband and remove him from the home.

Around that same time, Carolina stops talking to everyone: her silence goes on for months. Her distraught daughter takes her to a Spanish-speaking social service agency, where Carolina is given an emergency appointment to meet with Vivian, a Spanish-speaking, Latina Mestiza.[1] Prior to their first meeting, Vivian receives a brief summary of what had happened to Carolina.

Vivian and Ben identify a number of practice themes that arise from how the social worker (Vivian) provides help.

• Finding voice
• Finding oppression
• Finding resiliency
• Raising critical consciousness
• Standing up for client rights
• Developing solidarity for emancipation.

---

1 Latina refers to women from Latin America. Mestiza refers here to a bi-racialized woman having Indigenous and European ancestors.

When they examine these practice themes, they realize that these themes are also present in other situations in which they participate as counsellors. Though they also realize that while these themes may appear to be linear, they are not. Rather, they overlap and are often present simultaneously in various combinations. They suggest these themes, then, not as a mechanical toolbox, but as flexible guideposts for social service providers who want to deliver progressive social services. They believe too that Vivian's practice in this case contains components that are readily transferable to other practice situations.

Finding voice

In Vivian's first interview with Carolina, a long silence follows after Vivian briefly introduces herself. Carolina has brought along her knitting needles and a ball of wool, and starts to knit as soon as she is shown a seat in Vivian's office. During the silence, Vivian is attentive. Realizing that Carolina has not spoken a word for three months, Vivian uses non-verbal empathy to give Carolina as much emotional space as needed. Carolina continues knitting while she slowly looks around at the Latin American artifacts in Vivian's office.

Meanwhile Vivian's goal is to develop a therapeutic alliance with Carolina, as she does with others in her clinical practice. That approach means that for this first session Vivian refrains from using the usual direct approach of asking questions about the abuse. Instead, she uses non-verbal communication skills to express genuine concern and to provide reassurance that in this counselling session it will be safe for Carolina to find her voice. Taking her time, Carolina makes eye contact with Vivian, who continues to "tune in" to Carolina's needs.

Vivian's experience and intuition help her to assess the right moment to comment about the colour of the wool that Carolina is knitting with. In response, Carolina says a few words about the wool. Vivian then gently asks a question about the wool, to which Carolina replies. This interaction gradually grows into a conversation about knitting.

This respectful, non-threatening approach helps Carolina to engage in a conversation for the first time since her son-in-law's arrest. Based on her own cultural awareness, the social worker is able to "be present" to the client's communication needs. She neither rushes in with agency forms to fill out, nor imposes other agency procedures that interfere with the client's ability to find her voice.

Finding oppression

Once Carolina breaks her silence, it is important for the social worker to go on to build a warm, welcoming atmosphere, which will help the service user to gradually tell her own very personal and painful story. Carolina's narratives reveal that she accepts many of the other hurtful injustices that she has experienced throughout her life. During this early stage of weekly counselling sessions that continue for eighteen months, Vivian, exercising self-discipline, refrains from intervening with her own progressive perspective on what had happened. By allowing Carolina to tell her story in her own way, the worker learns about how the client gives meaning to her own experiences. This approach also allows for a deeper development of trust to evolve between the worker and service user. At the same time Vivian is making her own assessment by finding how Carolina's lived experience reflects multiple forms of oppression.

Finding resiliency

As a therapeutic relationship develops between them, Vivian helps Carolina talk about what kept her going despite experiencing the trauma of being repeatedly raped, her disgust of feeling trapped, her worry about her emerging symptoms of illness (weight loss and severe skin infections that continued despite prescribed medication), and her fears of putting her grandchildren in harm's way. Carolina speaks about being emotionally nourished by her loving relationship with her grandchildren, and being somehow spiritually strengthened through her own suffering to protect them. When survivors of oppression and trauma are able to find ways of holding on to their crushed sense of dignity, counsellors can help by recognizing and affirming these vital sources of resiliency.

Raising critical consciousness

Carolina speaks about her granddaughter being bullied by a boy at school, telling Vivian that the event does not matter because girls have no rights. By now, having provided clinical counselling to Carolina for a number of months, Vivian senses that a solid basis of trust exists between herself and Carolina. Vivian decides the time is right for her to tactfully challenge Carolina's attitudes by doing some critical education about gender equality. Vivian tells Carolina an abbreviated story about the women's liberation movement: how women organized themselves and pushed for changes in attitudes, practices, narratives, policies, and laws. By sharing this history of resistance to oppressive social relations, the counsellor is able to help Carolina expand her awareness. When Vivian asks Carolina if she will sign a consent form that gives the social worker permission to contact the school, Carolina agrees. Vivian meets with the principal, and the boy subsequently confesses and writes an apology to Carolina's granddaughter.

Standing up for client rights

Will Carolina testify in court? It is one thing for service users to find their voice in counselling sessions; it is quite another matter for them to speak their truths at public forums such as public hearings, court trials, or street rallies. Carolina wants to testify in court, but is stymied by her fears of the perpetrator. In response, the social worker, Vivian, is not neutral: she provides educational, emotional, and material support to assist her client, Carolina, to stand up for herself. In helping Carolina prepare for court, Vivian refers her to orientation sessions delivered in Spanish and sponsored by the court to demystify criminal court proceedings. Carolina asks Vivian to accompany her and her daughter to court.

Developing solidarity for emancipation

In court Carolina testifies and endures a tough cross-examination. The judge finds the perpetrator guilty and sentences him to prison. The court's verdict gives Carolina a liberating message of hope about abused women being vindicated. Meanwhile, Vivian teams up with a Spanish-speaking group facilitator and obtains management support for their co-facilitation of twelve sessions to a group of Latinas who have experienced abuse. Carolina is invited to join these sessions. The group is highly interactive (role-playing, story-telling) and culturally supportive (in Spanish, cultural foods, cultural activities). The sessions include critical education on such topics as sexual and emotional abuse, systemic oppression of male dominance, colonialism, internalized privilege, women's rights, and social justice. As a result, Carolina and other group members form bonds of solidarity with each other, and benefit from a new network of interpersonal support for their growing critical consciousness.

Bob Mullaly points out the value of such groups:

> There is widespread agreement [among many anti-oppressive and pro-gressive social work writers] that becoming part of a group process with other persons who are similarly oppressed is the most effective way for oppressed persons to (1) develop political awareness, (2) self-define a more authentic identity than the one imposed on them by their oppressors, (3) develop the confidence to "come out" and assert their more authentic identity, and (4) establish solidarity in order to take action against their oppression. (2010: 228)

As we reflect on the ways in which Carolina is helped, we may be struck by how group solidarity emerges from this progressive version of social work. In contrast with the more conventional forms of practice that shy away from political analysis, structural social workers are "case critical" in at least two ways: first, they are critical of casework and case management that ignore or diminish equity issues, and make all issues into individual problems; and, second, they apply critical consciousness to themselves by challenging the dynamics of privilege and oppression that play out in their own lives and the lives of others.

INDIGENOUS HEALING AND LIBERATION

Raven: We have discussed at various points in this book that Indigenous traditions and knowledge are increasingly being "centred" in social work discourses. The common theme that underpins this direction is Indigenization, which we now know to mean creating programs and interventions that are based upon Indigenous knowledge and that incorporate Indigenous intervention approaches.

An area where transformative approaches are urgently needed is in addressing lateral violence. Lateral violence is a term for the misdirection of rage and frustration stemming from oppression. Violence is misdirected away from the cause of abuse and indignities, and toward "safe" targets – family, friends, and community, because to lash out at the oppressor is far too dangerous (Fanon, 2008). Where there is lateral violence in Indigenous families, communities, and agencies (Bombay 2014), researchers are finding histories of inter-generational trauma (Menzies 2010) and historical trauma (Duran, Duran, Yellow Horse Braveheart, and Yellow Horse Davis 1998).

Lee Maracle (2003) describes lateral violence as "our anti-colonial rage working itself out in an expression of hate for one another." Indeed, anger is the most recognizable aspect of lateral violence, but there are many others. Lateral violence can include physical violence, verbal abuse, bullying and mobbing, substance abuse, suicide, and general social pathologies in communities. On the interpersonal level, laterally violent behaviour includes gossip, triangulation, complaining, manipulation, blaming, name-calling, chronic hostility and resentment, undermining, and sabotage (Jefferies 2007; NWAC 2011).

Children in residential schools and their parents were subjected to all of these behaviours, and they have been passed down from generation to generation within families and communities. Lateral violence issues have led to toxic work and community environments, leading people to recognize that interventions are needed to release this last vestige of residential school socialization.

Indigenous communities are looking to their traditions and traditional knowledges for interventions. Out of this, there is a promising and recent emergence of transformative healing methods. These newly emerging methods are premised on cultural context theory, which includes critical consciousness, empowerment, and accountability (Almeida and Lockard 2005). In response to community calls for interventions, scholars and practitioners, such as Rod Jefferies and Denise Findlay, have developed comprehensive training programs to develop awareness about lateral violence and help communities to address these issues.

Raven, one of the authors of this book, whose words opened this discussion, is one of the people who has developed a program to address lateral violence. The Transformative Accountability Model works to transform historical trauma and lateral violence into personal accountability and wellness. The model draws its strength from the Indigenous knowledge[2] foundation of Nehiyaw (Cree) laws that guide human conduct in relations to other people, animals, and the

---

2 Western philosophy uses the term "epistemology" for theories of knowledge, such as Indigenous knowledge.

natural world. In its essence, Transformative Accountability has three elements: the historical context, the traditional knowledge of ethical behaviour, and accountability practice.

• The *historical element* contextualizes colonization and establishes the basis for grief work as a core element of healing colonial trauma.
• The *traditional knowledge* piece reminds people about the ethical and moral nature of Indigenous lifeways.
• The *accountability* aspect encourages individuals to assume responsibility for their thoughts, words, and actions, not to over-look historical issues, but to transform their perceptions of it and the role they allow historical issues to impact upon their current well-being. By taking ownership of our current daily reality, we remember and reclaim our individual efficacy and personal agency in creating fulfillment, despite historical realities.

In her work with communities and agencies, Raven begins work-shops by first establishing the historical context. This situates lateral violence as a structural and systemic issue, as opposed to individual character flaws. For many Indigenous people, contextualizing family and community trauma within colonial history is, in itself, an empowering and liberating experience. It serves to "disembody" long-standing and internalized trauma; it also creates a space to place the shame and guilt individuals may experience if they recog-nize lateral violence in their own patterns of behaviour.

Lateral violence is treated as an outcome of multi-generational trauma, an insidious trauma that has seldom been acknowledged or mourned. To move beyond guilt and blame, individuals are sup-ported to recognize that multi-generational trauma and its outcome, lateral violence, may need individual and collective grieving; losses need to be mourned (Yellow Horse Braveheart and DeBruyn 1998).

In addition, Raven makes links between traditional Cree laws and contemporary notions of personal accountability. Transformative Accountability is defined as taking 100 per cent responsibility for thoughts, words, feelings, and conduct. In other words, Transforma-tive Accountability is taking a stance in life where we do not hold other people, places, or things responsible for our emotional state.

Many intergenerational survivors are empowered by the work of reconciling past experiences through contextualization and grief work and through embracing accountability. The approach is hard, but it is ultimately transformative. As one workshop participant said, "I'm slowly learning that adoption, residential schools, broken homes . . . we're all kind of damaged goods trying to make our way, to stand strong, to make our ancestors proud . . . but it's a darn bumpy walk sometimes" (Joanne R, personal communication, 2014 Adoptee Gathering, Ottawa).

LIBERATION AND SOCIAL SERVICES

In some parts of the world – particularly in police states rife with assassinations, HIV-AIDS pandemics, police repression, genocide, and extreme poverty – emancipatory efforts are extremely difficult and dangerous. At the same time, we can learn from the progress achieved through struggles, near and far. Baines (2011b) emphasizes that we can gain inspiration for our struggles at home by looking to "Third World and Indigenous experiments in participatory democracy, participatory budget and policy making, and new forms of collective social support." Indeed, she argues, "some of our best hopes for social justice lie in finding common ground and internationalizing our struggles" – that is, in finding ways of supporting and working in solidarity with the struggles for self-determination, peace, and sustainable development taking place around the world (Baines 2011c: 41).

The contested nature of social services in Canada is a small part of the global drama to transform all unjust structures into processes of equity, ecological sanity, authentic democracy, and to respect the diversity of multiple cultures and communities. Such transformation is being nudged forward by a liberated version of professionalism, beginning to take shape within social work in Canada and elsewhere.

Being fully liberated as a person is probably not possible within an overall system that remains highly oppressive. But it is still possible to be partly liberated, as a person and as a helper, as we push the boundaries to dismantle all oppressions. Part of that process consists of listening to what service users are saying. For example, two single-parent women who self-identify as Native and who experienced both good and bad service give clear messages about what they want from social service providers.

"Don't treat me as a number," one of them said. *"Take the time to show interest in my life. Don't tell me what to do, but help me figure out what I should do."*

"Be personal," said the other. *"Share a bit of your life with me, so I know who's working with me. Don't just hide behind your desk.*

"When helpers and people being helped know we're all in this together, there's not that thick line dividing us. Then we know we're here for each other. That's the kind of service I'm part of now – and it's great! It's changed my life for the better. I'm not shy to speak up any-more. I've found my voice, and now I can help others too."

As we listen to people who know about oppression from first-hand experiences, there is much we can learn about how to deliver social services in respectful, effective ways. A group of Queer activists, for example, offer some snippets of advice to social service providers:

- *Do your own work* – examine your own beliefs, attitudes, and knowledge about queer people, issues and communities. . . . Examine how you contribute to the oppression, marginalization, power-lessness and exploitation of queer people. . . . Eliminate heterosexist language from your spoken use. . . . Take the challenge to interrupt homophobic and heterosexist behaviours whenever you see them.
- *In work with individuals* – validate the stories of stigma and victim-ization and connect them to their historical, structural and political origins; listen to the coping strategies, frustrations, and anger and draw from them to develop potential actions that impact social con-ditions.
- *In institutions* – take active steps to create your agency as one where queer people and heterosexual allies would like to work and/or come for service; develop non-discriminatory and anti-harassment policies for the explicit protection of queer staff and clients; hire, retain, and validate the contributions of queer people.

(Brown, Richard, and Wichman 2010: 169–70)

These plus similar guidelines for social service work with all of the other distinctly disempowered populations need to be implemented throughout all social services in Canada. More than that, these guidelines for respectful practices toward everyone who experiences systemic oppression need to be implemented in all institutions, including private, public, and NGO (non-governmental organization) non-profit sectors. That includes all schools, banks, and media and online communication industries. Achieving this change would represent a significant step toward social justice.

As we listen and learn about what service users and their social movements see as important, our focus becomes the question of what should be the role of helpers. Jim Albert, a respected Indigenous Elder with Algonquin roots, has taught social work at universities for almost three decades. He is regularly asked to serve as an Elder at ceremonies, to conduct sweat lodges, fasts, and healing circles.

> We have to respect the autonomy of the persons asking for help as they are the only ones that can heal themselves. It's all about relationships. For our part in a helping relationship, we need to know who we are, to learn to respect ourselves in a fundamental way, and to be able to love ourselves. If we are on our own healing journey then we are better able to share our medicines and our skills with those who have asked for help. We have to be very careful that we don't take over someone else's problem, and [we have to] respect their ability to deal with it themselves.
>
> While we have to respect the autonomy of the individual we also have to recognize that we live in a world where people's rights are constantly being violated through the various forms of oppression that they experience. We need to walk with them and advocate with them and find ways to expose the oppressions and inequalities that they face. We need to walk with others who are on their healing journeys, to be good role models, and to be prepared to stand in opposition to oppressive practices and policies in the world around us.

Part of this work includes mainstream social workers seeking to practice from a decolonized perspective. Helping us to do that is the following "Pendulum of Social Work Practice."

THE PENDULUM OF PRACTICE: A TOOL FOR ASSESSING CULTURAL COMPETENCE

Many have questioned the value of a cultural competency tool by implying that if we "know" a culture then our practice will automatically be liberatory. But this is often not the case. Others criticize cultural competency for failing to engage with power. Whereas we can see some point to this argument, we find the model presented below addresses this criticism by combining Indigenous knowledges with critical practice, and so, is an exception.

Dr. Christine Fejo-King (2013), a Warramunga/Larrakia social work educator from the Australian Northern Territory, offers a traditional knowledge based cultural competence model called the Pendulum of Practice. This tool can aid social workers in completing critical cultural competence self-audits in social work practice contexts. The Pendulum of Practice model has two parts: the *spectrum of practice* (figure 9.1) as a visual assessment tool, and the *Competence Matrix* (table 9.1), which explains the spectrum levels of competence.

According to Fejo-King, "the Pendulum of Practice represents the social worker as a pendulum that can swing in both directions, dependent upon the context of practice. Their expertise, knowledge, and past experience first place them as the pendulum at a certain point when they enter a given context; but it is their willingness to learn that determines which way they, as the pendulum, will swing, as well as how far and how fast." She reminds us that because Aboriginal and other groups differ in various ways from each other, and because our competence shifts in each context in which we practice, social workers do not stay in exactly the same position on the spectrum when they move to a new practice context.

In the spectrum of practice figure (see figure 9.1), the bar on the bottom is the spectrum (or range) and depicts levels of cultural competence and safety. Social workers are represented by the pendulum and can quickly assess their competence in each new cultural or group context. A quick glance at the spectrum immediately directs our attention to self-awareness of our cultural competence.

Figure 9.1. Spectrum of Practice

| Harmful | Unaware | Cognizant | Effective | Experienced | Innovative |

COMPLETING A CULTURAL COMPETENCE SELF-AUDIT

Obviously, we all want to fall within the *experienced* and *innovative* categories in our self-assessments. But if we are honest with ourselves, we know the reality is that we will be competent with some groups and in some contexts, and in need of more skills and experience with other groups and in other contexts. The strength of this particular model is that we can apply it widely across a huge range of socio-demographic factors that affect people, such as culture and ethnicity, ability and disability, and mental health, to name only a few. It may be challenging for us as individual social workers to admit that in some contexts our level of competence falls within the "unaware" or even "harmful" categories. But when this is the case, it is important, in order to reduce harm, that we know this. We can use this model to help us become aware of our own issues that we may not know exist.

The *Competence Matrix* explains each of the spectrum competence levels (see table 9.1). The column headings summarize our level of cultural competence functioning as social workers and are arranged in order from least to most competent and safe. These enable us to critically evaluate and place ourselves within the spectrum of practice and to see where we can improve our practice.

Table 9.1
Competence Matrix

Spectrum Heading	Examples: "I am . . ."	Description: "I . . ."
Harmful	Discriminatory	• favour one individual or group above another
	Stereotypical	• classify all as fitting a certain mould
	Prejudicial	• am biased against; hold stereotypes to be true
	Racist	• see some as inferior
	Oppressive	• impose upon, rather than collaborate with
	Self-serving	• am unwilling to examine biases and attitudes toward group • resist or am defensive about self-audit
Unaware	Ignorant	• have no understanding of the people or group
	Willfully unaware and complacent	• ignore obvious signs and messages of bias • am unaware of biases and attitudes toward group • do not see problems that do not affect me personally
Cognizant	Aware	• have cognitive recognition, but this does not necessarily lead to positive action • can listen to other sides of the story
	Non-judgmental	• am aware but stuck in guilt or fear
	Ineffective	• am basically not getting the job done
Effective	Consultative	• ask for others' opinions and advice before acting

Spectrum Heading	Examples: "I am . . ."	Description: "I . . ."
Effective (continued)	Participatory	• ask for information about culture or group; have an inclusive approach
	Culturally considerate	• recognize that there are differences in culture, then act in culturally congruent ways
	Reflective	• think about my own practice and improve practice based on those reflections
	Competent	• engage and am aware and willing to get the job done
Experienced (Knowledgeable)	A source of information	• share information with the people who need it
	A source of empowerment	• take responsibility for cultural safety in practice contexts • recognize the strengths and capacity of others and help to enable them to use these to bring about change
	A challenger of inequalities	• speak out fearlessly, even to own employer or government, about injustices • internalize requests, consider, take responsibility and implement
	A listener	• recognize when the client/group is the expert and learn from them
	One who walks beside	• have a collaborative approach
Innovative	Able to be led by the people	• internalize group values and norms; have strong ethic of relationality with group

Spectrum Heading	Examples: "I am . . ."	Description: "I . . ."
		• recognize self as the student and support leadership shown by client or group; show constant willingness to learn
		• see the client as the expert, encourage them, and help them to empower themselves
	A person who fights wilful ignorance and complacency	• recognize the political and structural agendas of others; am willing to teach others
		• actively challenge inequities and harmful approaches
		• can categorize approaches that are more appropriate, see what could be done instead, develop proposals, and advocate for change (due to depth of knowledge and level of trust)

COMPETENCE MATRIX

To get the most out of this tool, Dr. Fejo-King recommends that we go through the Competence Matrix each time before entering any practice setting with marginalized groups. This will help us identify both our strengths and gaps in knowledge in broad terms. For example, when used during employment in a particular Indigenous practice setting, it can be used to guide us to improve our skills and practices in the local context, keeping in mind that our competence will vary. As an example, Fejo-King explains, "I, as an Aboriginal social worker from the Northern Territory, would rate well on the broad spectrum, but if I were asked to work with Torres Strait Islander people I would rate much lower because my knowledge and experience in that area is much less. In fact, even in the Northern Territory, I would rate much more highly with the Larrakia and the Warumungu (my mother's and father's people) than I would with the Tiwi or the Arunta."

The Pendulum of Practice, which includes the spectrum of practice visual assessment tool and the explanations in the Competence Matrix, supports anti-oppressive practice by providing a readily usable tool to engage in a cultural competence self-audit at any point in social work practice and with any group that we are new to.

SUPPORTING AND ACTUALIZING TRANSFORMATION

As this Pendulum of Practice illustrates, our activities in carrying out these roles are not restricted to formal job descriptions. We need to bring all of ourselves into our relationship with our work. Luisa Quarta spent some time as a clinical social worker at an agency that works with people who have developmental disabilities, and she describes her approach to practice in that job:

> For me it's important to understand that "social work practice" doesn't just mean what happens in the office between myself and a client. Yes, practice definitely includes that relationship, but it also includes my relationship with the agency, plus my relationship with community – from local to global spheres. And more, practice includes my relationship to myself. What I mean is – my willingness to enter into self-reflection, and to share this self-reflection with clients. I believe that when we do this personal sharing, it helps to break down the imbalance, the distance between clients and ourselves.

Other helpful models also exist to build liberatory practice. For example, Luisa Quarta worked at a social service agency with about one hundred and twenty employees. It was structured in what she calls "a racialized hierarchy." The workers who do housekeeping and clerical work are predominantly people of colour, and the clinical professional staff are predominantly White. She tells Ben (a co-author of this book) about a time when the agency had a new chief executive officer who set out to cut agency costs – and who also clearly wanted to be seen as being fair about it. According to Quarta, "he had the management prerogative of laying off people and that's what he did. He gave notice and targeted clerical and housekeeping staff for layoffs."

Quarta and her co-workers were members of a local of the Ontario Public Sector Employees Unions (OPSEU); she was president of the local. They saw clearly what was happening: at the same time as the agency management was planning to lay off members of the housekeeping and clerical staff, it was spending large sums of money on technology and consultants. *"We knew there were other ways to save money rather than throwing people out of jobs. We felt the layoffs devalued the importance of housekeeping and clerical staff to accomplishing our work. Without question, it would create hardships – some people to be laid off were single parents, women of colour."*

Under the circumstances the union saw the layoffs as immoral and decided to try to stop them. While management tried to de-personalize the layoffs, offering a rationale that offered no recognition of the people involved, the union insisted that the layoffs involved real people. One of the union's first steps was to invite the people threatened with layoff to come to a union meeting. It encouraged them to step forward, to tell their stories, give voice to their experience. *"This created spaces where professionals could learn, sometimes for the first time, about the details of the work done by these employees. The more that the professionals heard about the planned layoffs, the more that opposition grew to this way of cutting costs."*

Luisa and her co-workers came up with a plan of attack. At the next agency staff meeting every single one of them showed up wearing black tops as a symbol of protest against the layoffs. The agency managers, she says, *"were utterly shocked that the room was a sea of black. . . . The managers cut the meeting short, and two days later announced there would be no layoffs."*

When we heard the results, tears came to my eyes. Agency staff had never before experienced the power of a collective voice, and now were saying "we did it!" It was meaningful for me to be part of an experience where we made a material difference to people's lives. We actually prevented people from losing their jobs. We showed that collective resistance can work and that sometimes we can win.

That collective resistance – and the strategy involved – draws upon community organizing skills similar to those used by social workers and others within the wider community. Going up against the forces of privilege can be risky. People of privilege feeling threatened will typically retaliate, carefully hiding their own positions of privilege as they belittle or attempt to discredit our efforts. They may honestly believe that they favour social justice as they organize a political backlash to protect their privileges (Klein 2008 and 2014; Nasser 2015). Amid such contradictions, they may portray themselves as victims and complain about being unfairly treated, even silenced. This is not easy terrain, which is why activists always need the support of trustworthy allies along the way – which sometimes means creating our own support groups.

Support groups vary in how they get formed, how often they meet, how they function, and how long they last. A support group that Ben belongs to is small, consisting of half a dozen people who practice or teach in the social services.

Ben: We began as an activist group, tackling issues ranging from racism to professional elitism. Our activities have ranged from lobbying public officials to working with media, from sponsoring public educational events to joining large-scale street demonstrations. We meet once a month, which we've been doing for over twenty years.

One of our members, Judy Tsao, who works with homeless people, describes how our group provides support:

As the group evolved, our get-togethers created a space where we could vent our frustrations and receive encouragement from each other. There's a lot of pressure in our work, yet despite the complexities – I felt understood by other members. I felt we had shared values. As we got to know each other, there was relationship-building among ourselves, which to me is so important. The result was amazing – I found the group provided safety for us to express our concerns. It wasn't at all planned, the group seemed to evolve organically, as a few people moved on and new folks came in. We respect and like each other – we became friends. We'll brainstorm about issues and exchange information about resources. We'll go and support picketing social workers out on strike, but our main focus is to give each other support. Knowing I have that level of support adds to the strength I need to do my job.

Paul Agueci is another member of our group:

*As a person with a disability, I know the importance of support. At the
age of ten, I was in crisis, in a coma for three months. I had a huge struggle, and without support from my family and others – I'd be dead now.
I'm an activist because I've learned from that experience – people in the
disability community can't do it alone. Our survival depends on that support, and I believe that's true for others too. Whether it's people in feminist groups, unions, mental health organizations, or other community
networks – it's through support that people find their communal voice.
And we're finding that voice. That's what gives me hope. That's what
makes us strong."*

Hope is also echoed in the Idle No More movement whose vision
is to protect Treaty and land rights of Indigenous people, and also to
value and respect the principles of reciprocity and sustainability for
future generations. These values are shared by many others, including progressive social workers and helpers whose concerns move far
beyond the delivery of enlightened social services

These life-affirming values inspire and lift up human life as a
precious, sacred gift. The challenge remains: How do we move forward to carry out these values and principles? How do we challenge
ourselves to be vigilant in standing up for these principles? Since
most of us have experienced systemic abuse, many of us still continue to submit to such abuse, allowing these principles to be
silenced. By contrast, when we refuse to submit, when we stand up
and engage ourselves and others in healing and wellness, we
empower ourselves and promote social justice. In other words, striving for social justice means reaching for the well-being of ourselves
and others. By taking action with progressive activists locally and
globally, we join together, we resist. We mobilize. We reaffirm the
value of human life. We listen to Indigenous leaders such as Grand
Chief Ronald Derrickson:

In any negotiation there are things that you do not put on the table.
For Indigenous nations, as for all nations, this includes surrendering
our land. Instead, what Indigenous peoples in Canada can discuss is
what kind of usage of our land we can live with and under what conditions. (Manuel and Derrickson 2015: 229)

Derrickson makes a strong case that Indigenous nations must establish their own governments to receive royalties and other payments at fair and reasonable levels from the extraction of resources from the land by lumber, mining, gas, and oil industries. These payments will be based on these industries being required to obtain an Aboriginal as well as a provincial permit to operate, and that "Aboriginal permits will be issued only in an environmentally sustainable way . . . and will reflect not only our Indigenous values, but also an element of local control. . . . Our revenue, finally, will come from the wealth of the land." (232) Viable Indigenous economies based on their title of the land and its resources would mean that Indigenous communities would no longer have to depend on welfare. As that happens, then "governments would no longer have to waste the billions of dollars a year they currently pay to keep their colonialist and largely self-serving Department of Indian Affairs afloat. . . . The Department would be eliminated, along with the racist Indian Act, as Indigenous governments are funded through their Indigenous economies just as provincial governments exist on their own-source revenues" (233).

Banakonda

What does using the term *resources* really mean? The term is problematic. It suggests ownership of what are viewed as "objects." It negates or minimizes our place in, our relationship with creation, and the relationship between humans and the land. Such attempts to convert land and life into material objects do not comply with Indigenous ways of knowing and being in relationship with all life. Seeing ownership of land, that is, land as a *resource* is problematic, not only because it is a mainstream way of thinking. It also suggests you "can own" land, water, trees, animals. Such ownership violates the principles of equity, reciprocity, mutuality, interdependence, and the maintenance of balance. By contrast, Indigenous perspectives call each of us to honour those Seven Generations yet to come, and those ones who thought about us, remembered us, as they lived on this very land.

Sometimes we witness disagreements among leaders we support. We need to remember that neither Indigenous people, nor Anglo-Europeans speak with one voice. A challenge for Indigenous organizations, and also for mainstream social movements, is to arrive at some level of consensus to encourage potential supporters to join the rallying cries for justice. While the roles of leaders are not easy, neither are the roles of being supporters: there is a personal turbulence from the conflicting appeals for our allegiance and involvement.

Our observations are that the more ground we gain through our advocacy for new laws and policies to affirm our human rights, the greater the backlash against our credibility by defenders of the status quo. Backlash aggravates the lateral violence that Raven discusses earlier in this chapter. Similarly, among mainstream social activists, backlash aggravates jealousies, insecurities, and competition. When that happens, we believe it helps to pause and pay heed to cultural ways that Indigenous people are addressing lateral violence, as outlined by Raven. For non-Indigenous people, it is also worthwhile to pause and touch base with their own lived experience, their own insights, and their raised consciousness about how their lives intersect with the lives of others.

Here, all of us need to be open about receiving support from people who are our actual and potential allies, whether they be family members, friends, work colleagues, social movement activists, or other equity seekers. Moreover, this demonstrates the nature of mutual support: flowing sometimes from us toward others, and at other times from others toward us. Through this reciprocity, we may experience a strengthening of our inner resilience and personal agency, which affirms the urgency of our contributing to liberation, along with many others. Brazilian educator Paulo Freire, in his paradigm-shifting work *Pedagogy of the Oppressed* (2001) describes this as "the great humanistic and historical task of the oppressed; to liberate themselves and the oppressor as well" (28).

Under certain circumstances, when our resilience and inner agency are in harmony with growing public support for social and economic justice, including open support from progressive people inside institutions, we enter the daunting stage of escalating our challenge of the toxic and oppressive social relations addressed in this book. This effort is undoubtedly a tall order. At the same time, it flows naturally from our commitment to honour the voices of people who have been silenced for too long (Choudry 2015). The multiple layers of social and economic justice are closely connected with participatory democracy and with a transformation of power that calls for a basic democratization of material wealth.

We view wealth at the individual level, as the having of a "comfortable enough" life. Democracy, to be real, must be within the reach of everyone rather than being manipulated by excessively privileged, super-rich elites who now dominate the heights of our economic, political, and social structures. By contrast to the elitist democracy we experience today, participatory democracy challenges the environmental destruction and the consumerism associated with contemporary wealth appropriation. Our goals for participatory democracy are nothing less than to ensure that each Indigenous nation is respected as evidenced by our actions, that each person has a voice and is fairly treated, and that everyone has a "comfortable enough" life. Those then, are the challenges – for you, for us – not just for social service providers, but for everyone.

10 Nawây-pîkiskwêwina
After Words

Raven: It has been a great journey teaming up with Ben, Donna, and Banakonda to work on the seventh edition of *Case Critical*. The book has been part of my reading collection since I started my undergraduate social work education and so it is a tremendous honour to become part of the *Case Critical* team and to contribute to this edition. *Case Critical* is a seminal work in the Canadian social work literature and even though it is challenging to improve upon something that is already excellent in quality, I am confident that the seventh edition is even more remarkable in its scope and in the strength of its analyses.

The field of social work, and especially Indigenous social work, is evolving so quickly that we have added several discussions and references to the latest literature to ensure that the book highlights the most recent social justice issues. The result is a book that is contemporary and asks tough questions to encourage critical thought about prevailing social inequities and the need for justice.

For me, the most significant shift in this edition is Ben's invitation to participate to Indigenize this seminal social work book and, rather than writing about Indigenous issues himself, he asked Banakonda and me to step in and contribute. To me, this is the difference between the "talk" of being an ally, and the

---

Raven consulted with the Language Carrier Neal McLeod for the Cree "Nawây-pîkiskwêwina" to correspond with the English "After Words."

[Raven:, *continued*]

"practice" of it. Working on a team with allies who interrogate their own privilege, and respect the meaning of "voice" and "representation," is life-affirming in these current times where Indigenous and other racialized and marginalized groups are under intense pressures from the current neo-conservative social, political, and economic milieu.

I believe that this book will meet the interests of students, allies, and scholars alike. It is written clearly and comprehensively, and jam-packed with information that links historical information with contemporary situations. We ask many questions to trigger reflection and analysis about urgent issues facing all Canadians. Ideally, these questions and reflections will spur us all toward concrete actions that contribute to a more equitable and just society.

Kinanaskomitinawaw, mistahi,

Raven (Otiskewapit)

Donna: Banakonda calls the writing of this book a journey. I was on several journeys when Ben asked me to join this one; some wanted and some not. Co-writing the book was a very welcome journey. Ben's book and his contributions to making the world a better place are something I long admired and it was wonderful to be part of this impressive writing team. I had used Ben's book in my BSW years at University of Calgary and writing with Ben felt like coming full circle.

In addition to the joy of working with Ben, Raven, and Banakonda, the book offered me an important opportunity to be part of a social work project aimed at redressing some of the deep historical wrongs in Canadian nation building and social work knowledge building, specifically the many injustices perpetrated against Indigenous peoples. One of the book's main goals is to disrupt the singular white, colonial, elite narrative, and create a story that reflects and interweaves anti-oppressive Indigenous and non-indigenous perspectives. The book is a beginning contribution to that huge and ongoing project.

When the book writing project began, I had just completed an unwanted journey with breast cancer and was trying to regain my swagger and focus. More than ever, I wanted to help change the world and build social justice. Books such as *Case Critical* offer a way to marry activism with social justice practice, social activism, and scholarly work. These kinds of book projects create important spaces for further critical thought and action, and it was a journey I was happy to join.

During the process of writing this book, I was asked to accept a Chair at University of Sydney, and eager to learn new things and new ways to contribute to social justice, I said yes. I am taking the learnings from the journey of this book with me on my Australia journeys, and will certainly learn more there. It is eye opening and comforting to know that the kinds of conversations and lessons we are eager to advance in Canada about social justice social work are the same kinds of conversations and lessons that many social work students, practitioners, and academics are eager to advance in Australia. The struggle for social justice has many fronts and I am thrilled that I have had the opportunity to contribute to this one and to join with the many students and practitioners who will read, reflect on, and critically engage with the important issues we raise in the struggle for peace, fairness, and equity.

Ben: Working on this seventh edition reminds me that the values I hold in relation to social services, social programs, and society – are shared by many others. We envision a caring society that is engaged in dismantling the toxic relationship between Indigenous and non-Indigenous people, and making amends. We reach for co-operation rather than competitive individualism. We seek systemic fairness and equality in the context of participatory democracy. At the same time, I feel it is important to honour ceremonial, spiritual spaces that affirm our gratitude for the amazing miracle of life. I believe that revitalized, generous, and liberated social services can be built on these values.

[Ben:, *continued*]

The oppressive mess that contaminates our lives today, I believe, is largely due to police and military violence deployed to advance contemporary take-overs of Indigenous land, and to enshrine neoliberal policies and laws, which enrich the few at the expense of the many. No wonder that as social service providers, we witness pain, suffering, and despair among people seeking help.

In pushing for progressive change through non-violent ways, a key for me, is for each of us to reach out to other people who share our motivation to challenge oppression and exploitation wherever they exist. As we strive to develop relationships of trust, appreciation, and reciprocity, these relationships can grow from one-to-one to small groups, such as the nourishing and mutually supportive team that is producing this book: I so appreciate the outstanding work by Banakonda, Donna, and Raven for this project and beyond. I'm also grateful for the highly talented individuals connected with Between the Lines Publishers who are bringing our work to fruition.

When such work and their caring relationships multiply and thrive among many people, the stage is set for the next levels. We not only express solidarity with Indigenous leaders for justice, and with non-Indigenous social justice activists – we also join them. We not only align ourselves with emerging initiatives dedicated to the creation of cultural, economic, environmental, political and social justice – we also extend their reach. And as we do, we may catch a glimpse of an inviting future overflowing with seeds of liberation rising up from our caring relationships, inspiring the knowledge and the action we need for our liberation.

CAN WE GO WHERE WE HAVE NEVER BEEN? AN ANISHINAABE ELDER'S PERSPECTIVES

Banakonda

The colonization of Turtle Island and its people was and remains a violent and exploitive occupation. Woven into the fabric of the creation and unfolding of Canadian society, exploitation lubricates and facilitates the power dynamics, narratives, and relationships with the original people and the land. The resulting dispossession and oppression were born in the homeland of the settlers; paradoxically, that is why they left and that is what they brought to Turtle Island. This is a willfully ignored truth that compromises our social fabric, our ability to participate and cooperate. It severely undermines the reality of our economic interdependence and ability to share equitably with one another.

Colonization is reflected in the relationship between corporations and governments. The mega oil, gas, and other extractive industries and related financial institutions are central economic cogs running our society. This segment of society moves the whole economic system, treating people and the land as mere "recourses" to be exploited. As a result, respect, reciprocity, health, and well-being are at increasing risk, putting our very ability to survive in question. Conventional social work practice along with all social services and health practices in this country are systemically delivered with built-in determining factors that are in the way of progressive economic change. They serve the economic development as defined by the wealth accumulation of business corporations. Equity, reciprocity, and balance are not possible as long as we give priority to the needs of business corporations.

It is highly unlikely that corporate elites will ever be convinced to give up the power and wealth they have accumulated through misappropriation. At the same time,

[Banakonda, *continued*]

as we reach for well-being for all, control by these elites can be reduced. In shifting toward reciprocity, we remove our tacit consent to their domination. We can challenge the social/economic narratives that communicate an expectation of consumerism as essential to well-being and survival. Prevailing narratives drive the belief that we can meet our needs by simply buying more. We are constantly told through advertisements by governments and corporations that we need more, that we do not have enough, and we are not enough.

How then, do we as a society engage in transformative change that embraces equity, balance, and reciprocity? Standing up for kindness, for balance, for sharing, necessitates a consciousness about decolonization. A mindful, investigative, relational inquiry is required within oneself, within one's family, community, and society as a whole. It is a commitment we all need to make. Our language, our governance, and our overall narratives must change.

They must be re-imagined, re-spoken, and re-written. Only then will our relationship with each other emerge anew. Our relationships are with each other, the land, water, air, and all of creation. There is a circular unfolding of development and growth. Wholeness is always unfolding. Recognizing this is essential.

This is not about isolating the parts from the whole or focusing only on those parts in isolation. It is not about saying; "this is an Indian problem, it's them over there." It's not about saying the "trauma" is over there; it does not stand alone. It calls us to recognize the systemic source of trauma within the whole. The trauma is different for each of us, and it impacts all of us.

The interpretive implications as we emerge out of the domination of colonization, out of being a colony, must examine language repeatedly. The ways our identity has been held, renamed in the language, deceptively culling us into a continued colonized mandate, have had the impact of domination and disenfranchisement, reinforcing rather than liberating or transforming the cross-Canada narrative.

The implications for social work practice are profound. Social services have in fact violated their own code of ethics and principles, which call for giving priority to the needs of the individuals and families they work with. Sadly, in practice, social work has implemented oppression.

A far-reaching, intergenerational harmful example is moving children out of families and communities to residential schools, then to child welfare agencies as a way of breaking down the cultural and social fabric of Indigenous families and communities. This demonstrates the need for systemic change. Without this kind of change the problem continues to be recycled rather than transformed. Social work practice will otherwise continue to be a part of systemic oppression, causing displacement, disenfranchisement, and the pain and suffering that are its fallout.

Reconciliation must be seen in this context. The work of the Truth and Reconciliation Commission is about ending domination, ending systemic foundational control, making restitution, and pursuing reciprocity, co-operation, and equity. Inch by inch, we must remove domination and then rediscover what good social justice practice can really be. These practices need to be in line with the communities and nations we are working for and with. Furthermore, these practices must also be applied in our international practice as well.

The settlers of Canada and the Americas have been and are operating as though extracting is the sole purpose of being here. Where is the vision to build a civilization that is truly civil, honouring the original people as well as the newcomers and the generations yet to come? Can we rise and stand up to the challenge of creating a new landscape that truly takes up caring, loving residence on, in, and with the land that nurtures and cultivates all life?

[Banakonda, *continued*]

The harm caused by treating the "extraction of natural resources" as normal has spilled over to harm social work and social services. It has contaminated mainstream child welfare agencies by extracting Indigenous children from their families and communities at unprecedented levels, and which has not offered up wellness or any qualitative or quantitative improvement. Furthermore, racialized families and others living in poverty have also been subjected to these unproductive, extractive interventions. How do we hold up "wholeness"? What is our centre? How do we address the heart of this matter as a country, a society, as communities, families, and individuals?

Looking back over the life of this country and forward to the one we are reaching for together ignites the fire within us. As citizens, as governments, corporations, in health and human services, the experience, the act of looking back and looking forward can create an environment where change is possible. One looks back to look forward. Change, invites growth within one's relationship with self and others simultaneously.

From a mainstream perspective, the current trends of change have come to mean increased control, increasing exploitation and consumerism, without regard for our relationship with each other and the land. The focus and values are on "use" not relationship. This approach ignores our connection with creation, yet when we harm creation, we harm ourselves. Individualism, in itself, maintains that disconnect. Materialism rules our everyday life. Even education is a route to our ability to increase personal acquisition.

In our education institutions we conduct ourselves as if we are in silos, rarely connecting or relating to each other. We are more engaged in protecting turf and reproducing the harmful values of materialism and its partner, consumerism. This imbalance between ourselves and creation reveals an underlying reason for the conflict between Indigenous and Anglo-French-European societies.

In this model there are principles of cause and effect among isolated elements.

In the Indigenous worldview, there are interrelated, interconnected, and interdependent elements in relationships all the time. Indigenous beliefs hold that all life has a spirit. This belief in spirit and our relatedness also explains our belief in co-operation. You are not a great hunter without the co-operation of the animal you hunt. The interaction between Anglo-French-European and Indigenous peoples has historically been a catastrophe for Indigenous people. It remains deeply harmful and troublesome to this day. What is not understood is how mutual that harm is.

My grandmother shared a simple teaching with me that saved my life. She told me, when you are in a strong current it is folly to swim against it, swim with the current, at the same time, gradually move little by little out of it. I followed that teaching as a girl swimming alone in Lake Superior and I survived.

We have to swim with the current while we gradually move ourselves out. Or will we drown? It is easy to look at our contemporary situation as a strong current taking us down. What is the work of gradually moving out of this current? That work ahead of us, I believe, is the untangling of ourselves, each other, and our communities from consumerism, from materialism and the abuse of land, water, and life. We are all caught up in this unsustainable taking. To have a future, we need to see ourselves living with creation, exploring, creating new ways to sustain ourselves, each other, and all of creation.

What needs do we have to meet to move beyond repeating the wrongs in our practice, the wrongs in our society? How can we participate in lifting up a new vision of well-being that includes all of us, all of life? How do we respond and address the living of our lives together in a sustainable, equitable, life-affirming way?

I believe we can!

[Banakonda, *continued*]

My Indigenous knowledge, humble as it is, leads me to believe that the way to facilitate positive movement and growth is by the application of the following gifts and values:

the importance of shared
Vision

the importance of shared
Respect

the importance of shared
Kindness

the importance of shared
Honesty

the importance of
Sharing

the importance of
Co-operation

Emerging from the application of these principles
and values is the practice of
interdependence and mutuality.

In that practice of reaching for balance and harmony with each other, our experience strengthens our relationship with each other and the land. Maintaining harmony and balance is the preservation of diversity and of life itself. Justice is the way to move forward, however justice is not just for human life but rather for all of life. We truly are "all related."

In this way, within this vision, I am grateful for this opportunity to reflect on practice alongside of Ben, Donna, and Raven. There is indeed unending work ahead for us. I believe we must first re-imagine together, *before* we rebuild. What are *our* next moves? What ways do we engage in movement? How do we come to knowing and to facilitate understanding that will promote the emergence and application of wholistic practice?

Can we go where we have never been?

– Awnjibinayseekwe Banakonda Kennedy-Kish (Bell)

REFERENCES

Ntamkidwinan (page 1): Banakonda consulted with Anishinaabe Language Carrier Lorraine McRae, who helped find "Ntamkidwinan" to correspond with "First Words" in the title for chapter 1.

"Nawây-pîkiskwêwina" (page 185): Raven consulted with the Language Carrier Neal McLeod for the Cree words to correspond with the English "After Words" in the title for chapter 10.

o o o o

Aboriginal Committee, Community Panel. 1992. *Liberating our children, liberating our nations.* Victoria: Family and Children's Services Legislation Review, Government of British Columbia.

Abramovitz, Mimi. 1988. *Regulating the lives of women: Social welfare policy from colonial times to the present.* Boston: South End Press.

Absolon, Kathleen E. Minogiizhigokwe. 2011. *Kaandossiwin: How we come to know.* Halifax and Winnipeg: Fernwood Publishing.

Absolon, Kathy (Minogiizhigokwe). 2009. "Navigating the landscape of practice: Dbaagmowin of a helper." In *Wicihitowin: Aboriginal social work in Canada,* ed. Raven Sinclair (Otiskewapiwskew), Michael Anthony Hart (Kaskitemahikan), and Gord Bruyere (Amawaajibitang). Black Point, NS: Fernwood Publishing.

Academics in Solidarity with Chief Spence and Idle No More. 2014. "Open letter to the Right Honourable Prime Minister of Canada Stephen Harper and the Right Honourable Governor General David Johnston." *The Winter we danced: Voices from the past, the future, and the Idle No More Movement,* ed. The Kino-nda-niimi Collective, 230, 231. Winnipeg: ARP Books.

Adams, J. Roy. 2009. "Collective bargaining is about a great deal more than money: Democracy is missing when 70% of workers lack basic rights." *CCPA Monitor* 16 (4). Ottawa: Canadian Centre for Policy Alternatives.

Adamson, Nancy, Linda Briskin, and Margaret McPhail. 1988. *Feminists organizing for change: The Contemporary women's movement in Canada.* Toronto: Oxford University Press.

Aging Out. 2015. "Aging Out: Moving towards queer and trans* competent care for seniors." Qmunity, B.C.'s Queer Resource Centre. http://qmunity.ca.

Albert, Jim.1991. "500 years of Indigenous survival and struggle." *Canadian Review of Social Policy* 28.

Alinsky, Saul D. 1946. *Reveille for radicals.* Chicago: University of Chicago.

Alinsky, Saul D. 1971. *Rules for radicals.* New York: Random House.

Allan, Billie, and Janet Smylie. 2015. *First Peoples, second class treatment: The role of racism in the health and well-being of Indigenous peoples in Canada.* Toronto: Wellesley Institute. www.wellesleyinstitute.com.

Almeida, Rhea, and Judith Lockard. 2005. "The Cultural Context Model: A new paradigm for accountability, empowerment, and the development of critical consciousness against domestic violence." In *Domestic Violence at the Margins*, ed. Natalie J. Sokoloff , 301–20. New Brunswick, NJ: Rutgers University Press.

Anderson, Chris. 2014. *"Métis": Race, recognition, and the struggle for Indigenous peoplehood.* Vancouver: UBC Press.

Antone, Bob. 2013. "Haudenosaunee decolonization." www.youtube.com.

Aronson, Jane, and Dawn Hemingway. 2011. "Defining the future of social work." *Canadian Social Work Review* 28 (2).

Assembly of First Nations. 2016. "A declaration of First Nations." www.afn.ca.

Association of Black Social Workers/Nova Scotia. 2015. "Racism is killing us softly." 19 October 2015 and 21 March 2016. http://nsabsw.ca.

Baines, Donna, ed. 2007. *Doing anti-oppressive practice: Building transformative politicized social work.* Halifax, Canada: Fernwood Publishing.

Baines, Donna, ed. 2011a. *Doing anti-oppressive practice: Social justice social work.* 2nd ed. Halifax: Fernwood Publishing.

Baines, Donna. 2011b. "Anti-oppressive practice: Roots, theory and tensions." In *Doing anti-oppressive practice: Social justice social work,* ed. Donna Baines, 2–14. 2nd ed. Halifax: Fernwood Publishing.

Baines, Donna. 2011c. "An overview of anti-oppressive social work practice: Neoliberalism, inequality and change." In *Doing anti-oppressive practice: Social justice social work,* ed. Donna Baines, 25–48. 2nd ed. Halifax: Fernwood Books.

Baines, Donna. 2014. "What's new about the new austerity? Care work in the nonprofits." In *Orchestrating austerity: Impacts and resistance*, ed. D. Baines and S. McBride. Halifax: Fernwood.

Baines, Donna, and Bonnie Freeman. 2011. "Work, care, resistance and mothering: An Indigenous perspective." In *A life in balance: Reopening the family-work debate*, ed. Cathy Krull and Justine Sempruch. Vancouver: University of British Columbia Press.

Baines, Donna, and Pat Armstrong, eds. 2015. *Promising practices in long term care: Ideas worth sharing.* Ottawa: Canadian Centre for Policy Alternatives. www.policyalternatives.ca.

Baines, Donna, Ian Cunningham, Wayne Lewchuk, and Navjeet Sidhu. (forthcoming). "How could management let this happen? Gender, participation, and industrial action in the nonprofit sector." *Economic and Industrial Democracy*.

Baines, Donna, Sara Charlesworth, and Ian Cunningham. 2013. "Fragmented outcomes: International comparisons of gender, managerialism and union strategies in the nonprofit sector." *Journal of Industrial Relations* 56 (1): 24–42.

Baines, Donna, Sara Charlesworth, Ian Cunningham, and Janet Dassinger.

2012. "Self-monitoring, self-blaming, self-sacrificing workers: Gendered managerialism in the non-profit sector." *Women's Studies International Forum* 35 (5) September – October: 362–71.

Baines, T. Carol. 1998. "Women's professions and an ethic of care." In *Women's caring: Feminist perspectives on social welfare*, ed. Carol T. Baines, Patricia M. Evans, and Sheila M. Neysmith. 2nd ed. Toronto: Oxford University Press.

Bantjes, Rod. 2007. *Social movements in a global context: Canadian perspectives.* Toronto: Canadian Scholars' Press.

Barnes, Colin, Mike Oliver, and Len Barton. 2002. "Introduction." In *Disability studies today,* ed. Colin Barnes, Mike Oliver, and Len Barton. Cambridge: Polity Press.

Baskin, Cyndy (On-koo-khag-kno kwe). 2009. "Evolution and revolutions: Healing approaches with Aboriginal adults." In *Wicihitowin: Aboriginal social work in Canada,* ed. Raven Sinclair (Otiskewapiwskew), Michael Anthony Hart (Kaskitemahikan), and Gord Bruyere (Amawaajibitang). Black Point, N.S.: Fernwood Publishing.

Baskin, Cyndy. 2013. *Strong Helpers' Teachings: The value of Indigenous knowledges in the helping professions.* Toronto: Canadian Scholars Press.

Baskin, Cyndy. 2016. *Strong helpers' teachings: The value of Indigenous knowledges in the helping professions.* 2nd ed. Toronto: Canadian Scholars' Press.

Bates, Michelle. 2011. Evidence-based practice and anti-oppressive practice. In *Doing anti-oppressive practice: Social justice social work*, ed. Donna Baines, 146–61. 2nd ed. Halifax: Fernwood Books.

Bellamy, Don. 1965. "Social welfare in Canada." *Encyclopedia of social work.* New York: National Association of Social Workers.

Benjamin, Akua. 2007. "Doing anti-oppressive social work: The Importance of resistance, history and strategy." In *Doing anti-oppressive practice: Building transformative politicized social work,* ed. Donna Baines. Black Point, N.S.: Fernwood Publishing.

Bernard-Thomas, Wanda, ed. 2015. *Still fighting for change: Black social workers in Canada.* Lawrencetown Beach, N.S.: Pottersfield Press.

Bernard-Thomas, Wanda, and Veronica Marsman. 2010. "The Association of Black Social Workers (ABSW): A model of empowerment practice." In *Structural social work in action: Examples from practice*, ed. Steven F. Hick, Heather I. Peters, Tammy Corner, and Tracy London. Toronto: Canadian Scholars' Press.

Bielmeier, George. 2002. "Social work and sexual diversity." In *Social work in Canada: An introduction*, ed. Steven Hick. Toronto: Thompson Educational Publishing.

Birnbaum, R., and R. Silver. 2011. "Social work competencies in Canada: The time has come." *Canadian Social Work Review* 28 (2).

Blackstock, Cindy. 2006. "Reconciliation means not saying sorry twice: Lessons from child welfare in Canada." In *Reconciliation in child welfare: Touchstones of hope for Indigenous children, youth, and families.* Ottawa: First Nations Child and Family Caring Society of Canada.

Blatchford, Andy. 2015. "Canadian CEO pay climbs twice as fast as average worker's since 2008: Study." *Huffington Post*. Canadian Press. January 1. www.huffingtonpost.ca.

Bocking, Richard. 2003. "Reclaiming the commons: Corporatism, privatization drive enclosure of the commons," *CCPA Monitor* 10 (5). Ottawa: Canadian Centre for Policy Alternatives.

Bombay, Amy. 2014. "Origins of lateral violence in Aboriginal communities: A preliminary study of student-to-student abuse in residential schools." Ottawa: Aboriginal Healing Foundation.

Borel, Kathryn. 2016. "Complainant in Jian Ghomeshi case issues statement." *Toronto Star*. May 12, page 1. www.thestar.com.

Brealey, Ken. 2012. Outcomes report for the Indigenizing the Academy Conference, University of the Fraser Valley. August 26–28, 2012. www.ufv.ca.

Brittain, Melissa, and Cindy Blackstock. 2015. *First Nations child poverty: A literature review and analysis*. First Nations Children's Action Research and Education Service, a partnership between University of Alberta and First Nations Child and Family Caring Society of Canada. www.fncaringsociety.com.

Broadbent Institute. 2014. "The Wealth Gap: Perceptions and misconceptions in Canada." https://d3n8a8pro7vhmx.cloudfront.net.

Brotman, Shari, Bill Ryan, Shannon Collins, Line Chamberland, Robert Cormier, Danielle Julien, Elizabeth Meyer, Allan Peterkin, and Brenda Richard. 2007. "Coming out to care: Caregivers of gay and lesbian seniors in Canada." *The Gerontologist* 47 (4).

Brown, Marion, Brenda K. Richard, and Leighann Wichman. 2010. "The Promise and relevance of structural social work and practice with queer people and communities." In *Structural social work in action: Examples from practice*, ed. Steven F. Hick, Heather I. Peters, Tammy Corner, and Tracy London. Toronto: Canadian Scholars' Press.

Burgess, Christian. 1999. "Internal and external stress factors associated with identity development of transgendered youth." In *Social services with transgendered youth*, ed. Gerald Mallon. New York: Haworth Press.

Business Council of Canada. 2016. "About" http://thebusinesscouncil.ca.

Butler, Robert N. 2001. "Ageism." In *The encyclopedia of aging*. 3rd ed., vol.1 (A-L), ed. George L. Maddox. New York: Springer Publishing.

Calgary Anti-Racism Education. 2015. "STAND / Framing and learning anti-racism / Whiteness." www.ucalgary.ca.

Callahan, Marilyn. 2004. "Chalk and cheese: Feminist thinking and policy-making." In *Connecting policy to practice in the human services*, ed. Brian Wharf and Brad McKenzie. Toronto: Oxford University Press.

Campaign 2000: End Child and Family Poverty. 2015. "Let's do this: Let's end child poverty for good." National 2015 Report Card. www.campaign2000.ca.

Campbell, Carolyn. 2011. "Competency-based social work: A unitary understanding of our profession." *Canadian Social Work Review* 28 (2).

Canada Without Poverty. 2015. "Poverty: What do we do – Dignity for all."
    www.cwp-csp.ca.

Canada Without Poverty. 2009. *Poverty and parliament*. Ottawa. Summer.

Canadian Association for Social Work Education. 2014. "Standards for
    Accreditation: Domain III, Program Content, Curriculum." Ottawa.
    http://caswe-acfts.ca.

Canadian Association of Social Workers. 1932. *Social Welfare* 14 (6) March.

Canadian Association of Social Workers. 2003. *Child welfare project: Creating
    conditions for good practice*. Ottawa.

Canadian Association of Social Workers. 2016. "What is Social Work?"
    www.casw-acts.ca.

Canadian Broadcasting Corporation. 2013. "30,000 Canadians are homeless
    every night: 200,000 Canadians are homeless in any given year, national
    report says" June 19: CBC. www.cbc.ca.

Canadian Broadcasting Corporation. 2015. "Canada adds 12,000 jobs in Sep-
    tember but unemployment rate rises to 7.1%" *CBC News,* October 9.

Canadian Encyclopedia. 2015. Inuit Tapiriit Kanatami (ITK).
    www.thecanadianencyclopedia.ca.

Canadians for Tax Fairness. 2015. "Campaigns: Help us organize tax fair-
    ness" www.taxfairness.ca.

Canadian Labour Congress. 2014. "Employment Insurance is failing unem-
    ployed workers in Canada" Ottawa. http://canadianlabour.ca.

Canadian Network for the Prevention of Elder Abuse. 2016. "What is Elder
    Abuse – Responding to abuse – Learn what you can do about ageism."
    www.cnpea.ca and www.cnpea.ca.

Canadian Network of Women's Shelters and Transition Houses. 2014. "News
    and events: Shelter voices." March 5. http://endvaw.ca.

Canadian Union of Public Employees. 2016. "Federal budget 2016: CUPE
    summary and response." Ottawa: CUPE. http://cupe.ca.

Capen Reynolds, Bertha. 1951. "Social work and social living: Explorations
    in philosophy and practice." *Classics Series 1975, 1987.* Silver Spring,
    Md.: National Association of Social Workers.

Carniol, Ben. 1992. "Structural social work: Maurice Moreau's challenge to
    social work practice." *Journal of Progressive Human Services* 3 (1).

Carniol, Ben. 2005a. "Structural social work (Canada)." In *Encyclopedia of
    social welfare history*, ed. John M. Herrick and Paul H Stuart. Thousand
    Oaks, Cal.: Sage Publications.

Carniol, Ben. 2005b. "Analysis of social location and change: Practice impli-
    cations," in *Social work: A critical turn*, ed. Steven F. Hick, Jan Fook, and
    Richard Pozzuto. Toronto: Thompson Educational Publishing.

Carniol, Ben, and Vivian Del Valle. 2010. " 'We have a voice': Helping immi-
    grant women challenge abuse." In *Structural social work in action: Exam-
    ples from practice,* ed. Steven F. Hick, Heather I. Peters, Tammy Corner,
    and Tracy London. Toronto: Canadian Scholars' Press.

CARP: Canadian Association of Retired Persons. 2014. "600,000 seniors in Canada live in poverty, including more than 1 in 4 single seniors according to new Statistics Canada report." www.carp.ca.

Centre for Families, Work and Well-Being. 2013. "The gender wage gap in Canada." April 16. University of Guelph. www.worklifecanada.ca.

Chan, Bonnie. 2013. "An interview with Mia Mingus, Oakland champion of change, on transformative justice." http://oaklandlocal.com.

Chiose, Simona. 2015. "Education a way to reconciliation: justice." *Globe and Mail*, May 30. www.theglobeandmail.com.

Choudry, Aziz. 2015. *Learning activism: The intellectual life of contemporary social movements*. Toronto: University of Toronto Press.

Church, Kathryn. 2016. "My dinners with Tara and Nancy: Feminist conversations about teaching for professional practice." In *Teaching as scholarship: Preparing students for professional practice in community services*, ed. Jacqui Gingras, Pamela Robinson, Janice Waddell, and Linda D. Cooper, 75–89. Waterloo, Ont.: Wilfrid Laurier University Press.

Citizens for Public Justice. 2013a. "Fact sheet #1. After-tax incomes in Canada: Running hard to stand still." Poverty trends scorecard: Fact sheet series. www.cpj.ca.

Citizens for Public Justice. 2013b. "Fact Sheet #6. Wealth in Canada: Concentrated in the hands of a few." Poverty trends scorecard: Fact sheet series. www.cpj.ca.

Citizens for Public Justice. 2015. Michele Bliss. "Shouting it from the rooftops: We need a plan to end poverty in Canada." www.cpj.ca.

Cohen, Erminie Joy. 1997. *Sounding the alarm: Poverty in Canada*. Ottawa: Senate of Canada.

Cohen-Rottenberg, Rachel. 2015. "Doing social justice: 10 Reasons to give up ableist language." *Huff Post,* The Blog. December 28. www.huffingtonpost.com.

Copp, Terry. 1974. *The Anatomy of poverty: The Condition of the working class in Montreal 1907–1929*. Toronto: McClelland and Stewart.

Corrigan, Philip, and Val Corrigan. 1980. "State formation and social policy until 1871." In *Social work, welfare and the state*, ed. Noel Parry, Michael Rustin, and Carol Satyamurti. Beverly Hills, Cal.: Sage.

Cunningham, Ian, and Philip James, eds. 2011. *Voluntary organizations and public service delivery*, 15–36. London: Routledge.

Czyzewski, Karina, and Frank Tester. 2014. "Social work, colonial history and engaging Indigenous self-determination." *Canadian Social Work Review* 31 (2).

Dale, Jennifer, and Peggy Foster. 1986. *Feminists and state welfare*. London: Routledge and Kegan Paul.

Daley, Michael R. 2015. *Rural social work in the 21st century*. Chicago: Lyceum Books.

Dalhousie University. 2016. "Human rights, equity and harassment prevention – Glossary of terms." www.dal.ca.

Daly, Mary. 1978. *Gyn/Ecology: The Metaethics of radical feminism*. Boston: Beacon Press.

Daschuk, James. 2013. *Clearing the plains: Disease, politics of starvation, and the loss of Aboriginal life*. Regina: University of Regina Press.

Davidson, Carl. 2010. "U.S. Steelworkers plan to experiment with factory ownership: Union to link with Mondragon worker cooperative movement." *CCPA Monitor* 16 (8). Ottawa: Canadian Centre for Policy Alternatives.

Davies, Steve. 2011. "Outsourcing and the voluntary sector: A review of the evolving landscape." In *Voluntary Organizations and Public Service Delivery*, ed. Ian Cunningham and Philip James, 15–36. London and New York: Routledge.

Democracy Now. 2014. "Vandana Shiva, Winona LaDuke and Desmond D'Sa on a Global, Grassroots Response to U.N. Climate Summit." September 23. www.democracynow.org.

de Schweinitz, Karl. 1943. *England's road to social security*. New York: Barnes.

Diebel, Linda. 2016. "Cindy Blackstock, single mom to 163,000 kids: The activist has taken on the cause of Canada's First Nations children, who have been shortchanged by Ottawa. It's proven to be the biggest challenge of her life." *Toronto Star*, Canada, Politics, March 27. www.thestar.com.

Dreier, Peter. 2015. "Social movement politics IS coalition politics" *Mobilizing Ideas*. South Bend, Indiana: University of Notre Dame Center for the Study of Social Movements. https://mobilizingideas.wordpress.com.

Dumont, Onaubinisay James. 2006. Nipissing Social Service Worker Diploma Teaching Session.

Dunn, Peter A. 2003. "Canadians with disabilities." In *Canadian social policy: Issues and perspectives*, ed. Anne Westhues. Waterloo, Ont.: Wilfrid Laurier University Press.

Duran, Eduardo, and Bonnie Duran. 1995. *Native American Post-Colonial Psychology*. Albany: State University of New York Press.

Duran, Eduardo, Bonnie Duran, Marie Yellow Horse Brave Heart, and Susan Yellow Horse Davis. 1998. "Healing the American Indian Soul Wound." In *International Handbook of Multigenerational legacies of trauma*, 341–54. The Plenum Series on Stress and Coping 1998.

Egale. 2011. "What you should know about LGBTQ youth suicide in Canada." http://egale.ca.

Eldridge v. British Columbia (A.G.). 1997. 3 S.C.R. 624.

Elliott, Larry. 2004. "Pursuit of 'job flexibility' a dubious route to full employment." *CCPA Monitor* 11 (2) June. Ottawa: Canadian Centre for Policy Alternatives.

Ennis, Dawn. 2015. "Report: Antigay violence down, transphobic hate crimes up." November 17. Advocate. www.advocate.com; www.avp.org.

Fanon, Frantz. 2008. *Black skin, white masks*. New York: Grove Press.

Feehan, Richard, Maureen Boettcher, and Kathaleen S. Quinn. 2009. "The societal context of child sexual abuse." In *Structural social work in action: Examples from practice,* ed. Steven F. Hick, Heather I. Peters, Tammy Corner, and Tracy London. Toronto: Canadian Scholars' Press.

Fejo-King, Christine. 2013. *Let's Talk Kinship: Innovating Australian Social Work Education, Theory, Research and Practice through Aboriginal Knowledge*. Canberra: Magpie Goose Publishing.

Findlay, Peter. 1982. "The 'Welfare State' and the state of welfare in Canada." Paper presented at annual conference of Canadian Association of Schools of Social Work. Ottawa.

Finkel, Alvin. 1977. "Origins of the welfare state in Canada." In *The Canadian state: political economy and political power*, ed. Leo Panitch. Toronto: University of Toronto Press.

First Nations Child and Family Caring Society of Canada. 2014. Closing submissions. Canadian Human Rights Tribunal: Memorandum of fact and law of the complainant First Nations Child and Family Caring Society, 75. August 29. https://fncaringsociety.com.

First Nations Child and Family Caring Society of Canada. 2016a. "Who we are / What we do / What you can do." https://fncaringsociety.com.

First Nations Child and Family Caring Society of Canada et al. v. Attorney General of Canada (for the Minister of Indian and Northern Affairs Canada). 2016b. Canadian Human Rights Tribunal. http://decisions.chrt-tcdp.gc.ca.

First Nations Child and Family Caring Society of Canada et al. v. Attorney General of Canada (for the Minister of Indian and Northern Affairs Canada). 2016c. Canadian Human Rights Tribunal. http://decisions.chrt-tcdp.gc.ca.

Flint, John. 1974. *Cecil Rhodes*. Boston: Little Brown and Company.

Food Bank Canada, 2015. Hungercount 2015. www.foodbankscanada.ca.

Freedenthal, Stacey. 2015. "Speaking of suicide – Transgender people and suicide: The tragedy, and the hope." www.speakingofsuicide.com.

Frideres, James S. 1998. *Aboriginal Peoples in Canada: Contemporary conflicts*. Toronto: Allyn and Bacon.

Friedman, May, and Jennifer Poole. 2016. "Drawing close: Critical nurturing as pedagogical practice" In *Teaching as scholarship: Preparing students for professional practice in community services*, ed Jacqui Gingras, Pamela Robinson, Janice Waddell, and Linda D. Cooper, 89–107. Waterloo, Ont.: Wilfrid Laurier University Press.

Freire, Paulo. 2001. *Pedagogy of the oppressed*. New York: Bloomsbury Academic.

Furlotte, Kirk, Sarah Paterson, Áine Humble, and Jacqueline Gahagan. 2013. "Nova Scotia LGBT end-of-life resource inventory." *Fostering end-of-life conversations, community, and care among LGBT older adults*. www.dal.ca.

Gaetz, Stephen, Tanya Gulliver, and Tim Richter. 2014. *The state of homelessness in Canada*. Toronto: The Homeless Hub Press.

Galper, Jeffrey. 1980. *Social work practice: A radical perspective*. Englewood Cliffs, N.J.: Prentice-Hall.

Garossino, Sandy. 2016. "Borel's counterpunch blindsides Henein, knocks out Ghomeshi." *National Observer*. Opinion, May 12. www.nationalobserver.com.

Gauci, Rosemary, Emelyn Bartlett, and Colleen Grey. 2004. "Focus on the special needs of youth and their families." *Mental Health Matters*. Spring ed. Toronto Branch: Canadian Mental Health Association.

George, Purnima, Amra Munawar, and Zakiya Atcha. 2013. "Food insecurity: Impacts and social costs," *A community participatory action research project*. Toronto: Reh'ma Community Services.

George, Purnima, Brienne Coleman, and Lisa Barnoff. 2007. "Beyond 'providing services': Voices of service users on structural social work practice in community-based social service agencies." *Canadian Social Work Review* 24 (1).

Germain, Carel B., and Alex Gitterman. 1980. *The Life model of social work practice*. New York: Columbia University Press.

Gillis, Wendy. 2015. "Don't regulate carding – eliminate it, consultation told" *Toronto Star*. September 1. www.thestar.com.

Goar, Carol. 2010. "Historic moment for nations disabled." *Toronto Star*. March 17, A15.

Gosine, Kevin, and Gordon Pon. 2010. "On the front lines: The voices and experiences of racialized child welfare workers in Ontario." *Paper presented at the meeting of the Canadian Sociological Association*, Montreal, Quebec.

Graveline, Fyre Jean. 1998. *Circle works: Transforming Eurocentric consciousness*. Halifax: Fernwood Publishing.

Gregoire, Lisa. 2016. "Inuit leaders pleased Supreme Court will hear Clyde River case." News, *Nunatsiaq, Online*, Nunavut. www.nunatsiaqonline.ca.

Griffin Cohen, Marjorie. 2009. "Response to the recession: Rescue the economy, protect people, and plan for the future." *CCPA Monitor* 16 (1). Ottawa: Canadian Centre for Policy Alternatives.

Guest, Dennis. 1980. *The Emergence of social security in Canada*. Vancouver: University of British Columbia.

Guest, Dennis. 1985. "Social security." In *Canadian encyclopedia*. Edmonton: Hurtig.

Gutiérrez, Lorraine, and E.A. Lewis. 2012. "Education, participation, and capacity building in community organizing with women of color." In *Community organization and community building for health*, ed.M. Minkler, 3rd ed. New Brunswick, N.J.: Rutgers.

Gutiérrez y Muhs, Gabriella, Yolanda Niemann, Carmen González, and Angela Harris, eds. 2012. *Presumed Incompetent: The intersections of race and class for women in academia*. Logan: Utah State University Press.

Hadden, Jennifer. 2015. "Expansion, evolution, and impact of the global climate change movement" The Center for the Study of Social Movements at the University of Notre Dame. https://mobilizingideas.wordpress.com.

Hanes, Roy. 2006. "Social work with persons with disabilities: Helping individuals and their families." In *Social work in Canada: An Introduction*, ed. Steve F. Hick, 2nd ed. Toronto: Thompson Educational Publishing.

Hanes, Roy. 2012. "Exploring the social construction of disability in a cross cultural context." Paper presented, at United Nations Conference of State Parties – The UN Convention on the Rights of People with Disabilities. http://newsroom.carleton.ca.

Harding, Robert. 2006. "Historical Representations of Aboriginal People in Canadian News Media." *Discourse and Society* 17 (2): 205–35.

Harper, Tim. 2016 "Fiscal policy driven by discrimination." *Toronto Star.* January 27. www.thestar.com.

Hart, Michael Anthony (Kaskitemahikan). 2009a. "For Indigenous people, by Indigenous people, with Indigenous people: Towards an Indigenous research paradigm." In *Wicihitowin: Aboriginal social work in Canada,* ed. Raven Sinclair (Otiskewapiwskew), Michael Anthony Hart (Kaskitemahikan), and Gord Bruyere (Amawaajibitang). Black Point, N.S.: Fernwood Publishing.

Hart, Michael Anthony (Kaskitemahikan). 2009b. "Anti-colonial Indigenous social work reflections on an Aboriginal approach." In *Wicihitowin: Aboriginal social work in Canada,* ed. Raven Sinclair (Otiskewapiwskew), Michael Anthony Hart (Kaskitemahikan), and Gord Bruyere (Amawaajibitang). Black Point, N.S.: Fernwood Publishing.

Hart, Michael Anthony (Kaskitemahikan). 2015. "From cultural awareness to Indigenist practice: Critical perspectives on a spectrum of services." Presented at Creating A New Legacy, Aboriginal Mental Health and Wellness Conference. October 6–7. Brandon, Manitoba.

Hedges, Chris. 2015a. *Wages of rebellion: The moral imperative of revolt.* Toronto: Vintage Publishers.

Hedges, Chris, 2015b. "Wages of rebellion: Part I." www.youtube.com.

Hedges, Chris. 2015c. "The next debate: The system of global capitalism is breaking down." Interview by Rudyard Griffiths of the Monk Debates. *Globe and Mail.* May 23: F3. www.theglobeandmail.com.

Heinomen, Tuula, and Len Spearman. 2001. *Social work practice: Problem-solving and beyond.* Toronto/Vancouver: Irwin.

Hemingway, Dawn, Clarie Johnson, and Brenda Roland. 2010. "Addressing the immediate needs of service users as part of fundamental structural change: Complementary or contradictory processes?" In *Structural social work in action: Examples from practice,* ed. Steven F. Hick, Heather I. Peters, Tammy Corner, and Tracy London. Toronto: Canadian Scholars' Press.

Henry, Frances, and Carol Tator. 2010. *The Colour of democracy: Racism in Canadian society,* 4th ed. Toronto: Nelson Learning.

Henry, Jennifer. 2015. "Opinion: Decolonizing Canada," Montreal Gazette. May 31. http://montrealgazette.com.

Heron, Craig. 2012. *The Canadian labour movement: A short history,* 3rd ed. Toronto: James Lorimer.

Heschel, Suzannah, ed. 1996. *Moral grandeur and spiritual audacity: Essays by Abraham Joshua Heschel.* New York: Farrar, Straus, Giroux.

Hick, Steven F., Heather I. Peters, Tammy Corner, and Tracy London, eds. 2010. *Structural social work in action: Examples from practice.* Toronto: Canadian Scholars' Press.

Hill, Gus, and Alicia Wilkinson. 2014. "Indigegogy: A transformative Indigenous educational process." *Canadian Social Work Review* 31 (2).

Hobbs, Margaret, and Carla Rice, eds. 2013. *Gender and women's studies in Canada.* Toronto: Women's Press.

House of Commons, Canada. 1983. Minutes of the proceedings of the Special Committee on Indian Self-Government, 40. Oct. 12, Oct. 20.

House of Commons. 2008. Debates: Official report (Hansard), vol. 142, no. 110, 2nd session, 28th Parliament, June 11. www.parl.gc.ca.

Huffington Post. 2016. February 26 report by Canadian Broadcasting Corporation. "What Does Black Activism Look Like Today In Canada?" CBC News. February 5. www.huffingtonpost.ca.

Hulko, Wendy. 2015. "Operationalizing intersectionality in feminist social work research: Reflections and techniques from research with equity-seeking groups." In *Feminisms in social work research: Promise and possibilities for justice-based knowledge,* ed. Stéphanie Wahab, Ben Anderson-Nathe, and Christina Gringeri. London and New York: Routledge.

Hunt, Gerald. 2011. "Are we equal yet? Making sense of lesbian, gay, bisexual, and transgender issues in the workplace." In *Understanding and Managing Diversity,* ed. Carol Harvey and M. June Allard, 5th ed. Toronto: Pearson.

Irving, Allan. 1981. "Canadian fabians: The work and thought of Harry Cassidy and Leonard Marsh, 1930–1945." *Canadian Journal of Social Work Education* 7 (1).

Irving, Allan. 1989. "'The Master principle of administering relief': Jeremy Bentham, Sir Francis Bond Head and the establishment of the principle of less eligibility in Upper Canada." *Canadian Review of Social Policy* 23 (May).

Jefferies, Rod. 2007. "Lateral Violence in the Workplace." Video. AMC Conference, Winnipeg, MB. www.youtube.com.

Johnson, Patricia. 2014. "Constructing a bridge between two cultures: How Inuit Qaujimajatuqangit is essential to addressing the 'modern' child welfare system in Nunavut." *Canadian Social Work Review* 31 (2).

Johnson, Shelly. 2014. "Knucwente-kuc re Stsmemelt.s-kuc; Trauma-informed education for Indigenous children in foster care." *Canadian Social Work Review* 31 (2).

Justice for Girls. 2003. "Young women in prison speak out." *Publications and Positions.* www.justiceforgirls.org.

Kennedy-Kish (Bell), Banakonda, and Ben Carniol. 2017, in press. "A two-road approach to ethical practice." In *Social work ethics: Progressive, practical and relational approaches,* ed. Elaine Spencer, Jim Gough, and Duane Massing. Toronto: Oxford University Press.

Kennedy, Mark. 2015. "Teachings about aboriginals 'simply wrong' says Murray Sinclair." *Ottawa Citizen.* May 24. http://ottawacitizen.com.

Kinewesquao (Cathy Richardson). 2009. "Métis experiences of social work practice." In *Walking this path together: Anti-racist and anti-oppressive child welfare practice,* ed. Susan Strega and Sohki Aski Esquao (Jeannine Carriere). Black Point, N.S.: Fernwood Publishing.

Kinewesquao (Cathy Richardson), and Allen Wade. 2009. "Taking resistance seriously: A Response-based approach to social work in cases of violence against Indigenous women." In *Walking this path together: Anti-racist and anti-oppressive child welfare practice,* ed. Susan Strega and Sohki Aski Esquao (Jeannine Carriere). Black Point, N.S.: Fernwood Publishing.

King, Thomas. 2009. *All My Relations: An anthology of contemporary Canadian Native prose.* Toronto: McClelland and Stewart.

King, Thomas. 2012. *The inconvenient Indian: A curious account of Native people in North America.* Toronto: Anchor / Random House.

Kino-nda-niimi Collective. 2014. *The winter we danced: Voices from the past, the future, and the Idle No More Movement.* Winnipeg: ARP Books.

Klein, Naomi. 2008. *The shock doctrine: The rise of disaster capitalism.* Toronto: Random House.

Klein, Naomi. 2014. *This changes everything: Capitalism versus the climate.* Toronto: Alfred Knopf / Random House.

Klein, Naomi, 2015. "Coming live from the Sydney Opera House: Capitalism and the climate," *Festival of Dangerous Ideas.* September 5–6. https://youtu.be.

Klein, Seth, and Yalnizyan, Armine. 2010. "Reducing poverty, inequality will spur economic recovery." *CCPA Monitor* 16 (9). Ottawa: Canadian Centre for Policy Alternatives.

Kumsa, Martha Kuwee. 2007. "A Settlement story of unsettlement: Transformative practices of taking it personally." In *Doing anti-oppressive practice: Building transformative politicized social work,* ed. Donna Baines. Black Point, N.S.: Fernwood Publishing.

Kush, Larry. 2015. "Selinger delivers moving apology for Sixties Scoop." June 19. Winnipeg Free Press.

LaBerge, Roy. 2010. "New economy is needed to replace failed neoliberal system: Book review of *Beyond the bubble: Imagining a new Canadian economy*, by James Laxer." *CCPA Monitor* 16 (9). Ottawa: Canadian Centre for Policy Alternatives.

La Rose, Tara. 2009. "One small revolution: Unionization, community practice, and workload in child welfare." *Journal of Community Practice* 17 (1).

Ladd, Deena, and Trish Hennessy. 2009. "New labour: When workers unite for fair treatment – How to rid the uneasy world of part-time work of unfairness, low pay and exploitation." *Toronto Star.* July 11.

Lappin, Bernard. 1965. "Stages in the development of community organization work as a social work method." Ph.D. dissertation. School of Social Work, University of Toronto.

Latta, Ruth. 2009. "More equal societies do better: The bigger the income gap, the worse the social problems." *CCPA Monitor* 16 (2). Ottawa: Canadian Centre for Policy Alternatives.

Lawrence, Bonita, and Enakshi Dua. 2005. "Decolonizing antiracism." *Social Justice* 32 (4).

Leonardo, Zeus. 2009. "The color of supremacy: Beyond the discourse of 'white privilege.'" Foundations of critical race theory in education, ed. E. Taylor, D. Gillborn, and G. Ladson-Billings. New York: Routledge. http://cidocstudents2012.wikispaces.com.

Levine, Helen. 1982. "The personal is political: Feminism and the helping professions." In *Feminism in Canada: From pressure to politics*, ed. Angela R. Miles, and Geraldine Finn. Montreal: Black Rose Books.

Lightman, Ernie. 2003. *Social policy in Canada*. Toronto: Oxford University Press.

Lubove, Roy. 1965. *Professional altruist*. Boston: Harvard University Press.

Lundy, Colleen. 2011. *Social work, social justice, and human rights: A structural approach to practice*. 2nd ed. University of Toronto Press.

Macarov, David. 1978. *The Design of social welfare*. New York: Holt, Rinehart and Winston.

MacDonald, Judy E., and Gaila Friars. 2010. "Structural social work from a (dis)Ability perspective." In *Structural social work in action: Examples from practice,* ed. Steven F. Hick, Heather I. Peters, Tammy Corner, and Tracy London. Toronto: Canadian Scholars' Press.

Mackenzie, Hugh. 2010. "Debate over taxes dangerously one-sided and misleading." *CCPA Monitor* 16 (8). Ottawa: Canadian Centre for Policy Alternatives.

Mackenzie, Hugh. 2016. "Staying power: CEO pay in Canada." Ottawa: Canadian Centre for Policy Alternatives. January 4. www.policyalternatives.ca.

Madden, Jason, Nuri Frame, Zachary Davis, and Megan Strachan. 2016. "Another chapter in the pursuit of reconciliation and redress: A summary of Daniels v. Canada at the Supreme Court of Canada." www.pstlaw.ca.

Madison, Nora. 2009. "Abstract fluid identify and embodied selves: Virtual community and the narratives of bisexuality in online social networking sites." Open conference systems, Internet research 10.0. http://ocs.sfu.ca.

Mallam, Teresa. 2014. "Men help Take Back the Night." Prince George Free Press. September 25. www.pgfreepress.com.

Mallon, Gerald P. 1999. "Practice with transgendered children" In *Social services with transgendered youth*, ed. Gerald Mallon. New York: Haworth Press.

Mallon, Gerald P. 2015. Social work practice with lesbian, gay, bisexual, and transgender people, 3rd ed. New York: Routledge.

Mandell, D., J. Clouston Carlson, M. Fine, and C. Blackstock. 2007. "Aboriginal Child Welfare." In *Moving toward Positive Systems of Child and Family Welfare* ed. G. Cameron, N. Coady, and G. Adams. Waterloo, Ont.: Wilfrid Laurier University Press.

Manuel, Arthur, and Grand Chief Ronald M. Derrickson. 2015. *Unsettling Canada: A national wake-up call.* Toronto: Between the Lines.

Maracle, Lee. 2003. *I am Woman.* Toronto: Press Gang.

Marcus, Stephen. 1978. "Their Brothers' keepers." In *Doing good: The Limits of benevolence*, ed. Willard Gaylin. New York: Pantheon.

Mayer, Jane. 2016. *Dark money: The hidden history of the billionaires behind the rise of the radical right.* New York: Knopf Doubleday Publishing Group. www.democracynow.org.

Mazowita, Benjamin, and Marta Burczycka. 2014. "Shelters for abused women in Canada, 2012." Statistics Canada. Juristat 85-002-X. www.statcan.gc.ca.

McAdam, Sylvia. 2015. *Nationhood Interrupted: Revitalizing Nêhiyaw Legal Systems.* Vancouver: Purich Publishing Ltd.

McDonald, C. 2006. *Challenging social work: The institutional context of practice.* London: Palgrave Macmillan.

McGill University Equity Subcommittee on Queer People. 2010. "Recognizing heterosexism and homophobia: Creating an anti-heterosexist, homophobia-free campus." www.mcgill.ca.

McIntosh, Peggy. 1998. "White privilege: Unpacking the invisible knapsack." In *Re-visioning family therapy: Race, culture and gender in clinical practice*, ed. Monica McGoldrick. New York: Guilford.

McIntosh, Peggy. 2007. "White privilege and male privilege: A personal account of coming to see correspondence through work in women's studies." In *Intersections of gender, race and class: Readings for a changing landscape*, ed. Marcia Texler Segal and Theresa A. Martinez. Los Angeles: Roxbury Publishing.

McMurtry, John. 2009. "Taxation and poverty: Injustices built into our tax system hurts poor the most." *CCPA Monitor* 16 (2). Ottawa: Canadian Centre for Policy Alternatives.

McQuaig, Linda. 2016a. "Different tax rules for wealthy and powerful." *Toronto Star*. Opinion, June 9: A21. www.thestar.com.

McQuaig, Linda. 2016b. "Sander's populism is more transformative than Trump's." *Toronto Star*, Opinion, July 28: A17. www.thestar.com.

McQuaig, Linda, and Neil Brooks. 2012. *Billionaires' ball: Glutton and hubris in an age of epic inequality.* Boston: Beacon.

Meerai, Sonia, Idil Abdillahi, and Jennifer Poole. 2016. "An introduction to anti-Black sanism." *Intersectionalities: A Global Journal of Social Work Analysis, Research, Polity, and Practice* 5 (3): 1–18.

Mehler Paperny, Anna. 2014. "Canada's failing to prevent inmate suicides, watchdog finds." *Global News.* September 10. www.globalnews.ca.

Menzies, Peter. 2010. "Intergenerational Trauma from a Mental Health Perspective." *Native Social Work Journal* 7: 63–85.

Menzies, Peter. 2014. "Child welfare." In *Journey to healing: Aboriginal people with addiction and mental health issues – what health, social service and justice workers need to know*, ed. Peter Menzies and Lynn Lavallée. Toronto: Centre for Addiction and Mental Health.

Menzies, Peter, and Lynn Lavallée. 2014. *Journey to healing: Aboriginal Peo-*

ple with addiction and mental health issues – what health, social service and justice workers need to know. Toronto: Centre for Addiction and Mental Health.

Métis National Council. 2016. "Métis Nation Rights. www.metisnation.ca.

Meyer-Cook, Fiona, and Diane Labelle. 2004. "Namaji: Two-Spirit organizing in Montreal, Canada." *Journal of Gay and Lesbian Social Service: Issues in Practice, Policy and Research* 6 (1).

Mihesuah, Devon, and Angela Wilson, eds. 2004. *Indigenizing the Academy: Transforming scholarship and empowering communities.* Lincoln: University of Nebraska Press.

Mingus, Mia. 2010. "Changing the framework: Disability justice." *Resist. Newsletter.* November. https://leavingevidence.wordpress.com.

Mingus, Mia. 2013. "Beyond access: Mia Mingus on disability justice." Video interview. Equitable Education.ca. http://equitableeducation.ca.

Mingus, Mia. 2015. http://blog.sacha.ca.

Mojtehedzadeh, Sara. 2015a. "Workers face fewer full-time prospects: Shifting labour landscape sees 'notable' rise in Ontario's low-wage jobs, survey finds." *The Toronto Star,* February: 18.

Mojtehedzadeh, Sara. 2015b. "Labour group calls for closing loopholes that harm workers." *Toronto Star,* April 1.

Moran, Bridget. 1992. *A Little rebellion.* Vancouver: Arsenal Pulp Press.

Moscovitch, Allan. 1986. "The welfare state since 1975." *Journal of Canadian Studies* 21 (2).

Mullaly, Bob. 2010. *Challenging oppression and confronting privilege: A Critical social work approach,* 2nd ed. Toronto: Oxford University Press.

Murray, Kate M., and Steven F. Hick. 2010. "Structural social work: Theory and process." In *Structural social work in action: Examples from practice,* ed. Steven F. Hick, Heather I. Peters, Tammy Corner, and Tracy London. Toronto: Canadian Scholars' Press.

Mussell, Bill. 2014. "Mental health from an Indigenous perspective." In *Journey to healing: Aboriginal People with addiction and mental health issues – what health, social service and justice workers need to know,* ed. Peter Menzies and Lynn Lavallée. Toronto: Centre for Addiction and Mental Health.

Nasser, Shanifa. 2015. "Paris attacks backlash 'nothing new,' Canadian Muslims say, but public also supportive: Muslims are speaking out about Islamophobia, but also find encouraging signs of support." *CBC News.* November 24. www.cbc.ca.

Native Women's Association of Canada (NWAC). (nd). Aboriginal Lateral Violence Fact Sheet. 2011. www.nwac.ca.

Neu, Dean, and Richard Therrien. 2003. *Accounting for genocide: Canada's bureaucratic assault on Aboriginal people.* Halifax: Fernwood Publishing.

Neysmith, Sheila. 2012. "Caring and aging." In *Canadian social policy: Issues and perspectives,* ed. Anne Westhues and Brian Wharf, 5th ed. Waterloo, Ont.: Wilfrid Laurier University Press.

Ng, Winnie. 2015. "Trade unions and social work: Lessons from Canada." In *International Encyclopedia of the Social and Behavioral Sciences*, ed. James D. Wright, 2nd ed., vol. 24, 491–96. Oxford: Elsevier.

O'Neill, Brian. 2006. "Toward inclusion of gay and lesbian people: Social policy changes in relation to sexual orientation." In *Canadian social policy: Issues and perspectives*, ed. Anne Westhues, 4th ed. Waterloo, Ont.: Wilfrid Laurier University Press.

O'Neill, Brian. 2012. "Toward inclusion of GLB people: Social policy changes in relation to sexual orientation." In *Canadian social policy: Issues and perspectives*, ed. Anne Westhues and Brian Wharf, 5th ed. Waterloo, Ont.: Wilfrid Laurier University Press.

Ontario Advocate for Children and Youth. 2014. "Children's rights matter to us: Over 400 children and youth speak out." Findings from the first annual listening tour. Ontario Advocate for Children and Youth. http://provincialadvocate.on.ca.

Osborne, John. 1985. "The Evolution of the Canada Assistance Plan." www.canadiansocialresearch.net.

Oxfam, 2015. "Richest 1% to own more than rest of the world." Business Report, BBC. www.bbc.com.

Palmater, Pamela. 2014. "Why are we idle no more?" *The Winter we danced: Voices from the past, the future, and the Idle No More Movement,* ed. The Kino-nda-niimi Collective. Winnipeg: ARP Books.

Paris, Erna. 1995. *The end of days: Tolerance, tyranny and the expulsion of Jews from Spain.* Toronto: Lester Publishing.

Piven, Frances Fox, and Richard A. Cloward. 1979. *Poor peoples' movements: Why they succeed, how they fail.* New York: Vintage Books.

Pon, Gordon, Kevin Gosine, and Doret Phillips. 2011. "Immediate response: Addressing anti-Native and anti-Black racism in child welfare." *International Journal of Child, Youth and Family Studies* 3 and 4: 385–409.

Poole, Jennifer M., and Tania Jivraj. 2015. "Mental health, mentalism and sanism." *International Encyclopedia of the Social and Behavioral Sciences,* 2nd ed., vol. 15: 200–3. Oxford: Elsevier.

Poole, Jennifer M., Tania Jivraj, Araxi Arslanian, Kristen Bellows, Sheila Chiasson, Husnia Hakimy, Jessica Pasini, and Jenna Reid. 2012. "Sanism, 'mental health,' and social work/education: A review and call to action" *Intersectionalities: A Global Journal of Social Work Analysis, Research, Polity, and Practice* 1.

Popple, B. 1983. "Contexts of practice." In *Handbook of clinical social work,* ed. A. Rosenblatt and D. Waldvogel. San Francisco: Jossey-Bass.

Porter, Beth. 2015. "After the TRC – the path ahead: An interview with Commissioner Marie Wilson (Part I)." *A Human Future* 13 (3). Toronto: L'Arche Canada. www.larchecommons.ca.

Porter, Catherine. 2016. "'Myths of rape should be dispelled,' says judge in Mandi Gray case: Ontario Court Justice Marvin Zuker changed the landscape of sexual assault and the criminal justice system on Thursday." *Toronto Star.* July 21: 1. www.thestar.com.

Rebick, Judy. 2009. *Transforming power: From the personal to the political.* Toronto: Penguin.

Reid, Jennifer. 2010. "The Doctrine of Discovery and Canadian law." *Canadian Journal of Native Studies* 30 (2): 335–59. www3.brandonu.ca.

Richardson, Cathy, and Dana Lynn Seaborn. 2009. "Beyond audacity and aplomb: Understanding the Métis in Social Work Practice." In *Wicihitowin: Aboriginal Social Work in Canada*, ed. Raven Sinclair, Michael Anthony, and Gord Bruyere. Halifax: Fernwood Publishing,

Riley, Barbara. 1994. "Teachings from the Medicine Wheel: Theories for practice." WUNSKA Network Presentation: Annual Conference of Canadian Association of Schools of Social Work, Calgary, June 16.

Rossiter, Amy, and Heron, Barbara. 2011. "Neoliberalism, competencies, and the devaluing of social work practice." *Canadian Social Work Review* 28 (2).

Royal Commission on Aboriginal Peoples. 1996. *Looking forward, looking back: Report of the Royal Commission on Aboriginal Peoples*, vol. 1. Ottawa: Minister of Supply and Services Canada.

Rudin, Jonathan. 2014. "The Criminal justice system: Addressing Aboriginal overrepresentation." *Journey to healing: Aboriginal People with addiction and mental health issues – what health, social service and justice workers need to know*, ed. Peter Menzies and Lynn Lavallée, Toronto: Centre for Addiction and Mental Health.

Schmidt, Sarah. 2012. "UN envoy blasts Canada for 'self-righteous' attitude over hunger, poverty." *National Post,* News, May 15. www.news.nationalpost.com.

Scientific Steering Committee Website. 2014. "Putting DNA to Work." Daniel E. Koshland, Jr., Bruce M. Alberts, David Botstein, Christopher R. Somerville, Brian J. Staskawicz. www.koshland-science-museum.org.

Shapcott, Michael. 2012. "The housing justice project." Toronto: Wellesley Institute. http://housingjustice.ca.

Shewell, Hugh. 2004. *Enough to keep them alive: Indian social welfare in Canada 1973–1965.* Toronto: University of Toronto Press.

Shiva, Vandana. 2002. Preface, *Water wars: Privatization, pollution and profit.* Toronto: Between the Lines.

Sinclair, Raven. 2007. "Identity Lost and Found: Lessons from the Sixties Scoop." *First Peoples Child and Family Review* 3 (1): 65–82.

Sinclair, Raven. 2009a. "Identity or racism? Aboriginal transracial adoption." In *Wicihitowin: Aboriginal social work in Canada,* ed. Raven Sinclair (Otiskewapiwskew), Michael Anthony Hart (Kaskitemahikan), and Gord Bruyere (Amawaajibitang). Black Point, N.S.: Fernwood Publishing.

Sinclair, Raven. 2009b. "Bridging the past and the future." In *Wicihitowin: Aboriginal social work in Canada,* ed. Raven Sinclair (Otiskewapiwskew), Michael Anthony Hart (Kaskitemahikan), and Gord Bruyere (Amawaajibitang). Black Point, N.S.: Fernwood Publishing.

Sinclair, Raven. 2016. "Indigenous Transracial Adoption in Canada." In *Contemporary Issues in Child Welfare: American Indian and Canadian Aboriginal Contexts*, ed. J.D. Ned and C. Frost. Vernon: J Charlton Publishing.

Sinclair, Raven, Michael Anthony Hart, and Gord Bruyere, eds. 2009. *Wicihitowin: Aboriginal social work in Canada*. Black Point, N.S.: Fernwood Publishing.

Smith, Dianah. 2015. "Vignettes of the working poor: Invisible lives" *CPPA Monitor: Economic, Social and Environmental Perspectives* 21 (9).

Smith, Jackie. 2008. *Social movements for global democracy*. Baltimore: Johns Hopkins University Press.

Smith, M. Kristin, and Donna Jeffery. 2013. "Critical pedagogies in the neoliberal university: What happens when they go digital?" *The Canadian Geographer* 57 (3) Autumn: 372–80.

Social Work Action Network. 2015. "Mental health charter on inpatient adult psychiatric care." www.socialworkfuture.org.

SOS Society: Surpassing Our Survival. 2013. Take Back the Night. www.sossociety.net.

Special Senate Committee on Aging. 2009. *Canada's aging population: Seizing the opportunity*. Ottawa. www.senate-senat.ca.

Special Senate Committee on Poverty. 1971. *Poverty in Canada*. Ottawa: Information Canada.

Spivey, Donald. 2003. *Fire from the soul: A History of the African-American struggle*. Durham, N.C.: Carolina Academic Press.

Stanford, Jim. 2015. *Economics for everyone*. London: Pluto Press.

Stapleton, John, with Vass Bednar. 2011. *Trading places: Single adults replace lone parents as the new face of social assistance in Canada*. Mowat Centre for Policy Innovation, University of Toronto.

Statistics Canada. 2015. "Unionization rates falling, 1981–2014." Canadian Megatrends. (11–630-X). May 28.

Stephenson, Marylee, Gilles Rondeau, Jean Claude Michaud, and Sid Fiddler. 2000. *In Critical demand: Social work in Canada: Final Report*, vol. 1. Ottawa: Human Resources Development Canada, Canadian Association of Schools of Social Work, Canadian Committee of Deans and Directors of Schools of Social Work, Canadian Association of Social Workers, and Regroupement des Unités de formation universitaires en travail social.

Strega, Susan, and Jeannine Carriere. 2009. *Walking this path together: Anti-racist and anti-oppressive child welfare practice*. Winnipeg: Fernwood Press.

Strega, Susan, and Sohki Aski Esquao (Jeannine Carriere). 2009. Introduction. In *Walking this path together: Anti-racist and anti-oppressive child welfare practice*, ed. Susan Strega and Sohki Aski Esquao (Jeannine Carriere). Black Point, N.S.: Fernwood Publishing.

Strojeck, Sylvia. 2008. "From East to West: Tears, applause and defiance greet Ottawa's gesture." *Toronto Star*, June 12.

Struthers, James. 1983. *No fault of their own: Unemployment and the Canadian welfare state, 1914–1941*. Toronto: University of Toronto Press.

Sue, Derald Wing, Christina Capodilupo, Gina Torino, Jennifer Bucceri, Aisha

Holder, Kevin Nada, and Marta Equilin. 2007. "Racial microaggressions in everyday life: Implications for clinical practice." *American Psychologist* 62 (4), May-June: 271–86. www.consumerstar.org.

Suzuki. David, and Moola, Faisal. 2016. "Clyde River Inuit fight to protect territory and livelihoods from big oil." *Science Matters, A weekly blog by David Suzuki.* August 18. www.davidsuzuki.org.

Swanson, Jean. 2001. *Poor-bashing: The politics of exclusion.* Toronto: Between the Lines.

Swift, Jamie, Brice Balmer, and Mira Dineen. 2010. "A pebble in the shoe." *Persistent poverty: Voices from the margins.* Toronto: Between the Lines.

Teeple, Gary, and Stephen McBride. 2010. *Relations of global power: Neoliberal order and disorder.* Toronto: University of Toronto Press.

Texler Segal, Marcia, and Theresa A. Martinez, eds. 2007. *Intersections of gender, race and class: Readings for a changing landscape.* Los Angeles: Roxbury Publishing.

Thakur, Ramesh. 2004. "Why we shouldn't rush to war over Darfur," *The Globe and Mail,* Sept. 11.

Timmins, Vivian. 2015. "Honouring my spirit." *First Lady Nation; Stories by Aboriginal women,* ed. Linda Ellis Eastman, vol. 3. Prospect, Kentucky: Professional Women Publishing.

Tobias, John. 1991. "Canada's Subjugation of the Plains Cree, 1879–1885." *Canadian Historical Review* 64 (1983): 519–48.

Todd, Sarah. 2006. "Social work and sexual and gender diversity." In *Social work in Canada: An Introduction,* ed. Steven F. Hick, 2nd ed. Toronto: Thompson Educational Publishing.

Torjman, Sherri. 2015. "Cut the tax cut." *Caledon Commentary.* Ottawa: Caledon Institute of Social Policy. January. www.caledoninst.org.

Toronto Star, Editorial. 2016. "'Panama Papers': Crack down on tax havens." April 5: A12. www.thestar.com.

Trans Pride Canada, Style Guide. 2012. www.transpride.ca.

Trans Youth Family Allies. 2009. "TYFA resources for educators: Executive summary: Harsh realities – the experiences of transgender youth in our public schools." www.imatyfa.org.

Truth and Reconciliation Commission of Canada. 2013a. "Inuit and the Residential School System" www.legacyofhope.ca.

Truth and Reconciliation Commission of Canada. 2013b. "Where are the children? Residential school oral histories and survivor stories" www.wherearethechildrn.ca.

Truth and Reconciliation Commission of Canada. 2014. www.trc.ca.

Truth and Reconciliation Commission of Canada. 2015. *What we have learned: Principles of truth and reconciliation.* Library and Archives Canada. www.trc.ca.

United Nations, Office of the UN special adviser on the prevention of genocide (OSAPG). 1948. www.un.org.

Vaillancourt, Yves. 2012. "The Québec model of social policy, past and present." *Canadian social policy: Issues and perspectives*, 115–14. Waterloo, Ont.: Wilfrid Laurier University Press.

Vaillancourt, Yves, François Aubry, Muriel Kearney, Luc Thériault, and Louise Tremblay. 2004. "The Contribution of the social economy towards healthy social policy reforms in Canada: A Quebec viewpoint." In *Social determinants of health: Canadian perspectives*, ed. Dennis Raphael. Toronto: Canadian Scholar's Press.

Vancouver Media Co-op. 2011. "2011 and Reflecting on 11 Social Movement Successes" Blog January 3. http://vancouver.mediacoop.ca.

Vernon, Ayesha, and John Swain. 2002. "Theorizing divisions and hierarchies: Towards a commonality of diversity?" *Disability studies today*, ed. Colin Barnes, Mike Oliver, and Len Barton. Cambridge: Polity Press.

Vincent, Donovan. 2016. "The whistleblower: Sylvie Therrien, former EI fraud investigator." *Toronto Star.* January 30: IN1, IN4–5.

Weinberg, Merlinda. 2010. "The Social construction of social work ethics: Politicizing and broadening the lens." *Journal of Progressive Human Services* 21 (1): 32–44. http://ethicsinthehelpingprofessions.socialwork.dal.ca.

Wilkinson, Richard, and Kate Pickett. 2014. "The Spirit Level authors: Why society is more unequal than ever." The *Guardian*. March 9. www.theguardian.com.

Withers, A.J. 2012. *Disability politics and theory*. Halifax and Winnipeg: Fernwood Publishing.

Wright, Kristie, Shahina Sayani, Andrea Zammit, and Purnima George. 2010. "Envisioning structural social work practice: The Case of the grassroots youth collaborative." In *Structural social work: Examples from practice,* ed. Steven F. Hick, Heather I. Peters, Tammy Corner, and Tracy London. Toronto: Canadian Scholars' Press.

Wright, Ronald. 2000. *Stolen continents: Conquest and resistance in the Americas*. London: Phoenix Press.

Yellow Horse Braveheart, Marie, and Lemyra DeBruyn. 1998. The American Indian Holocaust: Healing unresolved grief. *American Indian and Alaska Native Mental Health Research* 8 (2): 60–82.